(Radnorshire Wildlife Trust), Martin Kitching (Northern Experience Wildlife Ltd), Sophie Lake (Footprint Ecology), Brian Laney, Andy Lawson, Hannah Lawson, Jono Leadley (Yorkshire Wildlife Trust), Jonathan Lethbridge, Durwyn Liley (Footprint Ecology), David Lindo (The Urban Birder), Simon Linington (RBG Kew), Sharon Lowen, Joseph Lynn, Graham Lyons, John Marchant (BTO), Jason Mitchell (RSPB), Nick Moran (BTO), Andy Musgrove (BTO), David Newland, Natalie Ngo (Butterfly Conservation), Malcolm Ogilvie (Islay Natural History Trust), Phil Palmer, Penny Pereira, Rob Petley-Jones (Natural England), Doug Radford (RSPB), Joanna Richards (Yorkshire Wildlife Trust), Mike Richardson, Christian Roberts, Roger Safford, Rachel Shaw (Lincolnshire Wildlife Trust), Alick Simmons, Helen Smith (www. dolomedes.org.uk), Bill Stow (Radnorshire Wildlife Trust), Tom Stuart, Adam Taylor (Essex Wildlife Trust), Mark Telfer, Richard Thaxton (RSPB), Howard Vaughan (RSPB), Kerry Vaughan (Suffolk Wildlife Trust), Mike Waller, Laura Watson, Rob Williams and Jessica Winder. My apologies to anyone inadvertently omitted.

I am grateful to photographer colleagues who supplied images for the guide. Those whose pictures have been chosen are thanked on page 234. At and around Bradt, I thank Hugh Collins, Rachel Fielding, Deborah Gerrard, Donald Greig, Chris Lane, Adrian Phillips, Janet Mears, Mike Unwin and – above all – my project manager, Anna Moores.

Finally, Sharon Lowen was my accommodation guru and personal 'trip advisor'. She and Maya Lowen were eager companions on research trips, and their tolerance of my writing days was a prerequisite for this book becoming reality.

Feedback request

Why not write and tell us about your experiences using this guide? Post reviews to ⓦ www.bradtguides.com or Amazon. You can send in updates on out-of-date information or suggestions for your own recommended wildlife-watching weekends to ⓣ 01753 893444 or ⓔ info@bradtguides.com. Any contributors will be thanked by James Lowen in future editions. We may also post 'one-off updates' at ⓦ www. bradtguides.com/guidebookupdates.

Introduction

Red deer rutting. Puffins strutting. Salmon leaping. Bottle-nosed dolphins jumping. Helleborines blooming. Beachcomber beetles burrowing. Natterjack toads churring. Otters cavorting. Bluebells carpeting. White-tailed eagles fishing. Fen raft spider hunting. Purple emperors gliding. Hairy dragonfly hawking. Adders writhing. Snakelocks anemones waving. Starlings swirling. Yews towering. Water voles munching. Grey seals pupping. And basking sharks cruising.

This book's aim is simple: to inspire and inform, so that you rush to experience the exhilaration of British wildlife – at any and every time of the year. It is uniquely designed to help you do so. In no previous publication has wildlife-watching been packaged into 52 short break-sized chunks. Whenever you have a weekend free to immerse yourself in the natural world, this book has a recommendation for you.

My guiding principle has been to offer something for everyone. The weekends cover the breadth of British natural history. Fritillaries and fungi feature, so too flycatchers and fish. You may already be a birder or botanist – and perhaps believe that to be your lot. But, by weekend 52, if not long before, I wager that this book will have enticed you to enjoy butterflies and beetles as well.

Small red-eyed damselfly has colonised Britain since the late 1990s. This is a male. (JL)

Some weekends are unabashedly pacy; others more relaxed. There are weekends for the novice, but also for the expert. Some weekends involve hill-walking, others a sedate stroll. There are boat trips, suggestions for snorkelling and sites for rockpooling. You visit woodlands and wetlands, heathlands and grasslands, meres and mires. Some excursions will see you on your hands and knees. Others will see you scanning skies, waves or wetlands. But all focus on some special component of British natural history. And all provide unforgettable wildlife experiences.

Top 5 weekends for...

... birds	Jan, 1; Apr, 2; Jun, 4; **Oct, 2; Oct, 4**
... bird flocks	Feb, 2; Aug, 3; **Nov, 4; Dec, 1; Dec, 3**
... large land mammals	Feb, 1; Feb 4; **Sep, 4; Oct, 1; Nov, 2**
... small land mammals	Mar, 1; Jul, 5; **Aug, 3; Sep, 1; Oct, 3**
... marine mammals	Jan, 4; Jul, 3; **Sep, 4; Nov, 3; Dec, 3**
... underwater life	Jun, 4; Jul, 4; Jul, 5; Aug, 2; **Oct, 5**
... reptiles	Mar, 2; Apr, 1; Apr, 3; Apr, 4; Jul, 2
... amphibians	Mar, 2; Apr, 4; May, 4; Jun, 3; **Aug, 4**
... dragonflies	Jun, 3; **Jul, 2; Jul, 3; Jul, 4; Aug, 4**
... butterflies or moths	May, 1; May, 4; Jun, 1; Jul, 1; Jul, 2
... other invertebrates	Apr, 4; Jun, 2; Jul, 3; Aug, 4; **Sep, 2**
... orchids	Apr, 4; May, 1; May, 4; Jun, 1; Jul, 1
... other plants	Mar, 3; May, 5; Jun, 2; **Aug, 1; Nov, 1**
... fungi or lichen	Feb, 2; **Sep, 4; Oct, 2; Oct, 5; Nov, 1**

▲ *May, weekend 2* offers the chance to see badger. (SH/FLPA)

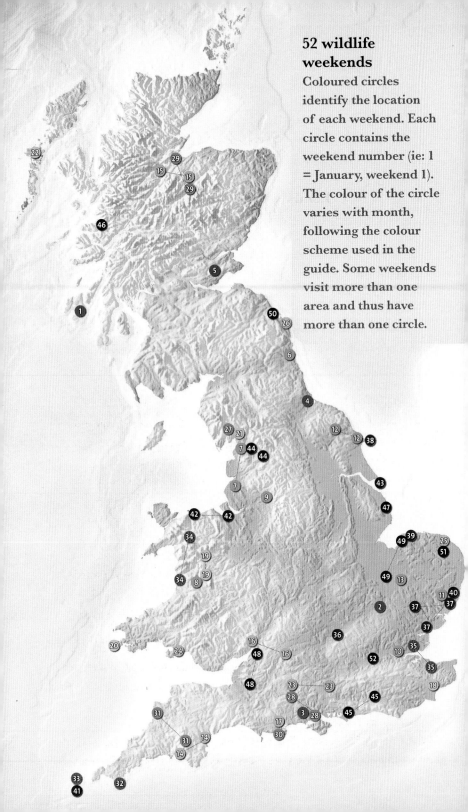

52 wildlife weekends

Coloured circles identify the location of each weekend. Each circle contains the weekend number (ie: 1 = January, weekend 1). The colour of the circle varies with month, following the colour scheme used in the guide. Some weekends visit more than one area and thus have more than one circle.

How to use this book

In this book, we suggest a year's worth of sublime wildlife-watching breaks – one for you to enjoy each weekend of the year. Eight months have four weekends; four (one per season) are indulged with a fifth.

About the weekends

Covering Great Britain *sensu strictu* (England, Scotland and Wales), the suggestions stretch from Cornwall to northern Scotland.

Our guiding ethos is to offer you outstanding wildlife-watching experiences in short-break-sized chunks. To help you 'prioritise', five **wildlife 'targets'** are suggested for each weekend. Should you prefer a more leisurely itinerary, simply pick and choose.

Fancy a weekend seeing both orchids and butterflies? Or reptiles and amphibians? See page 222 for a summary of the best weekends for combining different wildlife groups.

Practicalities

Each weekend includes access details for featured sites with unique grid references based on Ordnance Survey mapping (which you can key into an internet map provider such as Ⓦ www.streetmap.co.uk).

Each **suggested bases** section recommends a characterful, convenient B&B that caught the eye. Some accommodation providers have made a small payment to enhance their entries with a photograph and longer text.

Reserve websites usually provide comprehensive advice on accessibility for visitors with mobility issues – we provide only a rough assessment of overall accessibility (from ① easy to ⑤ hard). Weekends whose full itineraries might mean walking for at least 8km or a tough walk of 5km on at least one of the days are also identified: (🏃).

Each weekend reflects the seasonality of special creatures, but what if summer comes late or you can't make the specific weekend? A section on **flexibility** summarises your room for manoeuvre.

What's in a name?

Where no confusion is possible, we've used names in common parlance, rather than the formal moniker – hence badger rather than Eurasian

badger, for example. Scientific names appear in the *Index of target species* (pages 229–32) alongside each species' vernacular name.

Further information

This is not an identification guide or an ecological handbook, nor is it a comprehensive site guide or a gazetteer of nature reserves. For such publications, see *Further Information*, page 223–4.

Missing activities/species

Some popular wildlife-watching **activities** – bat walks, 'mini-beasting', moth-trapping, badger-watching – are largely absent. This is because they are less dependent on specific times than are the 'target' species so simply take opportunities to enjoy them wherever and whenever.

Finally, we are intentionally silent on particular wildlife species. Heeding guidance from conservationists, we omit certain sensitive species or sites. Should viewing arrangements change, we may be able to incorporate these into future editions.

▲ Shape-shifting clouds of feather: a murmuration of starlings as dusk encroaches. (JB)

Wildlife-watchers' codes of conduct

Responsible enjoyment of fauna and flora is essential; the welfare and conservation of the species comes first. Over and beyond legislative constraints (eg: it is illegal to disturb certain nationally scarce species), a series of codes of conduct exist to guide behaviour. The most well known is the Countryside Code (Ⓦ www.naturalengland.org.uk/ourwork/enjoying/countrysidecode), but others are listed below.

Butterflies Ⓦ www.purple-emperor.co.uk/page42.htm
Plants Ⓦ www.bsbi.org.uk/Code_of_Conduct.pdf
Birds Ⓦ http://tinyurl.com/crny83l
Seashore Ⓦ www.marlin.ac.uk/seashorecode.php
Fungi Ⓦ http://tinyurl.com/cpasnhc
Dragonflies Ⓦ http://tinyurl.com/dragonflycode
Photography Ⓦ www.rpsnaturegroup.com/page7.htm

Contents

▲ Short-eared owl (PM)

Contents

▶ Bee orchid (CM/FLPA)

Contents

◀ High brown fritillary (RP-J)

Contents

▲ Chough (PM)   xiii

Contents

1
Wild goose chases and whisky chasers

Islay, Argyll & Bute for barnacle goose, Greenland white-fronted goose, chough, otter, goose barnacle

> ❝ 6,000 'white-fronts' graze Islay's marshes, their shrill, musical vocalisations standing out from the canine calls of barnacle geese ❞

Fleeing the freezing Arctic in October, three-quarters of Greenland's barnacle geese and one-quarter of its white-fronted geese spend seven more temperate months nudging the North Atlantic on Islay in the Inner Hebrides. How better to start the New Year than a literal wild goose chase in the home of peaty whisky?

Some 40,000 barnacle geese spend January here, munching rich green grass in tightly packed flocks. When spooked – by peregrine, passing tractor or paranoia – the throng whooshes upwards, yapping and yelping, festooning the sky with monochrome forms. Should the panic pass, the feathered mass returns to ground, and your pulse rate returns to normal. Should the flock remain aloft, the horizon may entice them, pressing you into adrenalin-fuelled pursuit.

Few birds' names have such a curious etymology. Rather than a nod to the species's favourite food (herbivorous geese do not consume crustacea), the barnacle goose's moniker relates to its perceived genesis. For 600 years, this goose was conjectured to grow underwater in barnacle shells clinging to timber, then to emerge onto land in the

▲ White-fronted goose, fresh in from Greenland (WW/FLPA)

autumn. Only upon discovery of the goose's remote breeding grounds in the early 20th century did belief finally become myth.

No such legend surrounds Greenland white-fronted geese, but being privy to their 'skeins' is no less exhilarating. In January 6,000 'white-fronts' graze Islay's marshes and fields, their shrill, musical vocalisations standing out from the more canine calls of barnacle geese.

You bump into geese throughout the land of Lagavulin and Laphroaig, but the heftiest congregations are at RSPB Loch Gruinart, particularly around the visitor centre at Aoradh Farm. Using the car as concealment, also search west to Loch Gorm, north along minor roads beyond Ardnave, and east past Loch Indaal to roads south of Bridgend, and the A846 from Bridgend to Port Askaig.

As you search, expect the unexpected. Most winters, the gaggles woo vagrant interlopers into their midst. There may be a Eurasian white-fronted goose of the race breeding in Russia, pink bill distinguishing it from orange-billed Greenland brethren. Or perhaps red-breasted, snow or lesser Canada – the latter a wild bonsai cousin of the familiar denizens of our urban parks.

Catch your breath from the goose chase by imbibing Islay's wealth of other wildlife. The island's diversity reflects the coalition of habitats in an area just 40km by 32km. Sandy bays and shingle beaches rub shoulders with mudflats and rocky cliffs. Moorland and marshes brush against croftland and woodland. There's plenty to strengthen your resolve against succumbing to daytime whisky-tasting: after all, malts are what chilly evenings are for.

▲ On Islay, barnacle geese often graze in roadside fields: use your car as a hide to enable close approach. (JL)

Leading the wildlife supporting cast is another feathered speciality. Few places are better than Islay to see chough. And few crows are as fun to watch as these gregarious, red-billed 'aerobats' as they hang in the wind, then plummet with closed wings, only to pull out just before a crash landing, twisting upwards with a strident '*cheee-o*'. The beautiful beach and dunes at Ardnave and those at Machir Bay on the Rinns (or Rhinns) are good spots. Either area merits a proper meander.

At Ardnave snow bunting and twite nibble among spilled silage, and hen harriers make their rounds. The Rinns offer golden eagle and, increasingly, white-tailed eagle – 'flying barn doors' wandering from natal grounds on other Hebridean islands. Check bays for otters, pleasingly common along Islay's 190km of coastline. Peruse harbours at Portnahaven or Port Wemyss for grey seal and a few harbour seal. After Atlantic storms, in particular, search beaches for washed-up goose barnacles covering driftwood. Within an hour, you could see both barnacle goose and the shelled creature from which the bird was once thought to emerge!

Nearby Loch Indaal merits a full afternoon. Best known as a roosting site for barnacle geese, this sea loch hosts one of Britain's largest flocks of scaup, a smart seaduck. Good viewpoints are Blackrock, the A847 between Bruichladdich and Port Charlotte, and Bridgend bay; park only in laybys. You should come across great northern diver – particularly between Port Charlotte and Nerabus – Slavonian grebe, long-tailed duck and black guillemot, the latter colloquially known as 'tystie'. Look for 'white-winged' gulls from the icy north: the robust glaucous gull and the slighter Iceland gull. Oft-frequented spots are Bruichladdich, the river mouth at Uiskentuie and mudflats at Bridgend.

If you depart by ferry, save a half-day to explore east Islay *en route* to Port Askaig or Port Ellen. At Storakaig, near Ballygrant, red deer are fed in winter and give fine views from the road. Try the isolated moorland and towering sea-cliffs of the Oa for both species of eagle plus feral goats in their wilderness element: no domestic billygoatgruff these! Seek harbour seal in secluded bays between Lagavulin and Ardtalla, and roe deer anywhere in the lowlands. Even better, scour the coast for otters at Bunnahabhain (north of the distillery), Loch an t-Sailein, Clagghain bay or Craighouse. And weigh anchor with the yelping and yapping of geese in your ears.

Where to go: Travel details to Islay from mainland Scotland are summarised at Ⓦ www.scotland-inverness.co.uk/islay.htm. Car ferries run from Kennacraig, Argyll, two to four times daily in winter and take c2 hours to reach **Port Askaig** (◉ NR432694 Ⓣ 0800 0665000 Ⓦ www.calmac.co.uk). There are two flights daily from Glasgow (Ⓣ 0871 7002000 Ⓦ www.loganair.co.uk), and on two days per week from Oban (Ⓣ 0845 805 7465 Ⓦ www.hebrideanair.co.uk). **RSPB Loch Gruinart** is northwest of Bridgend, off the B8017 (◉ NR275672 Ⓣ 01496 850505 Ⓦ www.rspb.org.uk/reserves/guide/lochgruinart). View roosting geese at **Loch Indaal** from ◉ NR335620 or ◉ NR324627; other named viewpoints over the loch are accessible from the A847 or A846. **Ardnave** (◉ NR285730) is in the northwest of the island, at the northern end of Loch Gruinart. The minor road south of Loch Gorm leads to **Machir Bay** (◉ TR208635). Portnahaven and Port Wemyss lie at the southern tip of the Rinns; follow the A847 to its end. **The Oa** forms the southernmost point on Islay; access on minor roads southwest of the A846 at Port Ellen. For a guide to birding sites mentioned, see Ⓦ www.islaynaturalhistory.org/birding.

Suggested bases: Bowmore, Bridgend, Port Ellen and Port Charlotte (Ⓦ http://accommodation.islayinfo.com). **The Old Excise House** (Ⓣ 01496 302567 Ⓦ www.theoldexcisehouse.com) in Laphroaig offers two individually designed bedrooms with spectacular sea views.

Flexibility: Any weekend November to February should work well. Barnacle and white-fronted geese are present late October to March at least, with peak numbers of barnacle in the autumn. Chough, otter, feral goat and both eagles are resident.

Accessibility: ②

◀ Look for goose barnacle after winter storms. (DC)

2
Meres, fens and washes

Cambridgeshire for Chinese water deer, muntjac, Bewick's swan, whooper swan, hen harrier

> **❝A thousand or two swans honk and bugle their way to their watery roost ❞**

Fenland in midwinter is where fairies would live: a wondrous fusion of the remote and the magical. Following centuries of drainage, fragments totaling just 0.03% of Cambridgeshire's Fens remain. Fortunately, various consortia of the conservation-minded are rectifying this through visionary projects that will restore a vast fen and create Britain's largest reedbed. How different will a weekend wildlife-watching in 2050 be compared to one this January?

Open the weekend with a trio of RSPB reserves. At RSPB Fowlmere, 15km south of Cambridge, careful management has recreated meres and ditches, raised water levels, maintained reedbeds, grazed fen and wildflower meadows, and established stands of hawthorn, willow, alder and ash. In Tower, Reedbed or Spring hides try waiting for an otter to swim past, a sparrowhawk to buzz finch flocks, or a kingfisher to bullet through. Muntjac and fallow deer both occur, being easiest to see in fields to the southeast. Both are introduced to Britain but have become well established and are a treat to watch.

▲ Whooper swan families keep together throughout the winter. (DF)

Chinese water deer: face of a teddy bear but long canines of a vampire? (DT)

From Fowlmere, drive 30 minutes north to one of the charity's newer reserves. RSPB Fen Drayton is a fen in name only, and the reserve comprises carefully managed former gravel pits and reedbeds. You can have decent birding anywhere: various footpaths navigate the lake complex. Swavesey and Elney lakes host diving ducks such as smew and goldeneye. Elney and Holywell lakes are best for wintering bittern.

Finish at Britain's largest 'wash' – a habitat defined as grazing pasture subject to winter floods. At RSPB Ouse Washes, birding begins in the car park, a stronghold for the ever-declining tree sparrow. While you could easily idle away an hour watching the feeders, you have come to join the congregation of up to 50,000 wildfowl and waders.

Flooded fields teem with golden plover, lapwing and black-tailed godwit. Grazing ducks include thousands of wigeon, whistling away, and hundreds of the delectable pintail. But the reason to time your visit for the afternoon is to coincide with the arrival of wild swans. A thousand or two whooper swan and Bewick's swan honk and bugle their way to the watery roost, gleaming white against the blackening sky.

On day two, tour two of Britain's oldest reserves, both conserving Fenland's finest remnants. In 1910, the protection of Woodwalton Fen initiated England's Wildlife Trust movement, while the National Trust has managed Wicken Fen since 1899. To visit these reserves is to step back in time: they look, smell and feel old.

Precious though the past may be, it is the future that animates conservationists. The Great Fen project will create a 3,700ha wetland between Huntingdon and Peterborough, centred on Woodwalton. Wicken, meanwhile, is the core of a 100-year vision of habitat restoration that will protect land stretching 20km south to Cambridge.

At Woodwalton, ditches that mark old peat diggings interlace with a mosaic of fen habitats, ancient peatlands and moorgrass meadows. Walking the grassy rides, you might flush a woodcock from the willow carr or see lesser redpolls in the alders. Look for lesser spotted woodpecker amidst tit flocks roving the east of the reserve. From Rothschild's and Gordon's Mere hides, watch the reedbeds for bittern, bearded tit or marsh harrier and keep an eye out for an otter swimming the mere.

The star mammal is Britain's rarest and most localised deer. Non-native it may be, but our thousand Chinese water deer now form one-tenth of the world population and thus have global conservation significance. Woodwalton is the country's best site for this teddy-bear-faced yet bizarrely vampire-fanged herbivore. You may see a handful lolloping like giant hares, particularly from the high bank around North Hide or the western bank. The similar-looking but smaller muntjac is also present, so use willows as cover to get good enough views to distinguish them.

Wicken Fen lies between Ely's cathedral spire and the ivory towers of Cambridge. After lunch at the café, check nearby bird-feeders for finches, buntings and tree sparrows. Then wander across fen and lode ('Fennish' for river), along grassy rides and into hides to savour Wicken's wildlife. Wait by Burwell Fen for short-eared owl and barn owl. On Adventurers' Fen, look for brown hare. Harvest mouse occurs in sedge fields, but you need great luck even to glimpse one. Little Breed Fen and adjacent woodland are your best bet for muntjac. Wildfowl wintering on the meres and flooded fens include several hundred gadwall.

Look for bittern from West Mere Hide and marsh harrier pounding a beat around Verall's Fen. Tower Hide is also good for both species, so plan your walk to be here for the throes of daylight. As dusk encroaches, hen harriers arrive at their reedbed repose. The brown females and young birds are tricky to discern in the gloaming. In contrast, the powder-grey adult males glow as they glide by. A little larger than expected, but distinctly ethereal... Fenland fairies, anyone?

▶ Muntjac, Britain's smallest deer (PS/FLPA)

Practicalities

January weekend 2

Where to go: RSPB Fowlmere (☀ TL406461 ℡ 01763 208978 Ⓦ www.rspb.org.uk/reserves/guide/f/fowl mere) is south of the A10 between Cambridge and Royston. **RSPB Fen Drayton** (☀ TL352680 ℡ 01954 233260 Ⓦ www.rspb.org.uk/reserves/guide/f/fendraytonlakes, http://tinyurl.com/Fendraytonbirding) is off Fen Drayton road between Fen Drayton and Swavesey (☀ TL353680); follow signs to car parks at Holywell Lake (☀ TL342699) or Elney Lake (☀ TL339691). **RSPB Ouse Washes** (☀ TL471860 ℡ 01354 680212 Ⓦ www.rspb.org.uk/reserves/guide/o/ousewashes) lies east of Chatteris: from the B1093 at Manea, drive south on minor roads to Welches Dam. Access to **Woodwalton Fen National Nature Reserve** (☀ TL220873 ℡ 01487 812363 Ⓦ www.greatfen.org.uk/visit/ places/WoodwaltonFen), 13km north of Huntingdon, is from Chapel Lane, off the minor road that runs through Ramsey Heights. Park by the drain and cross the bridge. No dogs. **Wicken Fen** National Trust reserve (☀ TL563705 ℡ 01353 720274 Ⓦ www.nationaltrust.org.uk/wicken-fen, www.wicken.org.uk) is off Lode Lane, southwest of Wicken village. Finally, remember that meres, fens and washes are intrinsically wet places so be sure to wear wellies and stick to paths.

Suggested bases: Cambridge (Ⓦ www.visitcambridge.org), Ely (Ⓦ http://ely.org.uk), Littleport and Chatteris. **The Anchor Inn** (℡ 01353 778537 Ⓦ www.anchor-inn-restaurant.co.uk) at Sutton Gault has four bedrooms/suites in a 17th-century inn serving contemporary modern British cuisine.

Flexibility: Any weekend December to February should work, as long as the main winter floods have arrived. Wildfowl, including swans, harriers and bittern, are good throughout December to February. The deer are resident, but more easily seen in winter.

Accessibility: ③ 🚶

▲ Male hen harrier... or Fenland fairy? (GC)

3
Larking about

**New Forest, Hampshire for red deer, roe deer,
wood lark, great grey shrike, hawfinch**

As the sun periscopes above the coniferous canopy, a small bird floats into the air from an isolated tree. It spirals upwards on broad wings and then, at height, loops the loop as it whistles, trills and yodels an enchanting lullaby. Suddenly it pauses before plunging treewards. One of our finest avian songsters, simultaneously melodious and melancholy, the wood lark is also one of our scarcest. On a crisp January day, there are few better places than Hampshire's New Forest to be entertained by this vocalist.

England's oldest hunting forest became the country's newest national park in 2005, protecting its unique patchwork of ancient woodland, lowland heath, natural

> 66 Melodious yet melancholy, the liquid warble of the wood lark is one of Britain's finest bird songs 99

grassland and boggy mires. Best known as a summer escape, the New Forest is at its wildest in winter.

A fine place to start is Hawkshill Inclosure, midway between Brockenhurst and Beaulieu. As the sky pales above heath and forest, pine-dwelling finches emerge from roost sites. Heavy-billed and brightly hued, common crossbills recall parrots as they clamber through the canopy deftly using toes and crossed mandibles. Brick-red males and vivid green females vie for both conifer seeds and your attention, before flying up up and away to other feeding grounds. Smaller finches – jauntier but less confiding – quickly take the crossbills' place. These are siskins, delightfully striped in black, yellow, green and white.

▲ Wood lark: prime candidate for 'X Factor' among Britain's birds (DT)

January weekend 3

As the morning thaws, tramp the forest trails – pausing, gobsmacked, at the odd thigh-high nest of southern wood ants – and tread tentatively into the clearings to look for wood lark. Check prominent perches – lone trees, exposed bushes – and cock your ear for a liquid warble. If you find a lark, approach stealthily to get a good look at its intricate face pattern: russet cheeks, white eyebrow and slender moustache topped by an erectile crest.

Now turn your attention to deer. Five species inhabit the Forest, the native roe and red complemented by introduced sika, fallow and muntjac. At a push, fallow deer might deserve the title of honorary native, given that it was to hunt stags that William the Conquerer decreed England's first hunting forest in the 12th century. Nearly a millennium later, herds are easily stalked with camera rather than crossbow at Bolderwood Deer Sanctuary, 4km west of Emery Down.

Red deer are easily seen. Park at Puttles Bridge and walk west to view Ober Heath or look around the Burley Manor Hotel. Sika numbers are constrained to around 100 for fear of them interbreeding with red deer. To see them, try the heath/conifer interface between Brockenhurst and Beaulieu. You might bump into roe deer anywhere, often feeding in open grassland adjoining woodland. Roes are unique among deer in that pregnant females delay implantation of the fertilised embryo, presumably to time the kid's birth for optimum grazing opportunities.

On day two, head for open heathland south and west of Beaulieu Road station. Search the dry heath and spiky gorse for foliose lichen such as the genus *Cladonia* (the New Forest is a hotspot for lichenologists) and for Dartford warblers. This long-tailed insectivore confesses its presence with a scolding churr from within dense gorse clumps before finally popping out to examine its admirer from an exposed perch.

Another New Forest fan of prominent perches is the great grey shrike. The scientific name – *excubitor* – means 'sentinel', reflecting the species's predilection for vantage points from which to hunt beetles and buntings. Hampshire heaths are famed for wintering 'butcher birds' (the country nickname for shrikes), particularly in boggier areas adjoining willows and birches, the latter often adorned with birch polypore, a bracket fungus. Open land south of Beaulieu Road station is a classic site.

Take time here to enjoy stonechats as they lead you between exposed bushes in their quest for winter invertebrates. Pairs maintain contact

Increasing in size and complexity each year, the red deer stag's antlers serve as a status symbol. (CD)

with a staccato call recalling two stones being clacked together. Keep your eyes to the sky as well. Hen harriers regularly quarter the heaths, and peregrines frequently zip across.

For a complete shift in scenery, drive west to Blashford Lakes, north of Ringwood. Feeding stations in the willow, birch and alder woodland offer delightful views of siskin, lesser redpoll, other woodland birds and roe deer. Bitterns winter on Ivy Lake, and among the 5,000 wildfowl you may find scarcities such as smew.

As the light fades to grey, it's back south to Rhinefield Arboretum for a real treat. Shy to the point of being self-effacing, hawfinch is a cracker. Large-headed and strong-billed, with a staring eye, a plumage of pastels offset by striking black and white patches, and – on the male – a ruffle adorning iridescent wings, the hawfinch has it all. Cross the road from the car park, pass through the gate, and scan the tops of tall cedars for hawfinches consorting before going to roost. From sunrise with one special New Forest bird, to sunset with another.

Where to go: The **New Forest National Park** lies between Southampton, Fordingbridge and Christchurch (Ⓦ www.newforestnpa.gov.uk). Lyndhurst hosts the national park's main visitor information centre (Ⓣ 023 80282269 Ⓦ www.the newforest.co.uk). **Hawkhill Inclosure** car park (☀ SU353020) is north of the B3055, 6km east of Brockenhurst. For **Bolderwood Deer Sanctuary** (☀ SU242086), leave Lyndhurst south on the A35. After 4km turn west along Bolderwood Arboretum Ornamental Drive and park on the right after 4.5km. Burley Manor Hotel (☀ SU210033) is in **Burley**, which is signposted northwest off the A35, 1.5km north of the B3058 junction.

    Use the car park just west of **Beaulieu Road** station (☀ SU347065) and walk south and west. **Puttles Bridge** is 4km along Rhinefield Ornamental Drive, east of the A35 (☀ SU271029). **Blashford Lakes** is a Hampshire Wildlife Trust reserve (☀ SU151083 Ⓣ 01425 472 760 Ⓦ http://tinyurl.com/Blashfordlakes); access off Ellingham Drove, east of the A338, immediately north of Ringwood. For **Rhinefield Arboretum**, take the A35 south from Lyndhurst. After 3km, head southeast along Rhinefield Ornamental Drive towards Brockenhurst; Black Water car park is 1.5km further on.

Suggested bases: Beaulieu, Brockenhurst, Burley and Lyndhurst (Ⓦ www.newforestbedbreakfast.co.uk).

In Brockenhurst, **Daisybank Cottage** (Ⓣ 01590 622086 Ⓦ www.lymington. org/accomprofiles/daisybank.html) is a boutique B&B with delightful suites demonstrating a personal touch, thoughtful extras and a splendid breakfast.

Flexibility: Any weekend January to March should be successful; sun encourages wood larks to sing. Wood lark, Dartford warbler and the deer are resident. Hawfinch and (if present) great grey shrike occur between November and March.

Accessibility: ②

Seal of approval

**Cleveland for harbour seal, grey seal, glaucous gull,
long-eared owl, waxwing**

Wildlife and wilderness go hand in hand. But so can wildlife and industrial landscapes. Visual paradise it may not objectively be, but the smoke stacks, cooling

> **❝ Harbour seals frolic in channels or loll on exposed sandbanks ❞**

towers, chemical plants and nuclear power station of Teesside somehow vanish from your consciousness once you discover the faunal extravaganza in their midst. After a century of industrial pollution, a cleaned-up environment has been resurrected into the Teesmouth National Nature Reserve. The resulting juxtaposition of chemicals and creatures is nothing short of fabulous. Where else can you watch both Britain's seal species from a busy main road?

The tidal channel of Greatham Creek, bridged by the A178, is the Mecca for seals and their admirers. High tides are best, inspiring the harbour seal colony to frolic in the water or loll on the few exposed sandbanks. At the onset of the 19th century, a thousand seals inhabited Teesmouth, donating their name to one part of the estuary: Seal Sands. Chemical pollution of the waters caused them to desert the area for many decades, only returning in the 1980s. The harbour seal population now numbers 70 animals, the largest colony in northeast England. These are joined by 30 grey seals that visit regularly but breed elsewhere.

A short muzzle helps differentiate this harbour seal from grey seal. (DT)

Beneath and beside the industrial architecture, Teesmouth's natural bounty features pools and pastures, scrapes and shorelines, mudflats and marshes. There is more than enough for a full weekend of exploration, with the order of service being marshalled by tidal ebb and flow.

The RSPB has unearthed a gem of a reserve at Saltholme, creating a marvellous visitor experience for all. After refuelling in the café, enquire about viewing arrangements for the reserve's star winter visitor. Long-eared owls roost in the scrub around Haverton Hole, but are sensitive to disturbance – so enjoy only from the designated viewpoint.

Another thoughtfully sited panorama, the 'wildlife watchpoint', provides the best prospects of spying secretive species such as water rail and bittern as well as ducks such as wigeon, pintail and goldeneye. Brown hare is common on the reserve, even cavorting in the car park. As you return to the stunning visitor centre, check bushes around the feeding station as they often attracts flocks of fieldfare and redwing, the so-called 'winter thrushes'.

Seaton Snook is worth a wander. This samphire-rich shore is a haven for flocks of seed-eating birds such as snow bunting (avian snowflakes) and twite (cute and tawny-faced). If the flocks suddenly flurry, scan for merlin, an avian arrowhead that predates small birds. If you reach North Gare at high tide, check the breakwater for roosting waders including purple sandpiper, grey plover and turnstone.

◀ Look for a long-eared owl roosting by day. (PS/JT)

Seal Sands no longer harbours seals, and its estuarine shorebird population is but a shadow of its former glory. Nevertheless, it is worth visiting at low tide, when a few thousand waders – largely dunlin and curlew but also bar-tailed and black-tailed godwits – explore areas of the flats best suited to their particular feeding style. Ringed plovers pause and probe. Dunlin scurry and peck. Godwits stride and poke. Curlews lope and prod. There is much to enjoy.

Some Teesmouth denizens can be seen anywhere. Short-eared and barn owls hunt over a wide range, and you may bump into a red fox throughout the grazing marshes. A few peregrines winter, often resting on the Able UK floodlight towers between harrying the wildfowl of Dorman's Pool and beyond. January is a fine month to stumble across groups of scarce geese – perhaps Eurasian white-fronted – nibbling on grass at Seaton Common and elsewhere.

Carve out time for a couple of trips away from core Teesmouth. Hartlepool headland, particularly around the fish quay, is a magnet for marine birds. Red-throated diver and guillemot frequently seek shelter in the harbour, while seaduck including velvet scoter loiter offshore. Best of all, fish discards are a magnetic allure for gulls, so the fish quay is one of the best places in northeast England to see Iceland and glaucous gulls, winter visitors from Arctic latitudes.

A third 'white-winged' gull, Mediterranean gull, is sometimes present, but is more reliable at nearby Newburn, *en route* from Teesmouth. Rocky shores below the car park are also favoured by purple sandpiper and turnstone, so thoroughly deserve a stop. Check through the great crested grebes that throng offshore for red-necked grebe, a real prize of a winter visitor.

Finally, keep your eye on the local bird news in case you visit during a 'waxwing winter'. With its shocking pink mohican and bold eyeliner, the waxwing is the punkiest of birds. Breeding in Scandinavia, trilling flocks sometimes 'erupt' southwards to winter in eastern Britain. Urban areas replete with berry-rich bushes, traditionally around Middlesbrough, entice these pink posers to stay for weeks at a time. Delightful and dainty, flighty and flirty, waxwings provide a splendid counterpoint to the marine mammals that headline the weekend. 'Where's there muck...'

▲ Glaucous gull (JL)

Where to go: Teesmouth National Nature Reserve
(Ⓦ http://tinyurl.com/Teesmouth) lies midway
between Hartlepool and Redcar, c5km north of
Middlesbrough. Access is off the A178. For an overview
of sites, see Ⓦ www.teesmouthbc.com/main.aspx,
http://davebarlow.co.uk.

Heading 1.6km north along the A178 from the
A1046 junction in Port Clarence, turn east down a minor road to reach
Dorman's and Recreation Pools (⊙ NZ513226). Continue 600m north
along the A178 for **RSPB Saltholme** (⊙ NZ506231 Ⓣ 01642 546625
Ⓦ www.rspb.org.uk/reserves/guide/s/saltholme), which is 400m
south of the A178/A1185 roundabout. **Greatham Creek** is 2km north of
the RSPB reserve; park in the National Nature Reserve car park
(⊙ NZ507251) and walk 200m north to the seal-viewing platform.
From the creek, walk 700m east along the southern bank of Greatham
Creek to reach the hide at **Seal Sands** (⊙ NZ517255). From here walk
south to view **Long Drag** pools (⊙ NZ517251). Telescope essential.

For **Seaton Snook** (⊙ NZ535268), 500m northeast of the A178/
B1277 roundabout, turn east along Zinc Works Road. Park at the end,
follow the track then walk south through the dunes. Some 300m
further north on the A178, **North Gare** car park (⊙ NZ535282) is
signposted; the access road crosses **Seaton Common**. For **Newburn**
(⊙ NZ518319), park at Newburn Bridge, east of where the A178 crosses
the railway line. **Hartlepool Fish Quay** (⊙ NZ525338) is in the northeast
corner of Victoria Harbour, west of the A1049 at Hartlepool headland.

Suggested bases: Middlesbrough (Ⓦ www.visitmiddlesbrough.com),
Hartlepool (Ⓦ www.destinationhartlepool.com) and, a little further
afield but worth the trek, Yarm (Ⓦ www.yarm.com). Near Yarm
Judges Country House Hotel (Ⓣ 01642 789000 Ⓦ www.judgeshotel.
co.uk) is a quintessential English country hall with opulent, colourful
rooms in extensive grounds.

Flexibility: You should see most of the star wildlife November to
February. Harbour and grey seals are resident, but numbers are
highest June–September. January–March is best for glaucous and
Iceland gulls.

Accessibility: ② 🚶

5
Fife's seaduck fiefdom

Fife for scoter, purple sandpiper, white-tailed eagle, Mediterranean gull, otter

> 66 **Dense black rafts of scoter bob in the waves, here one moment, apparently gone the next** 99

Close January where you started: on the Scottish coast. This time your beat is east rather than west. Explore the wintry wildlife of the Kingdom of Fife: a land of geese, flanked by a sea of duck.

Spend most of the first day in Largo Bay, southwest of Kirkcaldy. There may be no finer location to watch the wintering seaduck for which Scotland is renowned. If the tide is high and the sun shining, start with the light behind you at the bay's eastern edge, Ruddon's Point. Look westwards for dense black rafts of scoters, mainly common scoter. A flash of white wings draws your attention to velvet scoters secreted among them. Check the flock carefully and you could even see surf scoter. There is no more regular British site for this North American visitor, with several birds present each winter since 1985.

Armed with telescope, you should also pick up divers and grebes. This is a great spot for black-throated diver, probably the smartest diver when in non-breeding attire. Before leaving, check Shell Bay for waders: knot, sanderling and grey plover forage on the beach, and purple sandpiper scurry across rocks.

▶ An adult white-tailed eagle in fish-grabbing plunge (JW)

January weekend 5

Now drive west to Lower Largo, mid-bay. From the car park east of the village, scan for red-breasted merganser, eider and other seaduck. There should also be red-necked grebe, albeit regrettably not in crimson summer finery. Check the stone pier behind Crusoe Hotel for roosting waders, particularly purple sandpiper. Then head west to Levenmouth. Scan the sea off Methil docks and power station for hundreds of long-tailed duck, the males adorned with the extravagant protuberance that gives the species its common name. Scaup are here too, usually just east of the sewage outflow. At your final Largo stop, gulls are the quarry. Shore Street at Buckhaven is Scotland's best site for the bandit-masked Mediterranean gull.

For what remains of the day, drive east to the photogenic harbours at Anstruther or Crail. Munch a late lunch of local fish. Then scan the gulls for possible glaucous or Iceland (both visitors from the Arctic), check the calm waters for sheltering seaduck and auks, and recce the rocks for purple sandpiper.

Having started day one on the coast, open day two inland – at Scotland's largest freshwater body. Just east of the M90 at Kinross, Loch Leven attracts numerous wintering wildfowl, notably pink-footed goose. Numbers peak at either end of winter, but a few thousand should still be around this weekend. The 'pink-feet' are accompanied by several hundred greylag goose. Unlike the feral ganders frequenting your local park pond, these are genuinely wild creatures hatched in Iceland.

Peak goose-watching time is dawn, when the nocturnal roost disperses. The best vantage point is RSPB Loch Leven. Here three hides, a visitor centre, coffee shop and cosy observation room afford great views over fields, marshes and lagoons. As well as geese and one-twentieth of Scotland's wintering whooper swans, Loch Leven hums with wintering wildfowl, notably goosander and shoveler. To appreciate duck diversity, examine the bills of this duo, which fall at opposite ends of the duck spectrum. The goosander's serrated 'sawbill' is perfect for seizing fish, while the shoveler's massive spatula perfectly sifts plant matter.

Two species with different Leven histories complete the avian cast. White-tailed eagles are recent arrivals. One or two birds from

18

a reintroduction programme in Tayside hunt on St Serf's Island. A much longer association with Loch Leven is likely for the large gang of cormorants. One of Leven's smaller islands is named Scart, an old Norwegian moniker for cormorant.

Loch Leven is not just about birds. Climbing Vane Hill, south of the visitor centre, you may see roe deer. Walk east from Kindatie car park to check the burns for aquatic mammals: conceivably otter, or water shrew. And search Levenmouth Plantation pines for red squirrel, recolonising the area in the absence of the pox that has ravaged populations elsewhere.

After lunch at the reserve café, return coastwards to the Eden estuary, north of the university and golfing town of St Andrews. At high tide, waders roost on the saltmarsh. Look north from the layby between Edenside and Guardbridge for greenshank and Scotland's largest flock of black-tailed godwit. You can also view the Eden from Coble Shore, 1km northeast, and Balgove bay. Both are good for 'pale-bellied' brent goose and pintail. Around the estuary mouth, Outhead car park is a viewpoint for harbour seal, seaduck (notably goldeneye and long-tailed duck) and the odd Slavonian grebe. As afternoon wanes, keep an ear out for the few thousand pink-footed geese that roost here.

If you are not yet sated with seaduck, finish the weekend by scanning waves at St Andrews. A few thousand scoter and scaup bob offshore, appearing and disappearing in the swell. An afternoon visit enables you to sift through them with the light behind you. Scan the bay until daylight has ebbed.

Practicalities

Where to go: Largo Bay is accessed at various points from the A917. For **Ruddon's Point** (❂ NO454004), leave the A917 at the crossroads just west of Kilconquhar Loch, following signs for Shell Bay/Kincraig Caravan Park. In the caravan park, turn left at the T-junction and continue for 400m to park. For **Lower Largo**, use the public car park east of the village (❂ NO423026). At **Levenmouth**, park at the car park by the River Leven mouth (❂ NO382004). At **Buckhaven**, Shore Street is south of the B944 (❂ NO370979). Anstruther (❂ NO569034) and Crail (❂ NO611074) are northeast of Largo Bay, along the A917.

View **Loch Leven** from car parks at Kirkgate Park (❂ NT127017), Burleigh Sands (❂ NT135042) and Findatie (❂ NT170994), and use these as a base for walks (Ⓦ www.lochlevenheritagetrail.co.uk/walks. html, www.nnr-scotland.org.uk/loch-leven). Also visit trails and hides at **RSPB Loch Leven** (❂ NT160990 Ⓣ 01577 862355 Ⓦ www.rspb.org. uk/lochleven). **Eden estuary** viewpoints and car parks include Coble Shore (❂ NO468194), Outhead (❂ NO495198) and Balgove Bay (park in the golf club's Eden Course car park). Scan **St Andrews Bay** from West Sands Road, east of the junction of the A91 and A915, from the British Golf Museum (turn right at the beach end of Golf Place), from the grassy bank between the museum and The Scores, or from East Scores, east of the Castle. Detailed information is at Ⓦ www.the-soc. org.uk/fife-coast-sites.htm.

Suggested bases: St Andrews (Ⓦ www.stayinstandrews.com), Kirkcaldy (Ⓦ www.scottishaccommodationindex.com/kirkcaldy.php), Leven and Anstruther. For general Fife accommodation, see Ⓦ www.visitfife.com/accommodation. **The Grange** (Ⓣ 01333 310842 Ⓦ www.thegrangeanstruther.com) at Anstruther is an elegant Edwardian house with south-facing views across the Firth of Forth.

Flexibility: The end of November through to mid March would work well, as the seaduck and other specialities occur throughout much of the winter.

Accessibility: ②

Touting for Tarka

Northumberland for otter, red squirrel, great variety of ducks, Mediterranean gull, red kite

> 66 **The diver eventually surfaces. Low-slung, head and back barely visible... it's an otter!** 99

From the comparative comfort of a hide overlooking a coastal pool, you spot a dog swimming. This cues a grumble about negligent owners and their pets invading a nature reserve. Then the 'dog' dives. You do a double-take, confused: canines are not known for sub-aqua pursuits. A minute later, the diver surfaces. It slinks low in the water, head and back barely visible. You finally twig what you are watching: not a dog, but a dog (male) otter!

Start your otter-watching odyssey at five reserves stretching the 10km of Druridge Bay: Hauxley, East Chevington, Druridge Bay Country Park, Druridge Pool and Cresswell Pond. Divide the day between them – and throw in a wild wander along the wintry bay.

The first two sites are prime real estate for otter (although favoured locations can vary between years). As *Tarka the Otter* aptly demonstrates, there is perhaps no better loved British mammal than this largely aquatic relative of weasels. There may be few areas where one is more easily seen. Individuals fish on the pools at any time of day, blithely ignorant of human admirers semi-concealed behind shoreline screens. Nationwide, otters have bounced back following withdrawal of the pesticides that caused their demographic decline. But even during this population crash, they never deserted Northumberland.

▶ Otter: as alert to danger as it is to the possibility of prey (EN/FLPA)

When the otter has slunk off, watch wildfowl. All Druridge reserves have freshwater pools – some relics from coal-mining operations that dominate the local landscape and economic history – which are a beacon to ducks. Meanwhile, the pools' proximity to the coast means you need not walk far to see ducks that prefer saltwater. With luck, you may see 16 of Britain's 19 regularly wintering species – a feat probably impossible anywhere else.

The trick is knowing what to look for where. In shallow freshwater and on flooded pasture (Budge Field at Druridge Pools, say), search for teal such as wigeon and pintail. Scrutinise deeper water for goldeneye, scaup and the three 'sawbills': goosander, red-breasted merganser and, after cold snaps, the punk-crested smew. Offshore, scan for scoters.

There are other waterfowl too. Two thousand pink-footed goose winter, often harbouring stragglers such as tundra bean or Eurasian white-fronted goose. A few whooper swan may be present. Inspect fields for grey partridge, a declining species in southern Britain but surviving in Northumberland. In February, members of the gamebird coveys flirt: males scamper like rotund clockwork toys as they court females with hyperactive, vocal displays.

Check reedbeds for grey heron, water rail and occasionally bittern. Particularly in late afternoon, watch open areas for barn or short-eared owls. And pause at the feeding station at Druridge Bay Country Park to photograph yellowhammer, tree sparrow, brambling and siskin among the commoner seed-eating birds.

▲ Flocks of wigeon whistle as they come into land. (DF)

At some point in the day, wander the rolling sand dunes and beach. The sense of space proffered by Druridge makes the weekend worthwhile in itself. Perusing the white-capped bay, look for grebes, divers and more seaduck. On the beach, sanderling and ringed plover scurry, halt and peck. Dunes provide hidden foraging grounds for larks, finches and buntings, notably the subtly delectable twite.

Day two begins at Newbiggin, a little way south of Druridge Bay. On the beach south of town, your target is Mediterranean gull. Adults may be assuming striking summer finery: a bold combination of black, white and scarlet. 'Med' gulls first wintered at Newbiggin in 1996; now up to a dozen do so. Easy viewing of the colour- and metal rings sported by many birds has revealed interesting life histories. Most emanate from the Low Countries – but some from as far as Poland and Serbia.

Travelling 4km west, you reach Queen Elizabeth II Country Park, another former colliery site. Particularly in cold weather, the lake can hold goosander, scaup and smew. Pink-footed and other geese throng in nearby fields. Worth calling in!

Plessey Woods Country Park, a pleasant riverside woodland for an hour's meander, lies 6km further southwest. The River Blyth presents another tout for Tarka, but seeing spraints (fishy faeces) is easier than animals. Whilst searching the river, however, you should encounter dipper and kingfisher; both have loud calls designed for audibility above rushing water. Red squirrel clings on: enquire at the visitor centre for locations of recent sightings. Easier to see are roe deer and woodland birds such as nuthatch, treecreeper and woodpeckers.

Finish the weekend in style by enjoying one of England's most successful reintroduction schemes. If you don't visit Gigrin Farm later this month (see *February, 3* pages 29–32), then treat yourself here to red kites. At Nine Arches viaduct in the lower Derwent valley southwest of Gateshead, up to 20 birds materialise during late afternoon to roost. Revel in close flyovers from these resplendent raptors, wreathed in the supine winter sun and tails twisting as they navigate the upcurrent of evening air.

▶ A young red squirrel: the species's population and range have declined substantially since the introduction of the non-native grey squirrel. (JL)

Practicalities

Where to go: All **Druridge Bay** sites (Ⓦ www.druridge bay.org.uk/about; Ⓦ www.nwt.org.uk/reserves) lie along minor roads east of the A1068 between Amble-by-the-sea and Ellington. From north to south: **Hauxley** (☀ NU285023); **Druridge Bay Country Park** (☀ NU272998 Ⓣ 01670 760968 Ⓦ http://tinyurl.com/Druridgebay); **East Chevington** (☀ NZ270990); **Druridge Pool** (☀ NZ275963) and **Cresswell Pond** (☀ NZ283944).

View **Newbiggin** south beach (☀ NZ310875) from the road east of the B1334. **Queen Elizabeth II Country Park** (☀ car park: NZ284894) is off the A189 immediately north of Ashington. **Plessey Woods Country Park** (☀ NZ245792) is at the junction of A192 and A1068 between Morpeth and Cramlington. For **Nine Arches viaduct** (☀ NZ181599), park in Winlaton Mill at the junction of the A694 and Mill Lane; walk southwest through Derwent Walk Country Park for 1km along the 'Red Kite Trail' to the viaduct. For a local wildlife guide, try Northern Experience Wildlife Tours (Ⓣ 01670 827465 Ⓦ www.northernexperiencewildlifetours.co.uk; see advert, page 219).

Suggested bases: Amble (Ⓦ www.visitnorthumberland.com/amble), Ashington (Ⓦ www.ashington-ne.co.uk), Morpeth (Ⓦ www.morpethweb.com) and Newbiggin (Ⓦ www.newbigginbythesea.co.uk).

Flexibility: Any weekend November–February would work well, but early in the new year, particularly after a cold snap, is best.

Accessibility: ②

Bedding down

Thistleyhaugh (Ⓣ 01665 570 629 Ⓦ www.thistleyhaugh.co.uk) is an ivy-strewn Georgian farmhouse located on the secluded banks of the River Coquet. The five luxurious, en-suite rooms will transport you back in time. Sate your appetite with four-course evening meals.

Whirling waders, gathering geese, aerial attacks

Lancashire for otter, raptors, pink-footed goose, starling roost, scarlet elf cup

"Huge avian congregations and an abundance of predators: welcome to Lancashire's winter hotspots"

A hectare's worth of pink-footed geese erupts into the air, spooked. A marsh harrier moseys by; it's no threat, but the geese take no chances. A seething mass of dunlin wheels above the estuary mud, scarpering. A peregrine pursues a laggard; the waders' hysteria is warranted. A football crowd of starling flecks the evening sky, shape-shifting. A merlin zips through; the murmuration loses a member. Huge avian congregations and an abundance of predators: welcome to Lancashire's winter hotspots.

If ever a wildlife site warranted a full-day visit, it is Martin Mere. One of the Wildfowl and Wetland Trust's premier protected areas, this was England's largest lake until drained in the 19th century. Nowadays, assiduous management has created seasonally flooded grasslands, lakes and scrapes. Wildfowl winter here in huge numbers. Astutely positioned hides offer mind-blowing views: bring your camera.

Although wild, the waterbirds are fed daily; enjoy the commotion from Swan Lake Hide or the Raines Observatory. Top billing goes to

▲ Barn owls routinely hunt by day during winter. (JL)

nearly 2,000 whooper swan – imposing birds with bills like roman noses – with the odd Bewick's swan mixed in. Early February sees 10,000 pink-footed goose roosting on the reserve, many of which graze the fields by day. Among thousands of wigeon and teal, savour several hundred pintail, an elegant duck that is elongated at both ends.

Shelduck occupy the middle ground between duck and goose, displaying characteristics of both. A thousand winter here, more than at any other inland site. On muddy or grassy terrain, look for brown hare and waders. A couple of thousand lapwing predominate, but there are up to 60 ruff too – one of England's largest wintering flocks. After lunch in the Mere Side Café, digest in the Janet Kear Hide. Among common finches and tits adorning the feeders, there might be willow tit, tree sparrow, treecreeper and brambling. A stealthy stoat may lurk nearby.

Refreshed, head back to the main action. Martin Mere excels for watching raptors hunt. If geese, ducks or waders suddenly vault skywards, flick your eyes around until you spot the darting shape or looming spectre that provoked the panic. The 'darter' could be a peregrine, merlin or sparrowhawk, the 'loomer' a marsh or hen harrier, short-eared or barn owl. Ron Barker Hide is the best vantage point: sit back and peer out until dusk halts proceedings.

Spend the next day at two renowned reserves near Carnforth, one hour north: RSPB Leighton Moss and RSPB Hest Bank at Morecambe Bay. Your order of visit hinges on tide times. Visit Hest Bank at least one hour either side of peak water, and schedule Leighton Moss around this.

The sandflats and creeks of Morecambe Bay provide vast and vital feeding grounds for 200,000 shorebirds. During the hour before high tide, spectacular swirls of dunlin and knot gather to roost at Hest Bank. The waders whoosh one way then the other, alternately shimmering black then white in a bid to bamboozle marauding peregrines. Palls of bar-tailed godwits and Britain's biggest congregation of piebald, orange-billed oystercatchers join the throng. As the tide retreats and exposes invertebrate-rich mud, examine the waders' different feeding strategies. The leggier and longer-billed the species, the more sedate its foraging and the deeper its bill penetrates the flats.

At Leighton Moss, start with the reedbed specialities for which the reserve is cherished. The northern hides (Public, Lower and Lillian's) are best. February is a great time to see bitterns along reedy fringes, particularly when freezing nights concentrate open water. In icy conditions, water rails – laterally flattened to manoeuvre between reed fronds – are compelled to break cover. Bearded tits skulk in winter, but you might spy one visiting grit trays along the causeway or the path to Lower Hide.

Otters are regularly seen here: a rumpus among the coots often signals their presence. The northern hides are best, at either end of the day. Pools fringed by tufted sedge attract ducks. Teal, shoveler and gadwall dabble on the edges; goldeneye and goosander dive in the open water. Red deer stags love the area around Griesdale and Tim Jackson hides, particularly in mild weather. As you walk the wooded path to these hides, look out for nuthatch, treecreeper, marsh tit and the enchanting scarlet elf cup fungus.

If time remains, wander south to view the saltmarsh at the Allen and Eric Morecambe hides. Wigeon and greylag goose graze here. Spotted redshank and greenshank leg their way across the pools. Peregrines hunt the ducks, and merlins chase small birds such as meadow pipits.

Be sure to return to the reedbeds for dusk to enjoy up to 50,000 starlings massing to roost. The flock behaves as if a single organism, changing direction and form as it seeks to confuse potential predators. This living smoke cloud produces its own breeze, rippling water and rushing air around you. A fitting finale to your Lancastrian weekend.

Practicalities

Where to go: **WWT Martin Mere Wetland Centre**
(⬥ SD428144 ① 01704 895181 Ⓦ www.wwt.org.uk/
visit-us/martin-mere) is signposted from the A59,
northwest of Burscough. No access outside visiting
hours. The entrance to **RSPB Leighton Moss** (⬥ SD478750
① 01524 701601 Ⓦ www.rspb.org.uk/reserves/guide/l/
leightonmoss) is off Storrs Lane in Silverdale, 10km north
of Carnforth. At Morecambe Bay, **RSPB Hest Bank** (⬥ SD467666
① 01524 701601 Ⓦ www.rspb.org.uk/reserves/guide/m/
morecambebay) is open at all times. The car park is just west of
the level crossing, off the A5105 3.2km northeast of Morecambe.
Details on Lancashire's birding hotspots are at
Ⓦ www.lancasterbirdwatching.org.uk/siteguide.

Suggested bases: Southport (Ⓦ www.visitsouthport.com), Lancaster,
Carnforth and Morecambe (Ⓦ www.citycoastcountryside.co.uk).
The Sun (① 01524 66006 Ⓦ www.thesunhotelandbar.co.uk) in
Lancaster is a boutique hotel and eatery offering modern rooms with
feature walls.

Flexibility: Any weekend between November and early March will be
exciting. Starling and scarlet elf cup can occur any time in this period.
January and February are best for whooper swan and raptors, but the
biggest goose numbers are in late autumn. Bitterns are most evident
after a cold snap. Otter is resident.

Accessibility: ①

Whooper swans at Martin Mere: a special experience (AB)

8 Kite-flying

**Powys for red kite, raven, dipper, polecat,
Wilson's filmy fern**

> " Kites plummet,
> adeptly grabbing a
> beefy morsel in their
> talons from amidst
> a seething, screeching
> mass of feather "

Two hundred years ago, they commonly scavenged scraps from the backstreets of London. Fifty years ago, persecution had reduced their range to isolated valleys in mid-Wales and their population to perhaps 100 individuals. Now, thanks to reintroductions by farsighted conservationists, they are once more a familiar and striking sight across Britain. Few birds have experienced such a demographic rollercoaster. Red kites are well and truly back.

That red kites can be now seen in several areas, however, does not make it any less special to enjoy these long-winged raptors in their core domain of Powys. And nowhere is more spectacular than at Gigrin Farm. Each afternoon, on a hillside between the Elan and Wye valleys, farm managers spread butchers' off-cuts over an open grassy area. Take your seat in one of several hides and enjoy the showtime that is mealtime.

First on the set – pre-empting the offal-bearing tractor – are carrion crows, rooks and jackdaws. If birds had lips to lick, these coal-plumaged corvids would surely be salivating. Listen for the coarse croak that signifies the arrival of their heftier brethren, ravens. On nearby

▲ Red kite stooping groundwards (JL)

fenceposts common buzzards bide their time. Secluded in distant trees, you may decipher the shape of a few kites, similarly sanguine about the bloody gifts on offer.

At last, the odd buzzard or kite, normally an adult, sheds inhibitions and stoops to the feast. Then, as if in response to a starting gun audible exclusively to avian ears, feathered hell breaks loose. From every direction, buzzards and kites rush in. The kites plummet, adeptly grabbing a beefy morsel in their talons from amidst a seething, screeching mass of feather.

Fully 600 birds – 400 of them kites – frequently attend this frenzied feast, and it can be hard to know where to look. Thrill to the kites' aerial acrobatics, as bird after bird swoops down, wings and legs outstretched, before wheeling and wiggling upwards. Or look up to the skies for bickering birds: some kites are pirates, pursuing others until they reluctantly release their meaty prize.

The more you look, the more you see. Adult red kites, resplendent in russet regalia. Immature kites, streaked below. Kites marked with coloured wing-tags so conservationists can track their movements. And kites with plumage anomalies: a bird with a few white wing-feathers,

▲ This red kite, undisturbed by the presence of common buzzards and ravens, has been wing-tagged as part of a research project. (JL)

or one in creamy, ghostly garb. One winter the throng even attracted a black kite, a vagrant from continental Europe.

Suddenly, after three hours, the meat and the meat-eaters are noticeable by their absence. The curtain on the Gigrin show has fallen, and you exhale for what feels like the first time in days. Time for a cuppa, perhaps. Or, equally, time to explore the rest of the farm.

Gigrin happens to be a prime site to get to grips with one of Britain's most elusive mammals. Polecats – ancestor of the domestic ferret – are resident at Gigrin, and have even bred beneath the hides. Your best bet is to enquire where on the farm the animals have been seen recently, and then ask permission to stay until dusk. But don't get your hopes up: polecats are elusive critters. You may have a better chance of seeing one bounce across the road on a dusk drive through Glasfynydd forest around Usk Reservoir, c30km southwest in the Brecon Beacons National Park in Powys. Such a nocturnal encounter would provide a fitting finale to the day.

Three options stand out for daylight hours on the second day. The first is to return to Gigrin: particularly worthwhile if the sun is shining or snow is lying on the ground, when the kites will be lit from above and below. You might also make time for a wander along the Woodland Trail, which passes a badger sett and should enable you to see woodpeckers and nuthatch, and watch the finches at the farm's bird-feeders.

The alternatives, both good for a rugged wander, are the Elan Valley and Nant Irfon. Nationally important for mosses and lichens, Elan blends ancient woodlands, upland mires and hay meadows. Nant Irfon is a spectacular rocky valley with moorland and oak woodlands. In both areas, look along the river for dipper and grey wagtail. In the woodland keep alert for the secretive hawfinch and listen for the 'chip chip' call of common crossbills. Search the darkest and dankest of mossy rocks for Wilson's filmy fern. And at Dol-y-mynach Reservoir in Elan, look for goldeneye and, if you're exceptionally fortunate, a flitting, hyperactive water shrew. But, above all, enjoy those kites.

▶ Dipper: a characteristic denizen of rocky rivers in Wales (ML/FLPA)

Where to go: Gigrin Farm (☀ SN980677 ☎ 01597 810243 ⓦ www.gigrin.co.uk) lies east of the A470, 1.5km south of Rhayader. The farm opens at 13.00, with feeding times of 14.00 (end October to end March) and 15.00 (end March to end October). A modest charge is payable for access to standard or more spacious photographers' hides. **Elan Valley** (☀ SN928646) is 5km southwest of Rhayader along the B4518. **Nant Irfon** (☀ SN844540) lies c12km along a minor road leading northwest from Llanwrtyd Wells towards Tregaron; park in the riverside layby west of the road.

Suggested bases: Rhayader (ⓦ www.rhayader.co.uk) and Builth Wells (ⓦ www.builth-wells.co.uk).

Flexibility: Kites are present all year, but numbers are highest in winter. The other target species can be seen year round.

Accessibility: ①

▶ You will need sharp eyes and considerable luck to chance upon a polecat. (SL/FLPA)

Bedding down

Rhedyn (☎ 01982 551944 ⓦ www.rhedynguesthouse.co.uk) is a retreat in the tranquil, bird-filled Irfon Valley 5km west of Builth Wells. It features delightful bedrooms with

exposed walls and neat touches; the friendly hosts cook fabulous food so be sure to take up the dinner option.

9 Dark Peak, white hare

Peak District, Derbyshire for mountain hare, red deer, goshawk, raven, red grouse

> **" If the mountain hare sees you before you spot it, it will arc away, white bottom bouncing "**

Hares and late winter go hand in hand (or is it paw in paw?). Fitting, then, that you spend the final weekend of the second month searching for long-legged, long-eared 'lagomorphs' (the collective term for hares and rabbits).

But there's a twist. It is not the well-known, widely distributed brown hare that you seek, but its wilder, scarcer, more patchily located and fell-dwelling relative: mountain hare.

The hare duo are quite different concepts. The mountain hare is an indigenous species – unlike its relative, which was introduced to Britain in the Iron Age. And unlike brown hares, mountain hares change plumage to maintain camouflage across the seasons: brown in summer, white in winter. And mountain hares are well named, occurring in Britain only above 500m altitude. But they are still hares – and so still 'box'!

The Peak District holds England's only mountain hares. The native population died out 6,000 years ago; current inhabitants are descended from animals introduced in the late 19th century to meet the hunting appetite of Victorian gentry. Today, mountain hares have again made their home in the rugged moorlands of the northern

▶ Mountain hare, clad in a snowy coat for winter. (JC/FLPA)

Goshawk: garbed like a sparrowhawk but the size of a buzzard. (PM/FLPA)

Peak District, named 'Dark Peak' in recognition of bleak heather-clad terrain atop millstone grit. The best site to find hares is Dove Stone Reservoir in the extreme northwest of the Peaks.

From the main car park, walk past the sailing club, cross the bridge, then turn right uphill towards Chew Reservoir. When you reach the boulder fields, start searching. As you walk, scan ahead of you to avoid the hare spotting you first. It will then burst up, white bottom bouncing, and arc away (unlike a brown hare, which slaloms).

Largely nocturnal, a mountain hare spends most daytime hours hunkering down in sheltered sunny spots, only black-tipped ears betraying its presence. Look beneath large rocks high on both valley slopes and on rocky outcrops above Whimberry Moss and around Alphin Pike. The joy of a late February visit is that most hares should still have white pelage that gleams against the dark, snow-free gritstone. Mountain hares are largely solitary, but gather in 'community groups' in early spring. So once you find one, you should come across several. With luck, you may even chance upon a female boxing away the attentions of libidinal males.

The concentration of herbivores attracts mammalian predators. Stoat and red fox are regularly seen hunting. There are avian carnivores too. Peregrines inhabit craggy outcrops and secluded ledges (look from the viewpoint near the picnic area, on the shore opposite the car park), watching for an inattentive pigeon. On the moorland tops, merlins pursue pipits.

You will need sharp eyes to spot these predators. For other birds, keep your ears pricked. High-altitude species are frequently detected on call, particularly in early spring when pair bonds need forming and territories defending. A bubbling call evokes the wildness of these hills. It emanates from a curlew, freshly returned from an estuarine winter. The gruff barks of a pair of raven may herald a plummeting display flight. Pairs develop their own unique set of vocalisations, thought to strengthen their bond and facilitate recognition at distance. A throaty exclamation signals a territorial male red grouse. It bursts into the air, stalls, then parachutes down, tail spread and wings whirring, before bowing, tail fanned and wings drooped. As you cross streams, listen for the strident song of a dipper: its high decibel count is a response to life amidst the noisy torrents.

After a wild walk on the hilltops, indulge in a warm bath, decent meal and comfy bed. Start the following day in the depths of the Dark Peak, to the southeast. Three reservoirs in the upper Derwent Valley – Ladybower, Derwent and Howden – offer good raptor-watching. On a fine day, a couple of hours skywatching from Stony Bank Corner (aka Windy Corner) should reveal common buzzard, sparrowhawk, kestrel, peregrine and raven. If you are lucky, you may spy a pair of goshawk 'dancing' high in the sky – although illegal persecution has depleted numbers to the extent that this is no longer a sure thing.

Once activity dwindles, try other habitats. Starting at the feeding station at Fairholmes, search the forests for siskin, brambling, nuthatch and perhaps common crossbill. If you are feeling energetic, follow the valley northwards from Slippery Stones, above Howden Reservoir. Check streams for dipper and red-breasted merganser. Search crags for raptors and raven; moorland for red grouse and perhaps mountain hare.

In the afternoon, pamper yourself with a gentle end to an otherwise rugged trip. The grounds of Chatsworth House are an archetypal English country estate. Open parkland and ancient trees beside the River Derwent are home to herds of red and fallow deer: enjoyable and pleasant, but feral creatures rather than truly wild. The contrast with your time watching hardy mountain hares could scarcely be greater.

◀ 'Go-back, go-back, go-back...': the unequivocal call of the male red grouse (KD)

35

Where to go: RSPB Dove Stone (☀ SE013036
① 01484 861148 Ⓦ www.rspb.org.uk/reserves/guide/
d/dovestone) lies 8km east of Oldham in the extreme
northwest of the **Peak District National Park**. Leave
Greenfield, southeast on the A669 then turn east onto
the A635 towards Holmfirth. After 500m, turn right
onto Bank Lane and follow signs to the reservoir
car park. The **Upper Derwent valley** lies north of
the A57 between Glossop and Sheffield. If the road is closed north
of Fairholmes National Trust car park (☀ SK173894), a shuttle bus
will run north to Howden Reservoir, passing Stony Bank Corner
(☀ SK168932). **Chatsworth Park** (☀ SK262702 ① 01246 565300
Ⓦ www.chatsworth.org) is along the B6012 off the A619 between
Bakewell and Baslow. Entrance fee payable.

Suggested bases: Mossley, Glossop and Bakewell (Ⓦ www.bakewell-
accommodation.co.uk). **Bird's Nest Cottage** in Glossop (① 01457
853478 Ⓦ www.birdsnestcottage.co.uk) has five en-suite bedrooms
set in a secluded woodland garden and offers spa treatments to boot.

Flexibility: Any weekend during February and March should work.
Mountain hares are resident, but easiest to see
when their white pelage contrasts with
a snow-free landscape. Goshawk
displays between February
and May, but particularly late
February and March.

Accessibility: ⑤ 🚶

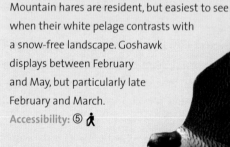

▶ Peregrine: a territorial
male calling. (JL)

10 From rifles to Ratty

Greater London & Kent for water vole, water shrew, harvest mouse, heronry, rook roost

Milling between estuary and lagoon, or meandering by reed-fringed channel, you hear it. *Plop*! Quiet, but unmistakable. The sound of mammal entering water. Specifically, the noise of spring's first water vole

> ❝ As adults whoosh into the treetop heronry, their serenity and curves transform into urgency and angles ❞

belly-flopping from bank to ditch. You have found 'Ratty', the rodent enshrined in cultural history through Kenneth Grahame's illustrated classic *The Wind in the Willows*.

Few British mammals have suffered as catastrophic a population crash as this denizen of well-vegetated dykes. The species has disappeared from 94% of former sites. Yet the resurgence has started, thanks to dedicated conservationists. RSPB Rainham Marshes, the organisation's diamond in the land of geezer, spearheads the recovery.

London's finest reserve, just west of the intersection of the Thames Estuary and M25 orbital motorway, Rainham harbours thousands of water voles. There is nowhere better to recce Ratty than these medieval marshes, which served as a firing range throughout the 20th century. Voles largely winter underground (resting but not hibernating) but by early March they should be out and about. Head clockwise around the reserve from the architecture of the award-winning visitor centre.

▶ Grey heron: a colonial breeder (JL)

Channels in the first 200m are prime terrain. Linger on bridges, watching for movement, ears pricked for that waterbound leap.

Vole enjoyed, wander the all-weather path that encircles a series of scrapes. The air resounds with whistling wigeon and piping teal. Lapwing rally by the thousand. After scavenging on the adjacent landfill site, gulls perform their ablutions. If identification challenges are your thing, sift through the gathering looking for two local specialities: yellow-legged and caspian gulls.

Where the path bisects reedbeds, loiter. Reed buntings feed prominently on reedmace. Bearded tits often winter, the moustachioed males brightening a dingy day. Cetti's warblers holler from reedy scrub. And, if you're really lucky along the northern boardwalk, you may bump into the rarely seen harvest mouse as it munches on reed heads.

Head to the Thames foreshore, where ducks, waders and gulls loaf. At high tide, pay particular attention to floating detritus, which a trio of pipits – meadow, rock and water – probe for small invertebrates while a water shrew, if you are lucky, may zip around hyperactively or a harvest mouse scurry into cover. Three amazing small mammals would make a remarkable morning!

After a restorative lunch overlooking estuary and scrapes at the snug visitor centre, cross the Dartford road bridge into Kent. On the Hoo Peninsula, RSPB Northward Hill offers viewpoints and trails over and through damp grassland, scrub and woodland. Bird-feeders by Bromhey Farm bustle with finches and tits; groups of redwing and fieldfare chatter nervously nearby. Scan from the marshland viewpoint for a miscellany of aerial predators: kestrel, marsh harrier, sparrowhawk and common buzzard, for sure. Peregrine and barn owl, most likely. And merlin and short-eared owl, quite possibly.

Drag yourself away east for two specific spectacles. Languidly flapping towards the wood are grey herons, dozens of them. Northward Hill hosts Britain's largest colony of our second-tallest bird. As adults whoosh into the treetop heronry, their serenity and curves transform into urgency and angles. Spend the last hour of light here, and then either stay put as darkness encroaches or return to the marshland viewpoint. It's time for the second spectacle: a cawing roost of 4,000 jackdaws and

▲ Rainham is probably the best place in Britain to see water vole. (JL)

rooks, black birds gathering on the marsh before streaming into the wooded obscurity. When silence finally descends, depart.

Next day, explore the Isle of Sheppey, the starkest wilderness within an hour of London. Bumping along the Elmley Marshes access track, you pass through swarms of lapwing and starling. Bleak skies heave with crying birds, the pandemonium prompted by a peregrine. Park at Kingshill Farm, then hike east to poolside hides, the path dividing grazing marshes from estuarine saltmarsh. Wigeon and teal forage by the thousand, pintail and shelduck by the hundred. A group of Eurasian white-fronted geese merges with a bevy of greylag. At high tide, waders roost on the pools: several hundred each of black-tailed godwit and grey plover, plus a few thousand dunlin. Falcons, harriers, buzzards and owls are enticed by these masses.

Back at your car, enjoy a half-hour respite from the windchill by driving to Sheppey's eastern tip, checking roadside fields for brown hare. Fields near Harty Church hold 'dark-bellied' brent goose, skylark and sometimes Lapland bunting. If you have time, walk north to the Swale National Nature Reserve for more of the same.

Your weekend culminates at the RSPB viewpoint at Capel Fleet, looking for the declining corn bunting while awaiting the arrival of roosting raptors: a score of marsh harriers and the odd common buzzard, hen harrier, merlin and peregrine. Better still, Capel Fleet is Britain's finest site for rough-legged buzzard, a rare visitor from Scandinavia with an addiction to Sheppey. Finally, as daylight evaporates, the rodent-eating nightshift emerges. Barn owl is a silent, beautiful and ethereal... killer. May Ratty be safely ensconced back underground!

Rooks congregate in large numbers prior to roosting. (DT)

Where to go: RSPB Rainham Marshes (☀ TQ552792
① 01708 899840 ⓦ www.rspb.org.uk/rainham
marshes) is in Purfleet: access is from the A1090 just
south of its junction with the A1306. For **RSPB Northward
Hill** (☀ TQ768765 ① 01634 222480 ⓦ www.rspb.org.uk/
northwardhill), head north on the A228 from the M2,
junction 1. Exit at High Halstow, then head west
towards Cooling. After 2km, the reserve is signposted to the right.
Elmley Marshes (☀ TQ924698 ① 01795 665969) is signposted from
the A249, north of the M2, junction 5. Use the old bridge rather than
the new flyover. For **Harty Ferry** (☀ TR015659), **Swale National Nature
Reserve** (☀ TR033672) and **Capel Fleet** (☀ TR023682), return to the
A249, then follow the B2231 east. Between Eastchurch and Leysdown,
turn south on a minor road signposted 'Harty Ferry Inn', which leads
to the eponymous pub on the Swale shore (☀ TR015659).

Suggested bases: Rochester (ⓦ www.cometorochester.co.uk),
Chatham, Gillingham and Sittingbourne (ⓦ www.iknow-kent.co.uk).
Sensitively renovated, the **Old Vicarage** (① 01795 886136 ⓦ www.
oldvicaragedoddington.co.uk) is a Grade II-listed property showcasing
period bedrooms.

Flexibility: Late February to mid-March is the best time; water voles
tend to be above ground February through to September. November
to February is best for water shrew and harvest mouse. Grey heron
breeds between February and May. Jackdaws and rooks roost
throughout winter. Raptors and geese are present October to March.

Accessibility: ②

▲ Look for harvest mouse along Rainham's northern boardwalk. (CD)

11

Serpents of the sandlings

Suffolk for adder, Dartford warbler, otter, brown hare, mossy stonecrop

> " Pausing to soak up the spring sun, you notice a fellow sunbather... an adder! "

The early spring sun proves simply too pleasant, so you pause on your heathland walk to soak it up. The morning air is further warmed by effortless southerly winds that whisper the evolution of the seasons. You bask. Then, with a grimace, you notice a dog turd a few metres along the sandy path. Suddenly, the 'turd' flicks out a tongue! Not coiled faeces, but a curled serpent. Like you, the male adder is lapping up solar rays, sprawling on sandy soil beneath a gorse bush.

Few places are better than the Suffolk sandlings to watch adders freshly emerged from winter slumber. And few sandling sites are as good for our only venomous reptile as sheltered, south-facing slopes on Dunwich Heath. Males vacate their winter den before females and stake out territories. Early in the season, the snakes are sluggish and often allow prolonged views. As the slopes heat up and cold-blooded bodies thaw, the serpents slither off to hunt. Time too for you to meander on.

Dominated by bell heather, the sandlings have hosted a remarkable avian comeback. Extinct in Suffolk by the 1920s, Dartford

◄ Two male adders dancing, including a melanistic form 'black adder'. (SB)

Boxing or not, brown hare is a particularly prominent feature of the March countryside. (JW)

warblers recolonised 70 years later. Today, the sandlings' population is vibrant. Dunwich and Westleton heaths form the warblers' heartland. You should see several fiery-eyed males scratching out a song atop a prominent perch and additional long-tailed, punk-crested forms flitting between heathery clumps.

In terrain peppered by birch or Scots pine, listen for the liquid lullaby of a wood lark or the *yaffle* of a green woodpecker. Damper areas occupied by birches offer further interest. Birch polypore wreathe dying trees. Once used to sharpen cut-throat razors (hence the alternative name, razorstrop fungus), this unmistakable white bracket fungus can reach 20cm in diameter. If you have a botanical bent, drop to your knees and scour the ground for the diminutive and rare mossy stonecrop at one of its sole sites outside Breckland (see *March, 4* pages 49–52).

Returning to the car park above Dunwich cliffs, the trail traverses the gorse-rich territories of a pair or two of stonechat. Near the coastguard cottages, a similar-sized, smoky-brown bird shivers its russet tail: a black redstart. A classic March migrant, only adult males are coal-black, so this is a female or immature. From the clifftop, look out to sea for harbour porpoise. Up to five of these (comparatively) pint-sized cetaceans regularly cruise offshore.

End the day as you started, relaxing in the sun. Park yourself on a cliff-top bench, imbibing the vista southwards towards RSPB Minsmere. Treat yourself to a literal overview of Britain's most renowned reserve, where you will spend day two.

With its majestic diversity of habitats – scrub and scrape, wood and reed, heath and beach – Minsmere is a splendid stage for celebrating the arrival of spring. The Mediterranean breeze has accelerated the arrival of a vanguard of summer migrants. A sand martin worries its way north. A chiffchaff sings its name from the scrub. On the beach, a wheatear bobs, flashing white.

And there are further signs of the shifting seasons. The pond near the visitor centre may host a libidinous ball of mating common toad. Woodland resounds with the territorial outpourings of resident birds. The first brimstone and small tortoiseshell wing across a sunny glade. On the 'levels' in the south of the reserve, male brown hares pursue a female, which boxes away their attentions: it is 'mad March', after all. Nearby, a Cetti's warbler explodes into song where bush meets reed.

It is the reedbeds that provide the day's major interest. To see all of Minsmere's reedy specialities, you must look in, on, beside and above the sea of sedge. Deep within this painstakingly managed habitat, a bittern 'booms' as if blowing across the top of a beer bottle. Wait a while at Island Mere or Bittern Hide and you should see one of these scarce herons feeding in the reedbed fringes or offering a deep-chested, heavy-winged fly-past. Parties of bearded tit perch on stems, *ping*ing to retain contact. In water sheltered by reeds – if you are patient – a family of otter may forage, unmolested and unwary. Up above, a marsh harrier pair displays. The male circles at height before tumbling towards the reeds. In established pairs, the female locks talons with her partner, and they flail downwards conjoined.

Mossy stonecrop JL

Once you have filled your boots, explore the rest of the reserve. Rabbits thrive in the sandy hollow near the visitor centre. Mossy stonecrop blazes paths red. A muntjac grazes beside wooded trails. On 'the Scrape', Minsmere's famous lagoon, avocets bleat through upturned bills: the RSPB's flagship species in its most iconic location. Nearby, stunning Mediterranean gulls display with head-bowing and mewing. As you leave for the evening, a herd of red deer hinds bumbles through the 'south belt' woods, pausing to observe you just as you paused in the Dunwich sun at the outset of the weekend.

Practicalities

Where to go: Both Dunwich Heath and RSPB Minsmere are signposted from the A12 northeast of Yoxford. For **Dunwich Heath National Trust Reserve** (☀ TM475683 ℗ 01728 648501 Ⓦ www.nationaltrust. org.uk/dunwich-heath), approach from Westleton, pass Westleton Heath on your left, turn right 1.5km before Dunwich onto Minsmere road, then continue 1.5km to the National Trust car park (fee for non-members). For **RSPB Minsmere** (☀ TM473672 ℗ 01728 648281 Ⓦ www.rspb.org.uk/ minsmere), leave Westleton village east on minor roads and follow signs. No dogs.

Suggested bases: Yoxford and Saxmundham (Ⓦ www.saxmundham. org), with villages including Eastbridge and Westleton. In Yoxford, try the remarkable **Old Methodist Chapel** (℗ 01728 668333 Ⓦ www. users.waitrose.com/~dfabrown/accommodation.htm) which offers a cosy bedroom with its own entrance.

Flexibility: Any March weekend would work. Adders emerge on sunny days from late February. Brown hares 'box' any time from late winter into late spring. The first spring migrants pass through in early March, but later in March is more reliable. Otter and Dartford warbler are resident; mossy stonecrop is easily seen in spring but does not flower until June.

Accessibility: ②

◀ Dartford warbler: a punk-crested colonist of the Suffolk sandlings (JL)

44

12 Daffs in t'dale

North Yorkshire for wild daffodil, common lizard, red grouse, goshawk, gannet

If a single swallow does not make summer, might a swathe of golden flowers hint that summer has, at last, started its journey. Welcome to one of Britain's most treasured floral displays, secluded in a valley deep in the North Yorkshire Moors. The collective carpet of wild daffodils, blooming into the mid-distance, is a sure sign that winter is ebbing.

> **❝Breathtaking blooms carpet the valley with gold into the mid-distance❞**

Don't be lulled into thinking that wild daffodils are identical to the 'daffs' in your garden, and thus not worth a visit. Wild daffs are a separate species, best distinguished from their cultivated cousins by paler yellow petals on uptilted flower-heads, with the brighter yellow corona (central protrusion) not tinged orange at its rim.

Once widespread across England and Wales, wild daffodil has declined drastically since the mid 19th century. It survives only in patchy populations, mainly in western Britain. In the east, displays such as that flanking Farndale's River Dove are the exception rather than the rule. Indeed, this distributional oddball prompts speculation that the dale's daffs stem from an old introduction, perhaps by monks.

Whatever their provenance, breathtaking blooms buoy the local economy through botanical tourism, with 30,000 people visiting the valley each spring. As flowers start to open in the first half of March, the third weekend should see a fine display while

▶ Wild daffodil, up close and personal (JL)

being a week or two shy of the peak – so you should pre-empt the hordes. Access is straightforward, thanks to a 'Daffodil Trail' looping around village and along valley, with longer walks of 5 to 15km available as you venture south from Low Mill towards Lowna.

The best daffodil belts lie between Church Houses and the bridge before Low Mill, and further south around (crowd-free) Dale End Bridge. As you walk, remember that the Dove's daffodils are wild plants rather than a horticultural exhibit: don't pick, and watch your step to avoid inadvertent trampling.

Keep half an eye out for the dale's other wildlife. Other early flowers should include wood anemone. Dipper and grey wagtail occur along river and stream: both are in song at this season. Climb to nearby moorland immediately west of the dale to look for red grouse: both Harland Moor and Rudland Rigg are good. Males should be in a territorial mood, rebuffing intruders – avian or human – with a strident '*go-bek... go-bek*' (anthropomorphically interpreted as the gamebird telling the interloper to 'go back!... go back!').

Get day two going by looking up for soaring raptors and down for sunbathing reptiles – from a single vantage point in Wykeham Forest. Success depends not merely on sharp eyes, but also on fine weather with at least moderate sun. If conditions are conducive, aim to arrive

▲ A blaze of wild daffodils flanking the River Dove. (AC/A)

at Highwood Brow by 09.00. But if the day dawns cool or damp, treat yourself to a lie-in instead.

Common lizard is the star reptile, with individuals frequently sun-worshipping on the watchpoint's wooden fence. Sheltered suntraps on the forest edge provide your best chance of adder or slow worm. This month, common toad and common frog hop towards pools that host mating frenzies, so you may bump into them anywhere. Of the raptors, you should see common buzzard, sparrowhawk and kestrel. Wykeham is also a reliable site for goshawk, particularly during its spring display, but views are often distant. Common crossbill and siskin typically fly overhead, calling.

When raptor activity dwindles and reptiles have slithered away, head to RSPB Bempton, north of the promontory of Flamborough Head. Chalk cliffs here host the southernmost seabird city on our North Sea coastline. Seabirds return from their maritime winter during February, and colonies should now be at full strength. As breeding activity peaks later in spring, you should again be ahead of the crowds. You may have tens of thousands of gannets and guillemots to yourself. What a treat: a private viewing of one of England's most special wildlife spectacles!

The show spoils you for choice. Gannet after gannet plummets into a sea soupy with auks. The razorbills and guillemots take off *en masse* to join their partners astride precarious ledges on vertical cliffs. Coming into land, they cross paths with kittiwakes. These endearing gulls with an onomatopoeic call return to their nests with a beakful of grass and mud. (Only a few puffins now breed: to see these clown-like seabirds, visit nearby Flamborough Cliffs Reserve, where paths are carpeted with a profusion of lemon-yellow cowslips.)

Before you head home, look for Bempton's other creatures. Brown hares box on the cliff-top fields. Weasels are frequently seen and harbour porpoises roll past on calm days. Tree sparrows – scarce nowadays so a treat to see – nest in the visitor centre eaves or jostle alongside corn buntings in the scrub. And, of course, it is early spring. And spring means migration. And migration may mean the first swallows. Given the proximity to the blooming daffs, perhaps our favourite hirundine at least confirms spring, if not summer?

▶ A gannet pair displaying, bills pointing skywards. (DE)

Practicalities

Where to go: **Farndale** (Ⓦ www.farndale.org/daffy)
is north of the A170 at Kirkbymoorside, between
Helmsley and Pickering. You can start a round walk
from any of three car parks: (from south to north)
Lowna Bridge (⊙ SE685910), Harland Moor (⊙ SE675928)
and Low Mill (⊙ SE672951). Additional informal car
parking is available in designated fields at Low Mill
and Church Houses (⊙ SE669974). Congestion is a problem in season,
so check whether the 'park and ride' bus service is operational from
nearby Hutton-le-Hole (Ⓦ http://www.northyorkmoors.org.uk/
moorsbus). Paths are frequently muddy.

For **Wykeham Forest**, leave the A170 at Wykeham and head
north. After 3km, you reach Highwood Brown viewpoint. Turn west
and continue 600m to the car park (⊙ SE936887), then walk 300m
north to the raptor viewpoint. **RSPB Bempton Cliffs** (⊙ TA197738
Ⓣ 01262 851179 Ⓦ www.rspb.org.uk/bemptoncliffs) is signposted
1.5km north of Bempton village, on the B1229 between Flamborough
and Filey. Seabird viewpoint is open March to October. For
breeding puffins, visit the Yorkshire Wildlife Trust's reserve at **North
Landing, Flamborough Cliffs** (⊙ TA239720 Ⓦ http://tinyurl.com/
flamborough). From Flamborough village, follow the B1255 northeast
to North Landing car park, then walk west along the clifftop path,
looking on cliffs and offshore.

Suggested bases: Pickering (Ⓦ www.pickering.uk.net), Scarborough
(Ⓦ www.scarborough.co.uk) and Filey (Ⓦ www.fileytourism.
co.uk). **Flamborough Rigg Cottage** (Ⓣ 01751 475263 Ⓦ www.
flamboroughriggcottage.co.uk) is 5km north of Pickering and offers
two tasteful bedrooms opening onto a courtyard in a delightfully
designed cottage.

Flexibility: Any weekend between March and early April should work.
Wild daffodil flowers are best early March to early April, peaking late
March. Reptiles emerge early March. Goshawk displays February–
May. Seabirds return in late February and stay until late summer. Red
grouse is resident.

Accessibility: ②

13
Wailing heath chicken run

The Brecks, Suffolk & Norfolk for stone-curlew, stoat, grape hyacinth, Breckland speedwell, fingered speedwell

This weekend may come immediately before April Fool's Day, but – whatever the title above might suggest – your focus is truth not spoof. You are indeed looking for the 'wailing heath chicken', an old Norfolk name for a truly bizarre bird. All three elements of the local moniker are somewhat apt. The bird's gangly legs and locomotion vaguely recall a domestic fowl. It inhabits lichen heathland and short, sandy turf. And its mournful call, frequently uttered by night, is very much the eerie wail of a banshee.

> " Gangly legs and goggle eyes; cryptic plumage and a banshee wail "

So what is it? Freshly returned from Mediterranean wintering quarters, the stone-curlew is a remarkable-looking wader. Goggle eyes reveal it to be a creature largely of the night; sandy plumage offers camouflage during daylight. Two-thirds of Britain's population breed in Breckland: a special bird in a very special part of East Anglia.

Breckland (or the Brecks) feels utterly different from anywhere else in Britain. Sandy or chalky nutrient-poor soils, human land-use stemming from the Stone Age and an arid, semi-continental climate create a unique mosaic of grassy heath, forest and arable land covering nearly 1,000km².

◀ Stone-curlew: no other British bird approaches it in appearance. (AS)

This uniqueness, in turn, kindles exceptional wildlife interest: wailing heath chickens headline an impressive bill.

As stone-curlews are sensitive to disturbance, most breeding sites are secret. So rather than try to locate your own, head to Weeting Heath's hides. Time your visit carefully: birds are most active early and late. With your eye in (no mean feat with this cryptically cloaked critter), you should enjoy prolonged views.

Weeting has plenty else worth watching. Rabbits, fenced in and used as a management tool, trim the grassland sward to the length demanded by stone-curlews. They attract mammalian predators, notably stoat (there may be no better place to watch it hunt) and red fox. Scanning the vicinity may reveal displaying lapwings, a little owl observing from an isolated pine and a wheatear bobbing near its rabbit-burrow nest. Stretch your legs along the 4km trail that winds through pine plantations and connects clearings. These are home to wood lark (stick to paths to avoid bothering this rare ground-nester), common crossbill, treecreeper and goldcrest.

Weeting is a must, but the panoply of cracking wildlife sites in such a small area makes selecting where else to go a tough decision. For ancient forest (and yellow star-of-Bethlehem), try Wayland Wood. For restored reedbeds (and 'booming' bitterns), RSPB Lakenheath excels. But for 'classic' Breckland, read on.

The Brecks' oldest reserve, East Wretham Heath, furnishes fantastic variety. Surface water in three small meres fluctuates with subterranean levels. If they are wet, look for common toad (perhaps 'balling' in their March mating orgy) and hunting grass snake. On heathland, particularly before mid-morning, search sheltered sunny spots for common lizard

Stoats are a major predator of Breckland rabbits. (JL)

and adder, wood lark and wheatear. In pine forests, goldcrest and common crossbill breed; a dusk visit may produce long-eared owl.

Breckland spring usually comes early, so check sandy turf for early forget-me-not, delicate flowers with five sky-blue petals. For another botanical treat, search rides carefully for mossy stonecrop, which has tiny flowers. Hugging winter-wet terrain, the stonecrop can be locally abundant around Thetford yet is otherwise absent from almost all of Britain.

Tiny, rare and localised: Breckland speedwell (JL)

These two plants hint at Breckland's floral majesty, which reaches its full steppe-like magnificence in the summer. Sixteen nationally rare or scarce flowering plants occur, of which 11 are Breckland specialities. By late March, grape hyacinth (the wild relative of your garden bloom), and fingered and Breckland speedwells should be flowering. All favour disturbed ground, so some sites are on roadside reserves adjacent to arable fields. Such is the case with grape hyacinth west of Brockley Corner, south of Thetford Forest Park. Remarkably, the most famous (and publicly accessible) site for the speedwells is on the Cloverfield housing estate in urban Thetford. Mossy stonecrop also thrives here. Enjoy – but tread carefully to avoid trampling.

Birdwise, Breckland is renowned for the swarthy, buzzard-sized goshawk. Normally reclusive hunters, pairs turn extrovert in early spring. Displaying duos 'sky dance' on fine days, circling high before plummeting to the canopy. As the best site unfortunately has no legitimate public access, try Mayday Farm. Scan the skies from the hide or the junction 500m further on. Lynford Arboretum is well known for wintering hawfinch: trees in the paddock near the southern car park are best. The immense bill of these bull-necked finches is so strong that the bird thinks nothing of cracking opening cherry stones.

Finish the weekend with a choice of mammals. For otter, try the river immediately east of Thetford town centre. Alternatively, if your journey home takes you along the A11, look for roe deer (particularly at Roudham Heath, northeast of Thetford) and muntjac (between Thetford and Barton Mills roundabout). Red deer is harder, but what a climax it would provide to your Breckland chicken run.

Practicalities

Where to go: Core **Breckland** (Ⓦ www.brecks.org) lies within an area bordered by the A11, A1065, A1075 and B1108. Weeting Heath and East Wretham Heath are Norfolk Wildlife Trust (NWT) reserves. **NWT Weeting Heath** (☀ TL757881 Ⓣ 01842 827615 Ⓦ www.norfolk wildlifetrust.org.uk/weeting) opens at the end of March, a week or two after the stone-curlews have returned; non-members pay. Leave Brandon north on the A1065, then turn left to Weeting; the car park is 2.5km west of the village. **NWT East Wretham Heath** (☀ TL913887 Ⓦ www.norfolkwildlifetrust.org.uk/ wildlife-in-Norfolk/reserves/East-Wretham-Heath.aspx) is off the A1075, 5km north of Thetford.

South of **Thetford Forest Park**, the roadside reserve for grape hyacinth (☀ TL 825713) is along the minor road connecting West Stow and Brockley Corner. In **Thetford**, the Cloverfield estate (☀ TL879833) lies at the junction of the A1066 and Rosecroft road; walk along the footpath called Green Lane. **Mayday Farm** (☀ TL795835) is west of the B1106, 4km south of Brandon; walk southwest to the radio mast and beyond. **Lynford Arboretum** (☀ TL822942 Ⓦ http://tinyurl.com/lynfordarb) is signposted along a minor road, 2km northeast of Mundford; use the southern car park for seeing hawfinch.

Suggested bases: Thetford (Ⓦ www.explorethetford. co.uk), Brandon (Ⓦ www.brandonsuffolk.com) and Mundford. Set in spacious gardens, **Glebe Country House** (Ⓣ 01842 890027 Ⓦ www. glebecountryhouse.co.uk) in Elveden (3km west of Thetford) has ten rooms of various sizes, individually decorated to match the manor-house style.

Flexibility: A weekend in late March or early April is best. The plants mentioned usually flower mid-March to early April. Stone-curlew is present late March through to September. Goshawk displays February to May, but peaks in March. Stoat is resident.

Accessibility: ②

◄ Grape hyacinth: cultivated versions eat your hearts out! (JL)

14
Sand and deliver!

Devon for sand crocus, sand lizard, wild daffodil, rockpool species, cirl bunting

A flower so petite that an adjacent blade of grass dwarfs it. A flower so localised that it occurs at just two British sites. A flower so rare that it flirts with national extinction. And a flower so reclusive that it remains

> **" What more quixotic a quarry than a flower so small, localised, rare and reclusive? "**

resolutely shut unless there is full sun. Such is the sand crocus. What more quixotic a quarry for your weekend?

Dawlish Warren, a sandy spit puncturing Devon's Exe Estuary, is a botanist's delight. Spend the morning on hands and knees as you search for rare plants. Sand crocus flowers in late March or early April. You should see them easily in short, sandy grassland that lines the compound by the visitor centre. But only if the sun shines will the lilac petals part.

Alongside the sand crocus, enjoy the delicate white flowers of both upright chickweed and subterranean clover, the latter so-named because – unlike other clovers – its seeds develop underground. Between the

▶ Get up close and personal with shore crab. (DP/FLPA)

visitor centre and main pond, look for early meadow-grass. Although early April is rather late for the throngs of mating amphibians, you should still see common toad at the pond itself.

Then walk to 'dune ridge', between the seawall and Warren Point. You may chance upon a stoat pursuing rabbits. Look carefully at sheltered sunny spots for the ridge's star species: sand lizard. Early April is a fabulous time to see this rare, stunning reptile, and the introduced population is thriving. Freshly emerged lizards bask for prolonged periods and allow close approach. The males are garbed vivid green as they gear up for the breeding season. Take care not to misidentify a common lizard, which also inhabits the ridge and can appear greenish.

Dawlish Warren holds one of the Exe Estuary's main high-tide wader roosts, best viewed from the hide overlooking the Bight. The principal participants are ringed plover, dunlin, oystercatcher, grey plover, sanderling and turnstone. At Warren Point, the distal end of the spit, the undisturbed dunes are home to skylark, and maritime plants such as sea spurge and sea-holly. Well worth the walk.

Depart Dawlish westwards for a late afternoon stroll at one of two Devon Wildlife Trust reserves. If you wish to see wild daffodils but did not venture to North Yorkshire in March (see *March, 3* pages 45–8), try the riverside at Dunsford. The bloom peaks in early March, but there should still be a reasonable display of these pale gold flowers in Cricket Pitch Glade.

The alternative walk is at Chudleigh Knighton Heath. Amidst the ling, bell heather and western gorse, there is a chance of adder absorbing solar rays before the evening chills. Peer into the depths of pools for great crested newt. But the site's speciality is somewhat smaller. Chudleigh Knighton is one of very few remaining English locations for narrow-headed ant. This globally threatened invertebrate has

▲ A pair of sand lizards basking in the wan sun of early morning. (JL)

disappeared from a swathe of southern England and has become truly rare. In heathland in the reserve's southernmost compartment, adjacent to the A38, look out for plate-sized anthills, and end the day as you started – on your hands and knees.

Spend day two at Wembury, in southwest Devon, which volunteers one of Britain's finest rockpooling experiences *and* one of its rarest songbirds. Spending the hour either side of low tide on the shore, indulge in an exciting activity oft-neglected since childhood.

The lowest tides (a few days after the new moon) expose the greatest expanse of rocky reefs and residual pools. The best gullies are those strewn with seaweed nearest the tideline. With careful searching, you should find a dozen or more species of marine marvel having emerged from winter sejourns in deeper waters. If you extract animals using a bucket (not a net), house them singly in a vessel containing seawater and repatriate the creatures to their lairs.

Beadlet anemone is common; one-third of its 7cm length comprises retractable tentacles. Yellow spots on a red column gives the strawberry anemone its name. Snakelocks anemone has purple-tipped tentacles 15cm long. Blue-rayed limpets, strip-lit with neon, cling to rocks. You may see five types of crab: common hermit, porcelain, velvet swimming, edible and shore. Small fish include rock goby, tompot blenny and common blenny. The last of these holes up under seaweed-covered rocks, relying on camouflage to elude detection.

As the tide rises, retreat to dry land. Replace pooling paraphernalia with binoculars. Harbouring sensitively managed coastal fields and hedgerows, Wembury is prime cirl bunting territory. No bird is more closely associated with Devon than this attractive, stripe-headed seedeater. A beneficiary of collaboration between conservationists and cultivators, cirl bunting populations have trebled in 20 years and are again looking healthy.

Seeing cirl buntings at Wembury requires patience. The valley footpath between village and beach is good. Likewise the coastal footpath and adjacent fields west towards Heybrook bay. Scan hedgerows and prominent perches, and listen for the dry rattling song. Once sated with southwest specialities, it's hometime.

▶ Sand crocus: a shy flower found solely at two sites in southwest England (BG/FLPA)

Practicalities

Where to go: Dawlish Warren (car park at ⊙ SX981787
① 01626 863980 Ⓦ www.dawlishwarren.co.uk)
comprises two nature reserves with open access. The
visitor centre should be your first port of call. From the
A379 Exeter–Dawlish road, follow signs east to Dawlish
Warren, pass under the railway bridge and park.
Dunsford and Chudleigh Knighton Heath are both
Devon Wildlife Trust reserves (① 01392 279244 Ⓦ www.
devonwildlifetrust.org/reserve) on the border of Dartmoor. You
can enter **Dunsford** at two points. For Steps Bridge (⊙ SX805883),
use the national park car park off the B3212 5km northeast of
Moretonhampstead, walk east to the bridge then follow the footpath
west. Alternatively, park 1km west of Boyland Farm
(⊙ SX784893), 3km west of Dunsford along the minor road to Clifford
Bridge, and follow the footpath south to reach Cricket Pitch Glade.

Chudleigh Knighton Heath (⊙ SX838772) is 2.5km southeast
of Bovey Tracey. There is open access at several points either side
of the minor road extending northwards from the A38 to north of
the B3344. **Wembury beach** (⊙ SX519484) lies south of Wembury
village, 8km southeast of Plymouth. Use the National Trust car park.
Footpaths lead along the coast and inland.

Suggested bases: Exeter (Ⓦ www.exeterviews.co.uk), Bovey Tracey
(Ⓦ www.devon-stay.com), Ashburton (Ⓦ www.
ashburton.org), Buckfastleigh (Ⓦ www.buckfastleigh.
org) and Ivybridge (Ⓦ www.ivybridge-devon.co.uk).
Luxurious **Kilbury Manor** (① 01364 644079 Ⓦ www.
kilburymanor.co.uk) in Buckfastleigh offers comfortable,
individually styled rooms.

Flexibility: Wild daffodil flowers early March to early
April. The short flowering window of sand crocus
(end of March to early April) limits flexibility. Sand
lizard is active mid-March to September, but is best
between April and May. Low tides are essential for
rockpooling. Narrow-headed ant and cirl bunting is
resident.

Accessibility: ④ 🚶

◄ Formerly widespread in England, cirl bunting is now
a Devon speciality. (A&GS)

15

Highland spring, famous grouse

Inverness-shire for capercaillie, black grouse, osprey, golden eagle, pine marten

Dawn on an isolated Scottish moorland. Rugged, remote and riotus. As the mist dissipates, you discern a cluster of swarthy, testosterone-fuelled gamebirds strutting their stuff. Black grouse! In a clearing amidst Caledonian pine forest, three turkey-sized birds spar. Capercaillie! On a

> **Head bowed and chest pumped, wings drooped and tail fanned, the black grouse mock-charge one another**

heather-clad incline, a red grouse beckons. On the rocky summit above, a pair of ptarmigan potter. This weekend, enter the Highland domain of Britain's famous grouse quartet.

Start – early – with black grouse at RSPB Corrimony. Grouse 'lek' (display) at dawn, and the action fizzles out within two hours. Parading grouse are susceptible to disturbance, so joining the RSPB 'minibus safari' enables you to enjoy the avian posturing from the seclusion of shared transport.

Ten males gather in a small arena. Each is velvet-black with a red skullcap and white undertail. Each has head bowed, chest pumped, wings drooped and tail fanned. Each coos and hisses hysterically as it mock-charges rivals. All this to court a demurely garbed female.

◀ Your best chance of pine marten is from a secluded hide in Rothiemurchus Forest. (MS/FLPA)

When the vim wanes, drive southeast to Findhorn Valley, a fine location to savour golden eagle. Pan across mountain tops and the overseeing sky for his or her soaring majesty. Clear weather is best; drizzle makes eagles sulk. Mammals provide an excellent sideshow. Scores of red deer command the wild, rocky skyline. (Quite some contrast to a sedate, tree-strewn English deer park!) Around Coignafearn Lodge, feral goat occurs. Although introduced, these creatures look, behave and 'feel' wild. Goats usually frequent flats by the river, but sometimes ascend the hillsides. Valley slopes sometimes hold mountain hare; lower down, the odd brown hare may lope past.

Leaving the glacial incursion, head south towards Aviemore. Pause at Slochd Summit, where a layby west of the A9 enables you to peruse heather for the protruding black-tipped ears that signify a mountain hare. By now this montane lagomorph has probably forsaken its white winter pelage for the brown fur of summer. Then onto Speyside.

As dusk drowns day beneath Caledonian pines, enjoy one of Britain's most reclusive mammals at point-blank range. From a wood cabin in the Rothiemurchus estate near Loch an Eilean, watch pine martens as they scoff food laid out each evening. Badgers and wood mice are also enticed by the buffet. A roe deer makes a doe-eyed appearance, before sloping off to graze. The canopy-level 'roding' display of a woodcock closes a fabulous day.

A second pre-breakfast start sees darkness retreat at Loch Garten Osprey Centre in Abernethy Forest. The centre offers a ringside seat at the bout of Britain's biggest grouse, capercaillie. With wings dangled,

A male black grouse displaying in the half-light of dawn. (os)

tail spread and neck outstretched, males broadcast an amazing vocal track that samples popping champagne corks, reverberating drum rolls and voluminous belches. A female approaches: tensions rise and squabbles break out between rival males.

When the sparrers lose interest and disperse, it's time to track down Loch Garten's other specialities. An osprey pair, recently returned from African winter quarters, prepares to be admired by 35,000 visitors over the summer. Around the centre there are red squirrels, bushy tailed and bright eyed. Above an understorey replete with juniper, blaeberry and cowberry, a purring call draws attention to Britain's most localised tit. The aptly named crested tit is a feathered bundle of energy.

An insistent, explosive call alerts you to crossbills. But which species? Elsewhere in Britain, they would be common crossbills. The Speyside situation is less clear. These wacky-beaked finches are most likely Britain's sole endemic bird, Scottish crossbill. But they could conceivably be parrot crossbill, a heftier colonist from Scandinavia.

On Loch Garten itself, a drake goldeneye throws its head back in display to a receptive, motionless female. Scan the loch; there's a chance of otter. As you hike through the forest, large domes of desiccated pine needles catch your eye. Look closely: the mounds are alive with their creators, thousands of wood ants. Speyside holds four species of these colonial wonders. Beneath the pines, look for the invertebrate citadels of northern wood ant (in old-growth forests) and Scottish wood ant (in younger stands). There are a few thousand of each!

Assuming favourable weather, spend the afternoon on the fell-fields of Cairn Gorm's ice-shattered mountain tops, picking your way between woolly fringe-moss and stiff sedge. Black grouse sometimes wander the valley near the ski-lift car park, and mountain hare inhabits the slopes where you ascend. At the top, a good site for Britain's final grouse duo – ptarmigan and red grouse – is Coire an t-Sneachda, a scree-filled basin southwest of the summit, 1.5km from the ski centre. Unlike capercaillie and black grouse, neither species leks, preferring solitary aerial displays. Uniquely among British grouse, but in similar vein to mountain hare that are often nearby, ptarmigan has different plumages for winter (white) and summer (mottled brown). And with this camouflaged gamebird you complete your grouse quartet in a fabulous Highland spring weekend.

Practicalities April weekend 2

Where to go: **RSPB Corrimony** (☀ NH383302

① 01463 715000 ⓦ www.rspb.org.uk/corrimony) lies
35km southwest of Inverness, off A831 between Cannich
and Glen Urquhart. Check website for black grouse
minibus safaris in April (booking essential, fee payable).
For **Findhorn Valley**, leave A9 at Tomatin, and take the
single-track road southwest, along the north bank of
the River Findhorn for 15km to its end at Coignafearn Lodge
(☀ NH680153). Scan the ridges at regular intervals. At **Slochd Summit**,
leave the A9 west towards Tomatin, cross the railway line and view
from the layby (☀ NH825263). Book the Pine Marten Hide near **Loch
an Eilean**, 12km from Aviemore through the Rothiemurchus estate in
Aviemore (① 01479 812345 ⓦ www.rothiemurchus.net) or through
Speyside Wildlife (① 01479 812498 ⓦ www.speysidewildlife.co.uk),
which also offers wildlife holidays and guiding (see advert, page 216).

The focal point of **RSPB Abernethy Forest** is Loch Garten
Osprey Centre (☀ NH978183 ① 01479 831476 ⓦ www.rspb.org.
uk/lochgarten), 5km east of Boat of Garten off the B970. Check the
website for 'caperwatch' arrangements. **Cairn Gorm** is 15km east of
Aviemore, along the B970 then a minor road; follow signs. Park in the
ski centre car park (☀ NH990061) and take the funicular.

Suggested bases: In the Cairngorms (ⓦ http://visitcairngorms.com)
these include Aviemore (ⓦ www.visitaviemore.co.uk), Grantown-on-
Spey (ⓦ www.visitgrantown.co.uk), Nethybridge (ⓦ www.nethy
bridge.com), Kingussie (ⓦ www.kingussie.co.uk), Kincraig (ⓦ www.
visitkincraig.com) and Boat of Garten (ⓦ www.boatofgarten.com).
In Boat of Garten, **Moorfield House** (① 01479 831646 ⓦ www.
moorfieldhouse.com) is a Victorian villa with six individually
designed, en-suite bedrooms.

Flexibility: Check ⓦ www.rspb.org.uk/datewithnature for black
grouse safaris and the capercaillie watch, but the former usually runs
on April weekends and the latter early April to mid-May. The Osprey
Centre usually opens 1 April. Ptarmigan, red grouse, mountain hare,
golden eagle and pine marten are resident, so any April weekend
should work.

Accessibility: ② (⑤ for Cairn Gorm element)

60

▶ Controversial incomer: wild boar in the Forest of Dean. (JD)

16

Snakes and snake's-heads

Gloucestershire & Wiltshire for wild boar, adder, goshawk, pied flycatcher, snake's head fritillary

> **" If a single snake's head fritillary has poise and presence, what to make of a meadow jammed with hundreds of thousands? "**

As you soft-foot from car park to viewpoint, the forked tongue of a pathside adder tastes the air, assessing whether you constitute friend, foe or – because it's that time of year – potential mate. This is your first of a possible trio of serpentine characters this weekend. A few steps later, you pass rootings of a wild boar, a once-native mammal again at large in Britain. Reaching a vista over extensive woodland, you scan for soaring raptors: here a common buzzard, there – yes, there! – a goshawk. Welcome to the Forest of Dean, a shard of the ancient wildwood that once carpeted southern England.

Survey slope and plain below New Fancy View (a tongue-in-cheek moniker for a former spoil heap?) for a fair chance of spotting a slumbering boar. The Forest's star mammal is also its most contentious inhabitant. Although boar once occurred naturally in Britain, the species died out in the 13th century. Britain's current feral populations – perhaps 5,000 animals in total – originate in escapes and deliberate releases. Decision-makers and local residents are split on whether to live alongside boar or cull them as invasives. But while their stay of execution persists, the chances of seeing Dean boar are fair.

While scanning for swine, watch fallow deer grazing below, listen for the croak of a passing raven and (aided by a telescope and assuming fine weather) watch raptors soaring above the treeline. This is Britain's best viewpoint for goshawk, one of the country's most elusive raptors: you could see half-a-dozen individuals.

When activity dwindles, the vicinity is packed with possibilities. For another shout at the wide-roving boar, explore Crabtree Hill or mooch around Boys Grave car park (also good for common crossbill). For crossbill and hawfinch, both seed-eaters with an impressive bill, try Parkend churchyard. Or, for hawfinch alone, check trees in paddocks opposite Speech House Hotel. As a bonus, the adjacent Cyril Hart Arboretum car park attracts nuthatch and treecreeper, and you might hear a firecrest singing. If an elegant duck tickles your fancy, look for mandarin at Cannop Ponds. Native to China, introductions have begat well-established populations across southern Britain. If Cannop fails you, try Mallards Pike ponds.

Wherever you go, leave time to enjoy RSPB Nagshead, a charming oak-dominated woodland. Lesser celandine, wood anemone and wood sorrel carpet the forest floor, and the Forest of Dean's mild climate means that tracts of bluebell should be emerging: a quintessential British sight. In trees above, a pied flycatcher sings, recently returned from Africa. On the forest edge, a tree pipit lilts in descending display flight. Check ponds for common frog (and thousands of tadpoles), and look out for grass snake. Late April is a great time to spot this serpent hosepiping across a pond or basking on its edge. Snake two of the weekend!

The next morning, drive an hour east into Wiltshire for the serpentine finale… If ever a flower – yes, flower! – were to embody poise and presence, it would be the snake's head fritillary. Its vertical stem reaches 30cm tall. At its apex the flower throws out two narrow, architectural leaves to counter the downwards arch of the upper stem. The pose culminates in a garnet bloom that is tubular when closed, turning bell-like when opened. It is the composite form – and the chequered, snakeskin-like pattern – that recalls a serpent poised to strike.

◀ Close-up of a snake's head fritillary (JL)

If a single snake's head fritillary has stature and grace, what to make of a meadow jammed with hundreds of thousands? Decide for yourself by visiting North Meadow at Cricklade, where three-quarters of Britain's population reside in damp, riverside fields. Mid-April is the peak flowering time, and it pays to spend a full day wandering and watching in wonderment as the serpents nod to the spring breeze, the intensity of colour transforming with the light. It is, after all, 'Fritillary Sunday', the sole day of the year that private fritillary meadows are traditionally open for public perusal.

At North Meadow, fritillaries are most abundant along the blue (river) and orange (reedbed) walks. With such an extensive, impressive floral tribute, it feels immaterial whether the plant is native to Britain or, as some botanists suspect, introduced in the 18th century. The spectacle is what counts – and the scarcity. Once so locally abundant that local children harvested blooms for sale at Covent Garden market in London, snake's head fritillary has declined rapidly to become a national rarity.

As you wander the trails look for other plants typical of winter-flooded grassland. You should spy the vibrant yellow marsh marigold in hedgerow ditches and the delicate lilac cuckoo flower (foodplant of the orange-tip butterfly) near the riverside. Water forget-me-not grows on damp terrain; look for curled dock, adder's-tongue fern and groups of cowslip too, as skylarks serenade you from above. But, above all, be hypnotised by the nodding and swaying of fields of flowering serpents.

▲ Thousands of snake's head fritillaries in Cricklade's North Meadow (PG)

Practicalities

Where to go: Most **Forest of Dean** sites are around Parkend, 6km north of Lydney on the B4234 (Parkend church: ☀ SO620076). From the B4226 Coleford–Cinderford road, turn south at **Speech House Hotel** (☀ SO620122). **Boys Grave** car park (☀ SO623109) is 1km south. **New Fancy View** (☀ SO628095) is 3km further to the west. **Mallards Pike Pond** (☀ SO638091) turn is left out of New Fancy View, then left again. **Cannop Ponds** (☀ SO608111) is off the B4234, but 2km west of the minor road from Speech House to New Fancy View. **Crabtree Hill** (☀ SO634135) is north of the B4226 between Speech House Hotel and Cinderford; explore forest tracks towards Woorgreens Lake (☀ SO630128). For **RSPB Nagshead** (☀ SO606085 ① 01594 562852 ⓦ www.rspb.org.uk/nagshead), leave Parkend west on B4431.

For **Cricklade's North Meadow** (☀ SU095945 ⓦ www.crickladein bloom.co.uk/fritillary_watch.html,) leave Cricklade on the minor road north towards the A419 and park at Weaver's bridge (☀ SU100945). Take the footpath west; avoid trampling (or picking!) flowers.

Suggested bases: Cinderford and Coleford in the Forest of Dean (ⓦ www.royalforestofdean.info) Gloucester (ⓦ www.thecityof gloucester.co.uk) and Cheltenham (ⓦ www.visitcheltenham.com).

Flexibility: Snake's head fritillary flowers early April to early May (best second half of April). Adders can be seen March–September. Pied flycatcher returns early April. Goshawk displays February to May. Wild boar is resident.

Accessibility: ②

Bedding down

The Bradley (① 01242 519077 ⓦ www.thebradleyhotel.co.uk), in the heart of Regency Cheltenham, is an award-winning boutique B&B in a listed townhouse with stunning contemporary rooms (including an exceptional junior suite), abundant antiques and *objets d'art*.

17

A rabble of reptiles

Dorset for eight species of reptile, natterjack toad, sika, early spider orchid, early gentian

> " Adders are feeling frisky, with mating pairs locked in procreational proximity "

Britain has six native reptiles. Yet you could see *eight* scaly-skinned, cold-blooded species this weekend. No, that is not a misprint. In addition to 'cleaning up' on our native creatures, try for two introduced lizards. And, to boot, look for the first orchids of spring: all 10,000 of them!

Start on Purbeck's limestone coast: steep white cliffs topped with plant- and invertebrate-rich grassland. Park in the quintessentially English Worth Matravers then mosey coastwards – across field, along hedgerow and through wooded glade – arriving at Winspit's clifftop quarry. Time to engage your reptile 'search image'.

Sheltered, sunny slopes are home to your first native reptile: adders bask on exposed areas in rough grass. The snakes look smart, having shed their skin: this annual ritual prompted Druids to revere adders as symbols of renovation. And they are frisky: you may spot two males intertwined in combat or a mating pair locked in procreational proximity.

The quarry and cliff base eastwards harbour common wall lizard, your first naturalised reptile. While argument rages as to whether some of England's wall lizards are native – Isle of Wight inhabitants have decent credentials – Winspit's inhabitants originate from a deliberate release decades ago.

▶ No reptile occurs further north in the world than common lizard. (PH/FLPA)

Walking the coast northeast, look skyward for peregrine and raven, and seaward for auks. Scattered cliffside nests of guillemot (plus razorbill, a few puffin and kittiwakes) denote the southern limit of the species's breeding range. Offshore, dorsal fins may break the surface: a bottle-nosed dolphin pod often ranges nearby.

Between Seacombe Cliff and Dancing Ledge (1–2.5km from the quarry), turn your attention groundwards. The orchid season has started, and the tonsured turf is littered with ten thousand or so early spider orchids, a nationally scarce plant with a velvety, chocolate and blue flower. Larger and vibrantly coloured, early purple orchid and perhaps green-winged orchid may be flowering. Other special plants abound. Early gentian, a delightful and rare spring flower, blooms on the downland at one of its few British localities. Wild cabbage commonly reside in cliffside quarries, ox-eye daisies gather in meadows, and Portland spurge sprawls over rocks.

Butterflies are good too. Wall and grizzled skipper bask on bare ground, green hairstreaks feed demurely on hawthorn and bramble, and an orange-tip flits past. If spring arrives early, you may even see small blue and Adonis blue on the coastal downland.

For the afternoon, explore Purbeck heathland at RSPB Arne. All Britain's native reptiles occur: ask wardens for the best recent locations. Common lizard is easiest: individuals bask on logs. Sand lizard – spring males a luminous green – favours firebreaks and exposed sandy patches on dry heath. A legless lizard, slow worm, often loiters under rocks or logs. Smooth snake – a scarce speciality of southern heaths – is hardest to spot; unlike adder, it sunbathes while partially covered by vegetation. If you can, join a guided walk; wardens know the best locations. As you wander, you may see 'refuges' laid out by herpetologists. Reptiles often warm up by snuggling beneath corrugated metal or felt squares. Resist the temptation to lift the 'tins' yourself. Doing so is frowned upon for non-specialists, and it is illegal to deliberately disturb smooth snake.

Other attractions proliferate. Sika is an Arne speciality, the deer often allowing close approach along the trail to Shipstal point. Dartford warbler pairs busily

◀ Britain's scarcest serpent: smooth snake (JL)

nourish their first brood. Heathland is great for ground beetles: one particularly striking, agile predator is green tiger beetle. And you could chance upon an enormous emperor moth.

The next morning, as sun warms air, try Wareham Forest for another crack at smooth snake and sand lizard. For the latter, check sandy, south-facing banks along coniferous forest rides around the triangulation point near Woolsbarrow hill fort. Examine vegetated banks for smooth snake. Adder and grass snake are here too.

Under an hour's drive east, the Bournemouth area offers three lizards (two non-native) and our rarest native amphibian. South-facing ravines at Boscombe and Southbourne Overcliff hold common lizard (native), common wall lizard and western green lizard (both introduced). Wall lizard is easy to see on ravine walls. Favouring scrub, green lizard is trickier – but worth it when you succeed. This large, vividly verdant reptile is stunning. Fossil records suggest that green lizard once occurred naturally in Britain; but then, so did lion! Look too for the aggressively named bee-killer digger wasp (or beewolf), a solitary wasp that predates honey bees to nourish larvae nestling in sandy burrows.

A few minutes away, Hengistbury Head hosts a star amphibian to complement the reptiles. Natterjack toad was once native here but died out. Reintroduced in 1989, it thrives again. Largely nocturnal, natterjacks emerge from burrows in the evening and run (rather than hop) to the margins of a shallow pool. As dusk descends, the males of Europe's noisiest amphibian churr, throat sacs vibrating. Let the toad chorus provide your weekend finale.

▲ Sika: browsing in Purbeck woodland (GKS/FLPA)

Practicalities

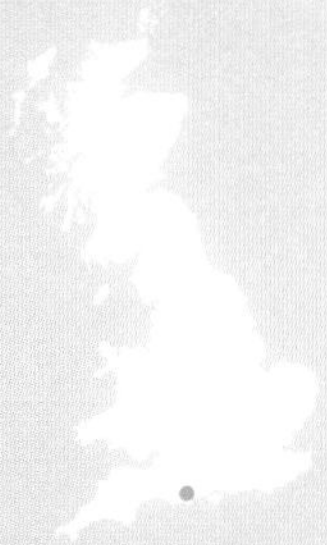

Where to go: For the **Purbeck coast** between Winspit and Dancing Ledge, park in Worth Matravers (⊙ SY974776). Walk south to the coastal quarry (⊙ SY977761), then northeast 1km to Seacombe Cliff (⊙ SY985766) and on 1.5km to Dancing Ledge (⊙ SY996769). Look west for puffins. Return by walking north then west along Priest's Way.

Durlston Country Park (⊙ SZ033774 ① 01929 424443 Ⓦ www.durlston.co.uk) provides another entry point and offers the same species (except wall lizard). Follow signs south from Swanage.

For **RSPB Arne** (⊙ SY971876 ① 01929 553360 Ⓦ www.rspb.org.uk/arne), leave Wareham southwards towards Stoborough, then turn west; follow signs to the car park. Check the website for guided reptile walks. For **Wareham Forest**, use Stroud Bridge car park on the minor road northwest of Wareham (⊙ SY889916). Walk 1km north to Woolsbarrow hill fort (⊙ SY893925). Alternatively, try **Morden Bog National Nature Reserve**. Park at Sherford Bridge (⊙ SY919926) on the B3075 north of Sandford, then walk west .

For **Boscombe and Southbourne Overcliff** local nature reserve (Ⓦ http://tinyurl.com/boscombecliff), drive east from Bournemouth along Boscombe Overcliff Road then Southbourne Overcliff Road. Park in roadside bays. Check coastal ravines between Boscombe Chine Gardens east to Grange Road, particularly Portman Ravine (⊙ SZ125913), opposite Wentworth Close. For **Hengistbury Head**, use the car park (⊙ SZ162911) near Hiker café. For natterjack toads, walk east past the Visitor Centre, bear right then left towards the Head. The pool (⊙ SZ168907) is marked with a board. Disturbing natterjack toad or smooth snake ('Schedule 1 species') is a criminal offence.

Suggested bases: Wareham (Ⓦ www.purbeck.org.uk), Swanage (Ⓦ www.virtual-swanage.co.uk) and Poole (Ⓦ www.pooletourism.com). **Gold Court House** (① 01929 553320 Ⓦ www.goldcourthouse.co.uk) is a Georgian townhouse with a delightful walled garden.

Flexibility: Early spider orchids flower early April to early May, early gentian March–June. Smooth snakes are best April–August. Natterjack toad calls April–June. April–May is good for lizards. Sika is resident.

Accessibility: ④ 🏃

18 Dukes and ladies

Kent for early spider orchid, lady orchid, bluebell, shingle plants, Duke of Burgundy

> **"Examine lady orchid blooms closely to see the 'lady', with her narrow 'arms' and frilled 'skirt'"**

Nowhere is quite like Dungeness, where you start a spring weekend dominated by floral displays. A Mecca for botanists and birders, this superficially desolate landscape hosts Britain's greatest sweep of coastal shingle, astride which a remote community scrapes a living from fishing.

If arriving early to find a southeasterly blowing, plonk yourself plus telescope on the beach and 'seawatch'. Ducks, waders and terns migrate past, and harbour porpoise linger offshore. The real prizes are black-throated diver and pomarine skua heading for the Russian tundra. If the action stops (or never starts), call it quits and turn 180°.

Dungeness shingle supports six nationally scarce plants among some 600 species (one-third of Britain's total). Specialised pioneer plants colonise the beach: look for Babington's orache, sea pea, sea-kale and wild cabbage. Older shingle ridges hold wood sage, prostrate broom, sea campion and sheep's sorrel. Further inland, where finer material accumulates, look for (early-flowering) Nottingham catch-fly with its fragrant, drooping white flowers that open only at night, or (end-of-season) shepherd's cress.

▶ Check out the frilled 'skirt' and 'bonnet' of this lady orchid. (RC/FLPA)

May weekend 1

Around the old lighthouse and nearby moat, search for migrant birds: probably a wheatear or reed warbler, but possibly something rarer. Keep looking upwards for a fly-over red kite or Mediterranean gull. Check for common lizard around the moat cottages, and small copper, a pugnacious butterfly.

In dense grey willow-dominated scrub to the northwest, migrant birds stay well concealed, so refrain from setting high avian expectations. Instead, inspect the ground and low vegetation for butterflies, notably small heath, grizzled skipper and brown argus, and moths including yellow belle. Check aspen for light orange underwing, a high-flying moth. Scan Long Pits – two rectangular freshwater ponds – for grass snake, great fen-sedge, a patrolling hairy dragonfly (the year's first dragonfly) or a vociferous marsh frog. The amphibian attracts a bloodsucking, wriggling, hermaphrodite parasite that is a national rarity. The best way to see a medicinal leech? Splash in shallow water, offering yourself as bait. (Or, perhaps, accept that the leech best remains unseen.)

Then drive inland towards Lydd. Scan the large pits flanking the road for feeding terns, waders and wagtails. In the car park west of ARC pit, look for tree sparrow then follow trails to further viewpoints. Overhead, hobbies – supremely aerodynamic predators – grab flying insects with outstretched legs and agile claws.

Walk or drive south along the entrance track to the RSPB reserve. Footpaths traverse vegetated shingle, reedbeds, damp grassland and pits. Brown-tail caterpillars litter brambles. Small, water-filled depressions hold smooth newt and (if you are really lucky) great crested newt. Standing well back from the pond and use binoculars to view the underwater world from above. Reedbeds around Hooker's Pit are excellent for marsh harrier, bearded tit and bittern. Sedge warblers treat you to close views as they announce territorial intent atop a prominent perch. Ditches are excellent for hairy dragonfly.

Day two is a plant extravaganza. On the toes of Dover's chalk cliffs, Samphire Hoe was created from Channel Tunnel spoil. The reserve's botanical luminaries are early spider orchids. Large numbers of these sumptuous flowers flourish on short turf by the railway line, within a few metres of the visitor hut.

As the morning warms, head half-an-hour inland for a charismatic butterfly and a suite of orchids. Bonsai Bank, a tiny but tremendous

▶ A quintessential British sight: a bluebell woodland in spring (PG)

reserve in Denge Wood, is a stronghold for Duke of Burgundy, a diminutive, early-flying butterfly. As you walk (along paths, to avoid trampling), check wayside hawthorn for green hairstreak and bare earth for dingy and grizzled skippers.

Even a fortnight ahead of their peak, Bonsai's orchid numbers and variety consistently amaze. Lady orchid – a stately species almost entirely confined to Kent – is spectacularly abundant. Examine blooms closely to see the 'lady', with her narrow 'arms' and frilled 'skirt'. Across the reserve, early purple orchid abounds, greater butterfly orchid stipples lower slopes, common twayblade is common and white helleborine flecks shadier areas. There are vertebrate attractions too. In the fortnight after nightingales arrive, these normally reclusive songsters are uncharacteristically extrovert.

Early May is peak bluebell season in Kent, so don't pass up the opportunity of viewing the county's finest display at King's Wood, a few minutes' drive away. Visitors throng the main bluebell carpet near Challock, so head instead to the North Downs Way near Chilham. Here the only crowd comprises lilac-blue flowers. Sit down and drink in.

For your floral finale, drive an hour west to Marden Meadow, south of Maidstone. Visiting these wondrous, unimproved haymeadows is to take a Tardis back in time. The ground is covered with tens of thousands of green-winged orchids, magenta petals radiant in the evening sun. By their side a similar number of ox-eye daisy and adder's-tongue fern vie for your attention, demanding their berth on a camera memory card already crammed with Kent's faunal and floral delights.

Practicalities

May weekend 1

Where to go: **Dungeness** contains a National Nature Reserve (Ⓦ www.dungeness-nnr.co.uk), an RSPB reserve and a bird observatory (☀ TR085173 ① 01797 321309 Ⓦ www.dungenessbirdobs.org.uk). Head southeast from the roundabout in Lydd. After 2km, **RSPB Dungeness** (☀ TR062197 ① 01797 320588 Ⓦ www.rspb.org.uk/dungeness) visitor centre is signposted to the right at Boulderwall Farm. The car park opposite gives access to Hanson's Hide. Continuing along Dungeness Road, you pass ARC and Burrowes pits before reaching the beach. Park at the old lighthouse (☀ TR089170).

Samphire Hoe Country Park (☀ TR293391 ① 01304 225649 Ⓦ www.samphirehoe.com) lies 1km south of Dover. Access is east of the A20. Early spider orchids favour the path by the railway line. **Bonsai Bank** in Denge Wood lies between Ashford and Canterbury. From Sole Street, follow Pennypot Lane north towards Thruxted. Park after 1km, where a track leads 1.5km northeast (☀ TR099501) to the reserve (☀ TR105510). For **King's Wood** (Ⓦ www.friendsofkingswood.org), continue north along Pennypot Lane to Thruxted, then turn west to Bagham. Turn south on the A28 for 500m then follow signs to Chilham. Leave Chilham south on Mountain Street. Park where the road turns east to Hurst Farm. Follow the North Downs Way to the wood, then head southwest into bluebell terrain. **Marden Meadow** is south of Maidstone (☀ TQ763445 Ⓦ www.kentwildlifetrust.org.uk/reserves/marden-meadow). From the M20, junction 7, take the A229 south to Staplehurst then, at the crossroads 800m after the railway line, head west 2.5km to the car park.

Suggested bases: Dymchurch (Ⓦ www.dymchurchonline.com), Hythe (Ⓦ www.hythe-tourism.com), New Romney (Ⓦ www.newromney.net) and Folkestone (Ⓦ www.discoverfolkestone.co.uk). Exclusive and intimate, **Centuries** (① 01303 266850 Ⓦ www.centuriesbedandbreakfast.com) is a 12th-century property in Hythe.

Flexibility: Early spider orchid and bluebell are best late April to mid-May, green-winged orchid late April to end May and lady orchid mid-May to mid-June. Duke of Burgundy flies mid-April to early June.

Accessibility: ③

Fantastic fish – and fishers

Radnorshire & Carmarthenshire for sea lamprey, brook lamprey, badger, osprey, wood warbler

> " Backed by statuesque mountains, Gilfach is Welsh woods and wild water at its finest "

Mid-Wales sparkles with semi-concealed jewels. One gem is Gilfach, a reserve-cum-working farm secluded in the Marteg Valley just north of Rhayader. Backed by the statuesque Cambrian mountains, Gilfach is Welsh woods and wild water at its finest. Its inhabitants are splendid too: crystal-clear streams host two fantastic fish, and the sessile oak stands shelter a trio of beautiful songbirds that epitomise the wildlife of the valleys.

Gilfach excels for leisurely exploration. Three trails connect a habitat mosaic: traditional hay meadows littered with anthills, pasture and wet flushes, damp oak forest, bracken-covered slopes, and birch-flanked river. Start early – in time for the dawn chorus, if your itinerary permits – and make for woodland near the river. Amidst the oaks, the flicker of flame-red tail draws attention to your first of the speciality avian triumvirate: common redstart. A vocal shiver marks out a wood warbler, glistening ivory and primrose. And, concealed in a carefully positioned hide, watch a male pied flycatcher returning to its nestbox with caterpillars for the incubating female.

▲ Listen for the shivering song of a wood warbler. (A&GS)

From the same hide, you glimpse a movement in the adjacent River Marteg. Your luck is in: an otter! As you idle away a riverside morning, look for dipper and grey wagtail on damp rocks. Peer into the river itself – particularly just upstream from Martbeg Bridge – for the fish duo: brook lamprey and bullhead. Primitive vertebrates, eel-like lampreys forsake jaws for a round sucker-like mouth lined with sharp teeth. May is spawning month, so you may witness libidinal activity. The bullhead's common name refers to its wide, flattened head. Males excavate a nest under a large stone, then (unusually among fish) take parental responsibility for safeguarding the eggs. Carefully lift likely-looking boulders and see whether a bullhead lurks underneath.

While probably too early, riverside hay meadows encompass a range of ancient grassland species, including the spherical yellow globeflower. In birches, look for tree pipit, siskin and lesser redpoll. Butterflies flit along old railway cuttings. While too early for small pearl-bordered fritillary, you should see small heath, the combative small copper and the luminous green hairstreak.

Elsewhere in the reserve, unusual ferns include moonwort and adder's-tongue, plus parsley fern in higher, rockier areas (with the vibrantly coloured mountain pansy on adjacent slopes).

Overhead you should see red kite, common buzzard and raven. For mouthwatering views of the former, set aside a couple of hours mid-afternoon to visit the kite-feeding farm at Gigrin, 6km south (see *February, 3* pages 29–32). While less impressive than winter (kites are busy breeding), Gigrin's spectacle is unmissable at any season.

Gilfach is the focus of the day, but if your departure point permits, start the morning 40km southeast. The River Wye at Boughrood Bridge south of Llyswen is renowned for spawning sea lamprey. Standing on the bridge, stare down into the water. Four times longer than brook lamprey, sea lamprey is parasitic during its maritime adult life, sucking at the flesh of living hosts. Adults return to freshwater to spawn: their last living act is to procreate. After mating, the female lays hundreds of thousands of eggs in a depression sucked out by the male from the gravel bed.

To round off the day, two options stand out. First, Nannerth Farm has a treetop hide sited above a badger sett: watch the

Green hairstreak: luminous yet surprisingly hard to see. (JL)

Ospreys, consummate fishers, have recently started breeding in Wales. (DT)

occupants emerge at dusk. Alternatively, bats frequent the lake in Llandrindod Wells at dusk on warm evenings. Daubenton's bat seizes insects over the water, with noctule high up and pipistrelles low down.

With all the fish about, Wales unsurprisingly attracts piscivorous predators. The most recent recruit is your major quarry on day two: osprey. Long restricted to Speyside in Scotland (see *April, 2* pages 57–60, and *July, 3* pages 117–120), this raptor has recently established isolated outposts elsewhere in Britain. In 2007, conservationists erected an artificial osprey nest-platform at the boggy Cors Dyfi reserve. A succession of ospreys have taken up residence, culminating in successful breeding in 2011. As you enjoy the osprey's waterborne pursuits, be mindful that you are watching an historic recolonisation in progress!

End the weekend 50 minutes east at RSPB Lake Vyrnwy, exploring more woodland, wild water and hills via a quintet of trails and hides. As at Gilfach, the 'oak trio' of pied flycatcher, common redstart and wood warbler are the avian highlights. Dipper and grey wagtail use the pool below the lake dam, while goosander and great crested grebe breed on the lake, and kites and buzzards cruise lazily around. If you have energy for a moorland yomp, you may be rewarded by hen harrier, merlin, red grouse or ring ouzel.

On your return, watch siskins on the feeder outside the reserve shop window. If you are carnivorous, combine watching with indulging in some of the shop's reserve-raised organic lamb. Sheep provide the reserve with a living mower and an income: your opportunity to contribute to the local economy and environment that has smothered you with wilderness and wildlife.

Practicalities

Where to go: **Gilfach Farm** (☀ SN965717 ① 01597 823298 Ⓦ http://tinyurl.com/gilfach) is a Radnorshire Wildlife Trust reserve. From Rhayader, take the A470 north. After 5km turn east towards St Harmon and Pantudwr. Park at Marteg Bridge or follow signs east for 1.5km to the visitor centre. There are three trails of various lengths (the 'Nature Trail' is best, and takes in the Otter Hide). For **Gigrin Farm**, see page 32. **Boughrood Bridge** (☀ SO130384) is 40km southeast of Rhayader. From the A470, 500m northwest of Llyswen village the B4350 crosses the River Wye east *en route* to Boughrood Brest.

Book badger-watching at **Nannerth Farm** (☀ SN945717 ① 01597 811121 Ⓦ www.nannerth.co.uk), northwest of Rhayader. **Llandrindod Wells** is 15km southeast of Rhayader. The lake (☀ SN063605) is in the southeast of the town, east of the A483. View from the west shore or the road (Prince's Avenue) encircling the remainder of the lake.

Cors Dyfi (☀ SN701985 ① 01938 555654 Ⓦ www.montwt.co.uk/cors_dyfi.html) is a Montgomeryshire Wildlife Trust reserve 5.5km southwest of Machynlleth. Travelling 4km south of Derwenlas, turn right after Morben Isaf caravan park and park at the reserve. Head east along the A458 to reach **RSPB Lake Vyrnwy** (☀ SJ016192 ① 01691 870278 Ⓦ www.rspb.org.uk/lakevyrnwy). Between Foel and Llanerfyl, head north on the B4395, then west on the B4393 to Abertridwr then Llanwddyn. When you reach the dam at the south of Lake Vyrnwy, turn west for the visitor centre.

Suggested bases: Llandrindod Wells (Ⓦ www.llandrindod.co.uk), Rhayader (Ⓦ www.rhayader.co.uk) and Builth Wells (Ⓦ www.builth-wells.co.uk). **The Old Vicarage** (① 01686 629051 Ⓦ www.theoldvicaragedolfor.co.uk) at Dolfor has four comfortable rooms with luxury textiles and an on-site restaurant.

Flexibility: Osprey occurs April – August, the 'oak trio' of birds April – June. Both lampreys occur from April but spawning is best late May. Small pearl-bordered fritillary occurs from mid-May; late May is more reliable. Badger, red kite and otter are resident.

Accessibility: ④

20
Pembrokeshire parrots, mystical Manxies

Pembrokeshire for Manx shearwater, puffin, gannet, bluebell, red campion

By day, puffins perform on a stage adorned with a lilac haze of bluebells and a red mist of campion, with a backdrop of translucent shimmering sea.

> **Air, turf and crevice resound with a bedlam of caterwauling, chuckling and croaking**

At night, a caterwauling of insane spirits trapped in the bodies of Manx shearwaters echoes across the misty island. Two contrastingly wild experiences in this weekend amidst the seabirds of Skomer.

Lying just off the Pembrokeshire coast, Skomer is a small island of 300ha. As you approach by boat, you realise that the sea surface is bristling with auks. Dense rafts of puffins, guillemots and razorbills slick the water, species intermingling as they rest between foraging trips. The boat scores through the sea, prompting auks to fly up and buzz past, their parting gift a wee wake of white water – a by-product of gaining momentum for take-off.

Once ashore at North Haven, there are bracken-covered slopes to explore, rocky coastlines to wander and flower-strewn plains to meander. Investigate sheltered bays and towering rocky stacks, windless gullies and exposed headlands. Numerous paths cross the island, carefully directed to leave sensitive wildlife areas undisturbed.

▲ Puffin: the 'Pembrokeshire parrot' sailing on an uplift of air. (JW)

May weekend 3

The scent of bluebell and red campion sweetens the air; sea thrift and sea campion itch to join them in the coming weeks. The bluebell display, particularly that lingering over the north of the island, may not be bettered in Britain. All the more so because there is no longer a tree in sight: Skomer's forest was chopped down thousands of years ago, but the normally woodland-loving bluebells have persevered.

Skomer's circumference comprises seacliffs, and seacliffs mean seabirds. Fulmar, kittiwake and guillemot cram onto the sheer, north-facing bluffs of The Wick. Escarpments opposite are home to puffins – thousands of them. Twee though the local nickname of 'Pembrokeshire parrots' may be, it certainly captures the species's comical essence with its parody of a bill, clown-like leer, excessive mascara and jaunty gait. Without pause, breeding puffins enter and emerge from burrows: Skomer has a honeycomb structure of underground nests.

Another excellent seabird site is High Cliff. Fulmars cruise past with barely a flicker of wing. Kittiwakes flutter overhead, the sun gleaming through translucent white wings. Auks belt unilaterally from sea to nest, single-mindedly speeding to avoid marauding gulls and peregrines. The seabirds' collective calls – more cacophony than chorus – bounce off the cliff, adding surround sound to the cinematic spectacle.

You can day-trip Skomer or – booking ahead – stay overnight in the Wildlife Trust hostel. Only by sleeping here can you truly experience Skomer's most singular seabird. As the light wanes, Manx shearwaters congregate offshore. Effortless ocean wanderers by day ('shearing' over the sea surface), 'Manxies' are ungainly creatures on land. Coming to shore is a chore, and also a risk. Stumbling towards their burrow, wings wilting, Manxies run the gauntlet of predation. To minimise the chances of becoming a gull's dinner, they return to and depart from the island only once darkness has descended.

Once sheltering safely in the underground burrow or rocky crevice that serves as their nest, the shearwaters celebrate by 'singing'. Air, turf and crevice resound with a bedlam of chuckling and croaking as thousands of shearwaters insist on their territorial claim. Upwards of 120,000 pairs nest

◀ Red campion: a feature of the Skomer spring (BG/FLPA)

Gannets are Britain's largest seabird – and one of our most striking. (JW)

here, one-third of the planet's population. As you tread carefully on the slopes above North Haven, the Manxies just keep coming, birds flopping around your feet or flapping past your ears. Spookily special.

The following morning, look for other creatures. Even forsaking seabirds and flowers, there's enough to enthrall. Grey seals loll offshore or bask on rocks: favoured locations are Garland Stone, North Haven, South Haven and Pigstone Bay. Rabbits are everywhere; the third denizen of the Skomer honeycomb. A chough, ragged and red billed, probes the turf for insects. A short-eared owl quarters the bracken, looking for common and pygmy shrews, or bank voles of a subspecies occurring only on Skomer. Breeding birds include oystercatcher (at West Pond), skylark and rock pipit, while migrants in transit favour sheltered valleys such as South Stream. If the night has been warm and humid, common toads may ply the paths. Another amphibian, palmate newt, breeds in the hostel garden pond. Skomer Head provides a vantage point to look offshore for cetaceans (harbour porpoise is regular) and gannets.

If you are unable or prefer not to stay on Skomer, do not despair. There are advantages to basing yourself on the mainland. Should the evening tide be high and the wind westerly, Manx shearwaters congregate through Jack Sound into St Bride's Bay. In such circumstances, the assembly can be seen from shore, dense rafts riding rollers. And you can spend day two on a boat, cruising around Skomer's sister islands of Grassholm and/or Skokholm. Skokholm's seabirds are similar to those of Skomer, but Grassholm has the added attraction of an amazing colony of 39,000 pairs of gannet. A cracking complement to a wonderful island weekend!

Where to go: Lying 3km off the Pembrokeshire coast, **Skomer** is a Wildlife Trust of South and West Wales reserve (☀ SM726095 Ⓦ www.welshwildlife.org/skomer-skokholm/skomer). Arrive by boat from Martin's Haven, 23km southwest of Haverfordwest and 3km west of Marloes. Use the dockside National Trust car park (☀ SM761089).

Weather permitting, transfers operate at least three times daily April to October (not Mondays, except bank holidays; Dale Sailing ① 01646 603109 Ⓦ http://tinyurl.com/dalesailings). Summer trips are popular so buy tickets two hours before departure. To protect Skomer's vulnerable terrain, only 250 people may land each day. Late arrivals may take a round-island cruise (no landings). The island is occasionally closed for wildlife monitoring; so be sure to check the Wildlife Trust website.

Lilac blooms greeting azure skies: bluebells on Skomer. (JB)

While day-tripping Skomer is straightforward, an overnight stay is needed to see *nesting* Manx shearwaters. Skomer's only accommodation is the Wildlife Trust hostel (ⓣ 01239 621600 ⓦ http://tinyurl.com/stayonskomer). West Hook Farm (ⓣ 01656 636424), 400m east of Martin's Haven, offers overnight parking.

View *rafting* Manx shearwaters in **Jack Sound** from Wooltack Point; take the footpath northwest from the car park. If birds are congregating in **St Bride's Bay**, walk east along the coast path. Dale Sailing offers an evening shearwater boat cruise from Milford Haven and a daytime cruise around the gannetry at **Grassholm** (as does Thousand Islands: ⓣ 01437 721721 ⓦ www.thousandislands. co.uk), plus a cruise around both **Skokholm** and Skomer. Landings on Skokholm are only permitted on Wildlife Trust open days, but you can stay overnight in the Trust's hostel accommodation (book as for Skomer; see above).

Suggested bases: On the mainland, Milford Haven and Haverfordwest, plus villages west of here towards the coast (ⓦ www. visitpembrokeshire.com).

Flexibility: Seabirds are present April to early July, (Manx shearwaters until end August). Grey seal numbers dwindle during April and increase from August. Bluebells flower from late April until early June, red campion from mid May to early July.

Accessibility: ④ 🚶

Bedding down

Fields Lodge (ⓣ 01646 697732 ⓦ www.fieldslodge.co.uk) is a contemporary boutique B&B in a rural location near Milford Haven, with four stylish bedrooms providing  sumptuously comfortable beds and containing thoughtful extras such as own-brand toiletries. This is all complemented by bountiful local organic fare.

Seabird colonies are arguably Britain's answer to the Galápagos, with oodles of wildlife at close range. Here puffins breeding on a coastal grassy slope attract the attention of an amateur wildlife photographer. (HH)

21

Limestone ladies

Cumbria & Lancashire for lady's slipper, coralroot orchid, pearl-bordered fritillary, Duke of Burgundy, natterjack toad

If you associate the word 'pavement' solely with pedestrian footfall along roadsides, you need to get out more. This weekend of Cumbrian geology and botany demonstrates why – and where. Britain is privileged to host a high proportion of one of the world's

> **An imposing orchid, lady's slipper is a spectacular blend of the tropical and the comical**

rarest habitats, and one threatened by the craze for garden rockeries: limestone pavements. Towering above the surrounding landscape, these castellations are outstanding for flora. And the pick of the bunch, so to speak, is Britain's most extravagant orchid, the lady's slipper.

An imposing plant, the lady's four lanceolate, purplish-brown petals guard a swollen pale yellow lip that recalls a clog (or 'slipper'); the result is somewhere between tropical and comical. So highly prized by collectors was this Cinderella of the orchids that it was picked and dug up to near-extinction in Britain. By 1930, just a single plant remained. That plant (in Yorkshire) is still going strong more than 80 years later and its seed has recently been harvested for a reintroduction programme that aims to establish sustainable populations on northern England limestone and to enable risk-free public viewing.

◀ Lady's slipper: no British orchid is more tropical in appearance. (RP-J)

Lady's slipper: a flourishing reintroduction scheme. (RP-J)

Among the ten chosen sites for lady's slipper is Gait Barrows. Here Natural England has deftly planted and cared for scores of plants. These now flourish and are enjoyed annually by 4,000 visitors who amble across pavement and through woodland via the Yew and Limestone trails. To appreciate the orchids' arresting splendour follow the purple-marked Yew Trail to post 4, c1km from the car park. As you kneel down to slipper height on the limestone pavement, thank the conservationists who have made your visit possible.

The surrounding pavement is a geology field trip in itself. Over thousands of years, rainfall has scoured out fissures ('grikes') in the limestone plateau, bequeathing blocks ('clints'). Each grike, drained yet damp, hosts its own particular plant community. Ardent botanists seek local specialities such as rigid buckler fern, limestone fern, lily-of-the-valley (with its snowy, bell-like blooms), angular Solomon's-seal and pale St John's wort.

Lepidopterists are also well served. In sunny glades in the southeast, look for Duke of Burgundy. This attractive, ever-rarer butterfly adores sheltered spots on nutrient-deprived soils. Similarly scarce is pearl-bordered fritillary. In late May this bright orange butterfly overlaps with the commoner and similar-looking small pearl-bordered fritillary, testing your identification skills. At first glance, the dingy skipper is appropriately named. Close examination, however, reveals a myriad markings; it is well worth scrutinising basking males. There are day-flying moths too: speckled yellow, and the verdant-winged cistus forester.

The Yew and Limestone trails meet amidst moist pastures in the south of the reserve. Here, scan the grass for the pink flecks of northern marsh orchid and ragged robin: the former as robust as the latter is scraggy. As you return to the car park along the exit track, check out the nesting mounds of southern wood ant; each citadel offers accommodation for 30,000.

Spend the remnants of the day leisurely exploring RSPB Leighton Moss (see *February, 2* pages 25–8). Reedbeds are alive with reed and sedge warblers, and marsh harriers quarter overhead. You may hear bittern 'booming' or bearded tit '*ping*ing'. Flocks of leggy apricots (black-tailed godwits) pause on their Iceland-bound voyage. Tiny fluffy balls on stilts (avocet chicks) wobble across the saltmarsh. If the sun is out, broad-bodied chasers zoom around. Non-breeding red deer herd around Griesdale Hide. Staying late increases your chances of a special encounter with an otter. Not bad for a postscript to today's target!

Next day, your itinerary traverses sodden terrain in two contrasting habitats: raised peat bog and coastal dune slacks. At Roudsea Wood and Mosses, a permit gives access to boardwalks crossing bogs at Fish House and Deer Dike Mosses. In wet woodland where limestone ridge cedes to raised mire, look for large yellow sedge at its sole British site. Where hare's-tail cotton grass nods in the breeze, scan for the pink flush of bog-rosemary, a relative of heather. And examine the mire at ground level for round-leaved sundew (a spiky red carnivorous plant) on the *Sphagnum* moss duvet, and common raft spider floating on a peaty pool.

Finish at the dunes of Sandscale Haws, Britain's finest site for arguably its most unassuming orchid. Unassuming does not, however, imply common – and the joy of locating a scattering of coralroot orchid amidst creeping willow in dune slacks stems as much from the species's national rarity as the notorious difficulty of spotting it. Joining a guided walk offers the best chance. If you can, linger until dusk to hear the nightjar-like churring of a natterjack toad chorus. Britain's rarest native amphibian is a pioneer species, breeding in ephemeral water bodies in young dune slacks. As you return to your vehicle by torchlight, let the toad's reverberations act as a *digestif* to a wonderful weekend of scarce plants, butterflies and birds.

▶ Round-leaved sundew: a meat-eating plant (JL)

Practicalities May weekend 4

Where to go: For **Gait Barrows National Nature Reserve** (☀ SD478776 ① 07747 Ⓦ http://tinyurl.com/ gaitbarrows, www.limestone-pavements.org.uk) leave M6 at junction 36, following the A65 north. At Crooklands, follow the B5282 west to Arnside. Head south from the railway station on a minor road, following this east for 2km. Take the first right and park after 300m. Walk southeast on the footpath and follow the Yew and Limestone trails. Permit needed for other areas (Ⓔ rob.petley-jones@naturalengland.org.uk). Check website for details of May's annual open weekend. The entrance to **RSPB Leighton Moss** (☀ SD478750 ① 01524 701601 Ⓦ www.rspb.org.uk/leightonmoss) is off Storrs Lane in Silverdale.

For **Roudsea Wood and Mosses** (☀ SD329827 ① 07747 852905 Ⓦ www.naturalengland.org.uk/ourwork/conservation/ designatedareas/nnr/1006126.aspx), leave the A590 at Haverthwaite. Take B5278 towards Cark. Immediately after crossing the River Leven turn right on a private road to the reserve car park. Access by Natural England permit only (email as above); stick to boardwalks. **Sandscale Haws** (☀ SD189750 ① 01229 462855 Ⓦ www.nationaltrust.org.uk/ sandscale-haws) is 5km north of Barrow-in-Furness. Leave the A590 following signs for Roanhead, then take minor roads northwest to the car park (☀ SD200756). Walk west to the dunes. It is worth phoning the rangers for directions to accessible orchids. Disturbing natterjacks toads (a 'Schedule 1 species') is a criminal offence.

Suggested bases: Kendal (Ⓦ www.visitcumbria.com/sl/kendal.htm) and Silverdale (Ⓦ www.visitlancashire.com/explore/arnside-and-silverdale-aonb). **The Drunken Duck Inn** (① 01539 436347 Ⓦ www.drunkenduckinn.co.uk) offers individually styled rooms, outstanding cuisine, cream teas on arrival and spectacular views.

Flexibility: Lady's slipper can flower early May to late June; coralroot orchid flowers late April to early June. Natterjack toad calls throughout April–May. Duke of Burgundy and pearl-bordered fritillary fly end April–early June.

Accessibility: ④ 🚶

22
Machair marvels, streaming skuas

Outer Hebrides for machair plants including orchids, corncrake, breeding waders, long-tailed skua, great yellow bumblebee

The air is fresh: moist with the spirit of the Atlantic. The ground is a paroxysm of pink and yellow: the machair in fragrant bloom. The slopes resound with bleating, whinnying and piping: the territorial calls of northern waders. From the iris beds slinks the sworn enemy of mechanised agriculture: the reclusive and rare corncrake. On the rocky shore a family fishes: otters no less. And through the sky above a pirate scythes: an Arctic skua signalling predatory intent. Welcome to North Uist: a small island at the heart of the Hebrides.

> **Where crushed-shell sand meets peat-based meadows, one of Europe's rarest and most diverse habitats develops: machair**

You are just an hour's flight from Glasgow, but could be in another world. Within 60 minutes you have exchanged hectic urbanity for simple crofting. All that breaks the ocean between North Uist and Newfoundland is the isolated seabird colony at St Kilda. So unwind. This weekend is about serenity and senses, about wildlife amidst wilderness. Relax, enjoy and imbibe.

The low western coastline of North Uist intersperses elongated white beaches with rocky foreshores. Where crushed-shell sand meets peat-based meadows, machair develops – one of Europe's rarest and most diverse

Magnificent machair: bounteous blooms nudging white sands and cobalt seas. (DT)

habitats with an amazing 45 plant species per square metre. In May, the blooms are largely white (eyebright, ox-eye daisy) and yellow (marsh marigold, lesser spearwort, common meadow buttercup and yellow flag iris), but the pink of emerging orchids brightens the dampest areas.

Orchid taxonomy is confused by flux (and identification by rampant hybridisation), so don't feel despondent if you are baffled by what you find. The stunted, squat marsh orchids have been considered a single-island endemic ('Hebridean marsh orchid', best found at Newton) but are now suspected to be an ecologically isolated form of Pugsley's marsh orchid. Whatever they are, they should be emerging now – as should common spotted, early marsh and northern marsh orchids.

While on your hands and knees, search for three special invertebrates. Belted beauty is a remarkable moth: the flightless female mimics the flowerhead of plantain. End May is the close of its season, so you will need luck to find one. Of five species of bumblebee found here, the star is great yellow bumblebee, one of the UK's rarest pollinators. Finally, the most striking of three dune snails is conical snail, housed in a towering spire of a shell.

Balranald Reserve captures much of what makes North Uist special. The reserve is renowned for one of Scotland's most important birds. Corncrake is locally common thanks to traditional farming techniques deployed by crofters. This migrant is easiest to see between late April and early June, before the sprouting flag-iris beds conceal pairs and their offspring. Even so, it is best located by call. The repetitive, harsh 'crex crex', enshrined as the crake's scientific name, resembles the sound produced when running fingers along the teeth of a comb.

Machair marvels, streaming skuas

The corncrake is just one voice in North Uist's choir. Singing skylark, corn bunting and twite abound, further indicators of amenable agricultural practices. Even more special are the breeding waders. On marshy grassland, snipe bleat, redshank chivvy and lapwing '*peewi*'. On machair, oystercatcher pipe and ringed plover peep. On moorland, curlew bubble and golden plover whistle. The sheer numbers and combined volume beggar belief. However, not all Uist waders are local breeders. Sandy stretches such as Vallay Strand are service stations for migrating groups of turnstone, purple sandpiper, sanderling and dunlin. Garbed in russet nuptial finery, these birds are still flocking north to nest.

While wandering, check the coast for marine mammals. Otter is widespread, families searching the shoreline or frolicking in the surf. Langass and Nam Feithean lochs are prime sites. Nearby, harbour seal lounge in seaweed-strewn shallows. Grey seal frequents more exposed sites.

If sea mist combines with onshore winds, seawatch from the promontory of Aird an Rùnair for a treat. The northwards passage of Arctic-breeding pomarine skua and long-tailed skua – the former replete with tail spoons, the latter with tail streamers – is a Hebridean speciality. There is no finer place or month to witness this migration – but weather conditions must be right.

For a change, explore the moorland interior along Committee Road. Short-eared owl, hen harrier and golden eagle will keep you enthralled. Red grouse and Arctic skua nest here, and lochs are home to nesting ducks such as wigeon and teal. Among the commoner breeding waders, look for two local, long-billed specialities: whimbrel and greenshank. A trio of divers occur. Black-throated frequents large lochs, great northern fishes offshore, and red-throated hurries between sea and small waterbodies. Lochs to scan include Scadavay and Skealtar. As you do so, a white-tailed eagle may cruise overhead, its massive form seemingly blotting out the sun, or a raven may croak its way past. Or they may not. By the end of this remote weekend, it won't seem to matter. You've relaxed. You've enjoyed. You've imbibed.

▲ The spring migration of long-tailed skuas is a North Uist speciality (HH)

Where to go: You can get to North Uist by car ferry from Uig on Skye or Tarbert on Lewis (T 0800 0665000 W www.calmac.co.uk). A more time-efficient option is to fly from Glasgow to the adjacent island of Benbecula, then cross the road bridge to North Uist (T 0871 7002000 W www.loganair.co.uk and W www.glasgowairport.com). **RSPB Balranald** (NF706707 T 01463 715000 W www.rspb.org.uk/balranald) is reached by turning west off the A865 towards Hougharry, 5km north of Bayhead. **Loch nam Feithean** (NF712704) lies just east of the visitor centre. From the visitor centre, walk west then southwest to reach **Aird an Rùnair** (NF687707). **Loch Langass** (NF841649) lies southeast of Langais Hotel, on a minor road south of the A867 northeast of its junction with the B894. **Committee Road** (midpoint NF788700) is the minor road cutting across the heart of North Uist between the A865 at Cladach a' Chaolais and the same road at Malacleit. **Loch Scadavay** (NF869673) and **Loch Skealtar** (NF896686) are in the northeast of the island, west of Lochmaddy and viewed by walking north from the A867. **Vallay Strand** (NF792736) is viewable from the A865, on the north coast 15km west of Lochmaddy. **Newton and Robach machair** (NF885775) lies in the extreme northeast of the island, northwest of the B893.

Suggested bases: Accommodation is scattered across North Uist (W www.visithebrides.com/islands/nuist, www.isle-of-north-uist.co.uk); Lochmaddy is the largest settlement. **Bagh Alluin** (T 01876 580370 W www.jacvolbeda.co.uk/b-b-bagh-alluin.html) offers spacious modern rooms with large windows that have a direct view of the machair.

Flexibility: The machair flowers late, and gets better during June and July. Orchid season starts in late May, but is best in June and early July. Corncrakes arrive from mid-April and are best seen before June when the vegetation grows too high. Skua passage can occur any week in May when weather conditions are conducive. Otter is resident.

Accessibility: ④ 🚶

23 Fluttering by flowers

Hampshire & Wiltshire for sword-leaved helleborine, musk orchid, frog orchid, Duke of Burgundy, pearl-bordered fritillary

> " Can't decide between early summer orchids or butterflies? Why choose? Do both! "

Early summer is all about orchids. Early summer is also all about butterflies. So this southern England weekend combines the best of both.

Chalk is the cornerstone of day one: impoverished soils peerless for striking plants and attendant insects. Start at Chappetts Copse in north Hampshire. This steep-sided beech 'hangar' is Britain's best woodland for seeing – in abundance – a declining and localised orchid. Up to 2,000 sword-leaved helleborines carpet the woodland floor. With stately stem, lissome leaves and spire of white, tulip-shaped flowers, these plants pose. Start looking as you draw up at this sylvan haven: plants even sprout along the roadside.

A further trio of orchid treats require sharper eyes. White helleborine is the sword-leaved's commoner cousin, but is outnumbered here. A very different concept is fly orchid: the flower has evolved to mimic its pollinator. This is not, as one might reason, a fly. Instead a male digger wasp is seduced into transferring pollen during a forlorn attempt to copulate with the

▶ Duke of Burgundy – one of our rarest butterflies (RCh/FLPA)

burnt purple and sky-blue flowerhead. Simply peculiar is bird's-nest orchid, which gathers in isolated clumps, lives a largely subterranean existence and subsists on nutrients derived from fungi. It is easy to dismiss this beige plant as a decaying broomrape. Up close, however, the flower's fan-shaped hood is undeniably that of an orchid.

As the day warms, head 15km northeast to Noar Hill, near Selborne. This reserve protects chalk downland at its finest. The ridges, banks and hollows of these medieval chalk workings are now speckled with rare plants and inhabited by 60% of Britain's butterfly species.

After an initial climb flanked by hedgerows, you reach the reserve. Yellow and pink garland the ground. Yellow swathes comprise cowslip, common rockrose, lady's bedstraw, horseshoe vetch and common twayblade (a lanky, diffident orchid). The pink is provided by common spotted, chalk fragrant and pyramidal orchids.

To reveal what makes Noar roar, investigate the short turf beneath the rich colour – and look low. The star orchids are tiny, if confusingly named. The large colony of musk orchid (in sheltered hollows) is nationally important, but don't expect it to smell of musk. (Any heady scents come from herbaceous thyme and majoram.) Frog orchid (on rims between hollows) is similarly petite, but only wild imagination could accuse it of resembling an amphibian. Early June marks the onset of both species' flowering season, so keep expectations as low as your eyes.

Noar has more. Fluttering around orchids are butterflies. Look for dingy skipper on bare earth, grizzled skipper on turf, small heath in short grass and green hairstreak anywhere. Best of all, if spring is late, Duke of Burgundy should still be flying. Sheltered hollows, including behind the visitor sign, are prime habitat.

When you leave Noar Hill, try to call in at neighbouring Selborne, the historic former home of famous naturalist Gilbert White. Remarkably, the village car park and adjacent pub garden are home to firecrests, perhaps Britain's most exquisite bird.

◀ A musk orchid, diminutive and delicate (JL)

Finish the day at Ovington, 10km northwest. Scan the River Itchen's shallows for innumerable fish, including trout and Atlantic salmon (returned seafaring) and the odd pike. If the air is still, watch the spectacular emergence from the water of hundreds upon hundreds of green drake mayfly. And then watch trout rise to snatch them!

Sword-leaved helleborine. (JL)

Start day two with a respiratory challenge near Winchester, ascending the steep slopes of St Catherine's Hill for chalky fare. This Iron Age hill fort is overlain with plant-rich grassland, strewn with kidney vetch and rock-rose. Check the fort's crewcut turf for musk and frog orchids then scour south-facing slopes for the tiny white flowers of the amusingly named bastard toadflax. Brown argus and small blue flit over the ground, and an early marbled white may belt past.

Today's main destination is Bentley Wood, 45 minutes' drive west of Winchester. One of Britain's top butterfly sites, Bentley attracts groups of wildlife-watchers in early July when purple emperor emerges (see *July, 2* pages 113–16). In early June, your targets are the blaze of orange provided by a quartet of butterflies. The star is pearl-bordered fritillary, a species in increasing trouble. Early June draws a line under this rarity's flight period – so individuals may be tatty – but has the advantage of being early in the season for two other targets: small pearl-bordered and marsh fritillaries.

Pearl-bordered fritillary frequents the 'eastern clearing' and adjacent wooded rides, feeding on bugle. The other fritillaries inhabit the clearing's damper areas, and Duke of Burgundy patronises drier, tussocky parts. Then head to Hawksgrove car park, looking for 'pearls' in drier parts of the western clearing and nearby leaf litter. If you have time, wander across the road to Blackmoor Copse. This reserve holds further pearl-bordered fritillaries, particularly in coppiced areas with pathside bugle and common spotted orchids.

Can't decide between early summer orchids or butterflies? Why choose? Do both!

Practicalities

Where to go: **Chappetts Copse** (◉ SU654230
Ⓦ www.hwt.org.uk/data/files/ReserveMaps/
chappet.pdf) is a Hampshire & Isle of Wight Wildlife
Trust reserve 13km west of Petersfield. At West Meon,
leave the A32 towards East Meon. After 1.5km turn south
into Coombs Lane. Park south of the reserve. For **Noar Hill**
(◉ SY740320 Ⓦ http://tinyurl.com/noarhill), leave
Selborne south on the B3006, immediately turning west towards
Newton Valence. Take the first left for limited roadside parking
(◉ SU838323). Walk uphill; a display board greets visitors. **Ovington**
(◉ SU561319) lies 3km west of New Alresford. From the A31
roundabout, take the B3047 north towards Itchen Stoke then
immediately west to Ovington. From the Bush Inn, walk north to the
River Itchen. **St Catherine's Hill** (◉ SU485275 Ⓦ www.hwt.org.uk/
pages/st-catherines-hill-r.html) is southeast of Winchester. Leave
the M3 at junction 10. At the A31 roundabout, head west towards
Winchester. After 600m park by the River Itchen.

Bentley Wood is 10km east of Salisbury. Leave Winchester
northwest on the B3049 to Stockbridge, then continue west on the
A30. Just after the A343 junction, turn south to East Winterslow then
West Dean along Tytherley Road. Bentley Wood eastern car park
(◉ SU256293) is signposted. Walk back east 100m, then north to the
'eastern clearing'. For the western wood, head northeast from East
Grimstead towards Winterslow. At the Farley turnoff, head east to a
car park and the 'western clearing' (◉ SU237286) or park on the verge
to access the adjacent **Blackmoor Copse** reserve (◉ SU234288
Ⓦ http://tinyurl.com/b3s2uab).

Suggested bases: Winchester (Ⓦ www.visitwinchester.co.uk) and
Petersfield (Ⓦ www.visitpetersfield.com). **The Old Vine** (Ⓣ 01962
854616 Ⓦ www.oldvinewinchester.com) in Winchester, is a Grade
II-listed, 18th-century inn and restaurant.

Flexibility: Early June is best for all targets. Sword-leaved helleborine
flowers early May to early July (best end May). Duke of Burgundy and
pearl-bordered fritillary are best in May. Musk and frog orchids are
best from mid-June. Mayfly and fish emerge late April–late June.

Accessibility: ④

24 Fens and flora

Glamorgan for fen orchid, early marsh orchid, fabulous flora, fen raft spider, beachcomber beetle

> " Luminously pale green needles with a whirl of delicate white flowers, fen orchids hide in boggy slacks "

A handful of regions in Britain pack such varied habitat into such a petite area that prioritising wildlife-watching locations can be challenging. The Gower Peninsula, Britain's first Area of Outstanding Natural Beauty, is one. Complementing Gower by locating two of Britain's rarest and most enigmatic creatures – its slightest orchid and heftiest spider – makes this weekend even more exciting.

Gower blends landscapes as varied as saltmarshes and dunes, foreshore and ancient woodland, moorland and limestone cliffs. One way to enjoy the gamut of habitat is to allocate a half-day to each of three thrilling reserves.

Oxwich Bay is a neat introduction to all things Gower. East of the car park, the dune slack flora is stunning. Round-leaved wintergreen and dune gentian nestle amongst a horde of orchids, including thousands of common twayblade and pyramidal orchid and scores of bee orchid, the latter our most familiar species. In damper slacks, including near the marsh lookout, early marsh orchid and southern marsh orchid abound.

On short grass, look for tiny butterflies: brown argus and small blue are both blues in taxonomy if not colour. The strandline is one of scant British sites for beachcomber, a striking and nationally scarce beetle that resides reclusively under driftwood. Should you fail to see it (as is likely), console yourself with

▶ The delicate whirls of a fen orchid (JL)

sea-holly, sea spurge and the rosy and ivory trumpets of sea bindweed.

In scrubby areas bordering reedbeds, yellow flag iris entices the eye and Cetti's warbler heralds the ear, while a hairy dragonfly patrols is reedmace-lined channels. In ash-dominated woodlands such as Nicholaston Wood, look for stinking hellebore, and scarce trees such as rock whitebeam and small-leaved lime. Keep an ear out for both marsh and willow tit, a conundrum of a species pair. Consider returning at nightfall, hoping to strike lucky with lesser or greater horseshoe bat.

Spend the afternoon west along the undercliffs between Port Eynon and Worm's Head, searching for limestone plants that occur at few other British sites. At the base of the cliffs, there is thrift, spring squill, sea stork's-bill, rock samphire and buckhorn plantain. Portland spurge occurs where the maritime community grades into calcareous grassland and heathland. Among limestone specialists, hoary rock-rose and bloody crane's-bill stand out, with the purple-flowered basil thyme on grassland. The beach at Port Eynon holds sea stock, for which the British distribution is restricted to Glamorgan and Devon. Finally, immerse yourself in wonderfully diverse clifftop bryophytes: get down low to enjoy streaky feather-moss, sand-hill screw-moss and frizzled crisp-moss. Fabulously different!

Among birds, you will not fail to see raven, but keep an ear out for the cawing of a relative that has recently recolonised Gower: chough. Another returnee is peregrine, perhaps seduced by seabird colonies at Worm's Head: kittiwake, guillemot, razorbill, fulmar and shag all breed. And keep alert for an entirely new avian arrival: Dartford warbler now breeds in the extensive gorse.

A single Gower day cannot suffice, so spend an additional morning at Whiteford Burrows. Flora is similar to Oxwich, but the dunes are larger, wilder and more bountiful, with carpets of bog pimpernel and great drifts of southern marsh orchid and the *coccinea* subspecies of early marsh orchid. The new slack in the southwest and grazing exclosures further north are particularly productive.

Your botanical targets are dune gentian (nationally scarce), round-leaved wintergreen (strangely seductive), variegated horsetail (largely

▲ Beachcomber beetle, beach combing (JWi)

prostrate) and adder's-tongue (a cunningly disguised fern). Gower butterflies include both the tiny and timid (small blue) and the big and bold (dark green fritillary). The damp slacks host a spectacular day-flying moth: scarlet tiger, dozens of which spiral upwards in their mad mating display. The star invertebrate, however, is dune tiger beetle, a scarce, hyperactive predator that scurries along the upper strandline.

A Gower dune speciality that you are unlikely to see is fen orchid, recorded from both Oxwich and Whiteford but probably now locally extinct. Fortunately – and despite a 99% decline since 1980 – this enigmatic Lilliputian plant persists at Kenfig, just off Gower, so head there for the afternoon. The orchid's luminously pale green needles underpin a whirl of delicate white flowers. They secrete themselves in boggy slacks, particularly along the 'Yellow Trail'. Ask at the visitor centre for the whereabouts of accessible plants; some are off-limits. Whilst searching, admire the pink haze of southern and early marsh orchids, heath and common spotted orchids, plus classic dune slack flora such as adder's-tongue, green-flowered helleborine and common twayblade, butterflies such as small blue, and birds such as Cetti's warbler.

If both daylight and energy remain, finish the weekend in style a short way back towards Swansea. Britain's largest arachnid (7cm from toe to toe), fen raft spider, walks on water thanks to its hairy legs. Strikingly striped, this globally threatened invertebrate frequents only three sites nationwide. Along the southern edge of Pant y Sais Fen, look for nursery webs in greater tussock sedge between towpath and the peaty Tennant Canal. Fabulous fens + fantastic flora = wonderful weekend!

Pink rafts of thrift line the Gower coast. (JL)

Practicalities June weekend 2

Where to go: The **Gower Peninsula** lies southwest of
Swansea. For **Oxwich Bay National Nature Reserve**
(☀ SS512874), turn south off the A4118 towards Oxwich.
Park at the reserve centre. The best dune slacks are
around ☀ SS507877. There are three access points for
South Gower Coast National Nature Reserve. From east
to west: park at Port Eynon (☀ SS467848) at the south
end of the A4118; at Pitton on the B4247 (☀ SS427877) then walk
southwest 1km; or at Rhossili (☀ SS416879) at the west tip of
the B4247. The coast is so floristically rich that it is worth walking
the whole 10km section then catching a bus back. For **Whiteford
Burrows National Nature Reserve** (☀ SS446956) take the B4295 from
Gowerton to Llanrhidian, then follow minor roads to Landimore,
Cheriton and Llanmadoc. Use the village car park (☀ SS440936), then
walk northwest to Cwm Ivy then northeast to the dunes.

For **Pant y Sais Fen National Nature Reserve** (☀ SS696945)
leave the M4 at junction 42, heading southwest on the A483. At the
roundabout turn north onto the B4290. Park sensibly by the canal and
walk east along the towpath (☀ SS712939 to SS719942). Intentionally
disturbing fen raft spiders is illegal. For **Kenfig National Nature
Reserve** (☀ SS793817 ☎ 01656 743386) leave the M4 at junction 37,
towards Porthcawl. At the roundabout turn onto the B4283. Once you
leave North Cornelly, turn left at the crossroads. From the car park
(☀ SS802810) walk west. There is useful detail on these reserves at
Ⓦ www.first-nature.com/waleswildlife/index.php.

Suggested bases: Mumbles, Rhossili and Port Eynon, but
accommodation is scattered across the peninsula (Ⓦ www.the-
gower.com/home/interactive.htm). The boutique **Blas Gŵyr**
(☎ 01792 386472 Ⓦ www.blasgwyr.co.uk) in Llangennith has
individually designed rooms named and coloured after plants.

Flexibility: Fen and marsh orchids flower throughout June. Fen raft
spider can be seen from April to early October, with females easiest
to see once they have built nursery webs in late June. Look for
beachcomber beetle from April to July.

Accessibility: ④ 🚶

25 Swallowtails and amazons

Norfolk Broads for swallowtail, Norfolk hawker, natterjack toad, nightjar, crane

> ❝ Powering past with wings of lacy lingerie, swallowtails are restless ❞

This weekend is all about water, in its abundance and (near-)absence. Visit saturated fens, reed-lined broads and tiny pools in arid dunes. Norfolk's Broadland comprises a mosaic of open water, sodden fen, reedbeds, marshes and carr woodland – all topped by big skies and distant horizons.

Broadland's flagship creature is the swallowtail, Britain's joint-largest and most localised butterfly. See it at Hickling Broad, a short sail from the setting of two books in *Swallows and Amazons*, the children's series by Arthur Ransome. Start along the Weaver's Way footpath, south of the broad. Swallowtails particularly occur between the hide overlooking Rush Hill scrape and Waggonhill plantation. Most restless on warm, sunny mornings and evenings, swallowtails power past before plunging to slurp nectar from a yellow flag iris, ragged robin or thistle.

Dragonflies abound. Red-eyed, blue-tailed, azure and large red damselflies inhabit iris beds lining the dyke. Four-spot chasers nestle alongside black-tailed skimmers in drier vegetation. Top of the pops is a 'dragon' almost as constrained in range as swallowtail: Norfolk hawker.

▲ Is there a more beautiful British butterfly than the swallowtail? (PF)

Males of this East Anglian speciality patrol low over grazing-marsh ditches, clashing over territorial rights.

With two target species under your belt, try the Norfolk Wildlife Trust reserve on the north shore of Hickling Broad. This offers further opportunities for swallowtail, particularly along the western boardwalk near the landing stage (check for otter too). Nearby, keep an eye out for fen mason wasp at one of its few British sites. The trails traverse varied habitats; pause in hides – particularly Bittern Hide – to check reeds for the reclusive brown heron and peruse pools for grass snake. Scan Hundred Acre Marsh, a breeding-season haunt of the common cranes for which northeast Norfolk is famous (see *December, 1* pages 199–202).

Make time for a unique Broadland experience: exploring Hickling from the water aboard an electric boat, which transports you to an otherwise inaccessible hide and magnificent canopy tower (the best view in this flat county?); the latter may produce intimate views of purple hairstreak and white admiral. As you float silently and serenely through reeds and channels, bearded tits betray their presence by calling. Marsh harriers and hobbies are everywhere, the former quartering low, the latter hawking high. And – of course – swallowtails hurry by with wings of lacy lingerie.

If the evening is dry and mild, and particularly if there has been rain, spend an exceptional evening at Winterton Dunes. The beach protects one of Britain's healthiest colonies of little tern, an irrepressible seabird. Then scale the dunes inland to where piddling pools (some natural, most purpose-built, all fenced off to safeguard from dogs) huddle in heathy hollows.

▲ The nocturnal chorus of male natterjack toads carries hundreds of metres. (DM/FLPA)

Choose a pool and wind down. A cuckoo calls before roosting. A roe deer grazes. A woodcock 'rodes' in display flight. As the sky thickens, a nightjar churrs in front of the woods, deeper inland. As dusk becomes dark, a different churring pulses from the pool: a chorus of male natterjack toads. Using binoculars or night-vision equipment, scan the shallows for this rare amphibian. Each squeaky rattle is produced by an inflated vocal sac that gleams white in the gloom. Marvellous.

The next day, explore further south. Upton Fen is magnificent, offering the best of Broadland wildlife in a primeval setting. The air bristles with dragonflies: on a warm day, they are everywhere. Norfolk hawker is common, even in the clearing by the car park. One step down in size, the hairy dragonfly is one notch up in abundance. Among numerous damselflies, look closely to distinguish variable damselfly, a scarce insect with a disjunct distribution.

Among other aerial attractions, hobbies dash overhead, ready to seize errant dragonflies that have whirred too high. Marsh harriers monitor the reedbeds; swallowtails occur in further-flung parts. Where wood segues into fen, look for Chinese water deer in the heart of its British range. Savour damp meadows teeming with yellow flag iris and ragged robin. And look carefully for southern marsh orchids, including a recently described form previously thought to be Pugsley's marsh orchid, a rare northern species.

Across the Broads as a whole, there is plenty more for botanists. Interesting plants include marsh helleborine, great fen-sedge, skullcap, bog-rosemary and round-leaved wintergreen. There is even the odd fen orchid colony (a very rare species that you can target elsewhere; see *June, 2* pages 95–8. The sensitive sites inhabited by this mysterious plant are not made public, but stay alert to occasional open days.

Strumpshaw Fen rounds off the weekend. Less wild than Upton Fen, this RSPB reserve has become very popular for those seeking swallowtails. The best area for swallowtail is the footpath and boardwalk in the north of the reserve, including around the obvious, flower-rich (but private) garden. As you walk, check dragonflies for Norfolk hawker and scarce chaser, and areas of open water for otter. In Broadland, wherever there is water there is wildlife.

▶ Nightjar: a cryptically plumaged creature of the night (DT)

Practicalities

Hickling Broad Norfolk Wildlife Trust
(NWT) reserve lies off the A149 4km south of Stalham.
From Hickling village, follow brown signs east to the
visitor centre where you may book boat trips (☀ TG428222
① 01692 598276 ⓦ www.norfolkwildlifetrust.org.uk/
hickling). For the Weaver's Way footpath at the south
of the Broad, follow the minor road southwest from
Hickling village. At the junction with the A149, turn sharp left onto
Reynolds Lane. Continue for 1.5km, parking in the obvious layby on the
right (☀ TG413208) by the signpost for Weaver's Way. For **Winterton
Dunes National Nature Reserve** (☀ TG495205 ⓦ http://tinyurl.com/
wintertondunes), park at the beach (☀ TG498197; check closing
times) northeast of Winterton-on-Sea, off the B1132. For little terns,
walk north along the beach for 1km. For natterjacks, walk north along
inland paths for 1.5km until you see the fenced-off pools.

For **Upton Fen** (aka Upton Broad and Marshes) NWT reserve
(☀ TG380136 ⓦ http://tinyurl.com/uptonfen), take the B1140 from
Acle towards South Walsham. After 3km, take the third right (Mill
Road). At a four-way junction, take the 'no through road' (Low Road)
to the car park. **RSPB Strumpshaw Fen** (☀ TG341065 ① 01603 715191
ⓦ www.rspb.org.uk/strumpshaw) is signposted from the minor road
between Brundall and Strumpshaw, sandwiched between the A47
and the River Yare. For possible fen orchid 'open days', check the NWT
website.

Aylsham (ⓦ www.visitaylsham.co.uk), Acle
(ⓦ www.acle-village.info), Martham and Brundall, and there
is accommodation in villages as well (ⓦ www.norfolkbroads.
com/accommodation). **Sutton Hall** (① 01692 584888 ⓦ www.
suttonhallnorfolk.co.uk) offers two luxurious bedrooms with four-
poster beds in a sympathetically refurbished country hall.

Swallowtail usually emerges late May, but mid-June to
early July is best. Norfolk hawker flies June–July; variable damselfly,
May–July. Natterjack toad is active April to June: warm, dry evenings
following damp days are optimal. Orchids are good all June. Nightjar
is present mid-May to to August; crane is resident.

③

26

Island intensity

Northumberland for seabird colonies including roseate tern & puffin, 'Lindisfarne' helleborine, grey seal, ballan wrasse

> **From great flotillas of auks on the sea to a snowfall of terns on the islets, this is seabird showtime**

Hard hats, ubiquitous on building sites, are not well-known attire for birders. But on this weekend, heads need protection. If you happen not to be equipped like a construction worker, an umbrella may serve you well. Welcome to an Arctic tern colony, where 'sea swallow' parents divebomb at will and strike with force. This makes for doubly exciting wildlife-watching.

One of Britain's most intimate wildlife experiences is to wander amidst the Farne Islands' huge colony of ground-nesting seabirds. This Northumbrian archipelago stakes a claim as Britain's answer to the Galapagos. Boardwalks weave between numerous nests: Sandwich terns on the left, Arctic terns to the right; here a shag, there a kittiwake; and puffins everywhere. Birds are so close that you may prefer a wide-angle lens to a telephoto.

Licensed companies run boats from Seahouses to the Farnes, landing on Inner Farne and/or Staple. Visits to each island take three hours; if you can, combine both islands in a single six-hour excursion so you can spend as much time as possible ashore, communing with the colony.

▶ Guillemots clinging to a rocky outcrop. (JL)

Roughly 40,000 pairs of seabirds breed on these low, rocky outcrops. Half are puffins, a third guillemots. There are a couple of thousand pairs of kittiwake, a delectable gull with an onomatopoeic cry. There are about half this number of Arctic tern, feisty creatures with an insatiable appetite for Iron Man migratory feats. There are 500 pairs of Sandwich tern, and smaller quantities of razorbill, fulmar and common tern. From great flotillas of auks on the sea to a snowfall of terns on the islets, this is seabird showtime.

And the attractions are not solely avian. The Farnes are one of the best places to get up close and personal with grey seals. Some 4,000 animals dwell here, and are easily seen lolling in breakwaters or lumbering on land. The more adventurous wildlife-watcher can get closer still, by investigating (and being investigated by) the seals underwater. At The Hopper, a dive near Longstone Island, an encounter with a bull that tips the scales at 300kg or an inquisitive youngster is unforgettable.

Several companies run dive boats, enabling qualified divers to profit from long summer days and investigate the Farnes' underwater world. Although most trips focus on wrecks, some visit marine life-packed refuges. Dolerite pillars descending 15 fathoms, the Pinnacles are strewn with plumrose anemone and a profusion of soft corals such as dead man's finger. Varied fish life includes ballan wrasse and conger eel. There are cold-water specialities such as Norwegian topknot (left-eyed flatfish!), Yarrel's blenny, lumpsucker and the spectacular wolf fish. Look on and between rocks for shrimps, nudibranchs, spider crabs, brittlestars, sun stars and sea urchins. Underwater life rocks.

▲ A maelström of Arctic terns on the Farnes (OS)

Islands are also the order of day two. Combine another offshore boat trip with a pilgrimage to one of England's most historic sites. The sequence of excursions depends on the tide: you need high water for the ride from Amble to Coquet Island, but low tide to cross Lindisfarne causeway and reach Holy Island.

Coquet offers a seabird experience distinct from the Farnes. Landing is not permitted, so there's neither a risk of treading on terns nor of being attacked by them. Instead, enjoy a profusion of puffins on the sea, big bills and inflected eyebrows on display. There are a few grey seals, while Sandwich, Arctic and common terns commute overhead. But, best of all, as you pass in front of Coquet's tern terraces, look for its avian star. Roseate tern is Britain's most endangered seabird, and 98% of the country's population breeds on Coquet. It is also the most sublime of our seafarers, with its seemingly endless tail streamers and rosy blush to the breast.

Crossing the causeway onto Holy Island, with its distinctive castle growing ever nearer, is a magnificent experience in itself. Eiders abound; the local name of Cuddy's duck honours St Cuthbert who ran Lindisfarne's monastery in the 7th century. But your principal quarry is smaller, rarer and more enigmatic.

Botanists differ on whether the helleborines on Holy Island (aka Lindisfarne) are dune helleborine or a separate species, Lindisfarne helleborine. In the former case they are pretty scarce; in the latter, they occur nowhere else in the world and are exceptionally rare, with fewer than 300 plants. Either way, these orchids are worth seeing; late June marks the start of their short flowering period. Search The Snook at the west of the island. Helleborines grow both among creeping willow shrubbery and open marram grass, particularly on the raised, slightly steeper slope around the dune slack perimeter.

If your luck is out, console yourself with thousands of northern marsh orchid, hundreds of marsh helleborine and a scattering of early marsh orchid. You may strike lucky with an early-blooming green-flowered helleborine, the delectable round-leaved wintergreen or, among butterflies, a bright orange dark green fritillary. Best of all, there's no further need for that hard hat.

▲ Kittiwake – arguably our cutest-looking breeding gull (JL)

Practicalities

Where to go: Visit the **Farne Islands** (⊙ NU230370
① 01665 720651 Ⓦ www.nationaltrust.org.uk/farne-
islands, http://farnephoto.blogspot.co.uk) on licensed
landings from selected boat operators between May
and July. Boats depart **Seahouses** harbour (⊙ NU221321).
Companies such as Billy Shiel's Boats (① 01665 720308
Ⓦ www.farne-islands.com) and Serenity Tours
(① 01665 721667 Ⓦ www.farneislandstours.co.uk) run several
daily tours on small boats, lasting from 2½ hours for a single island
(Inner Farne or Staple) to six hours for a multi-island trip. Dive
tours are operated by Sovereign Diving (① 01665 720760 Ⓦ http://
sovereigndiving.co.uk/diving.html) and Farne Islands Diving Charters
(① 0191 2970914 Ⓦ www.farne-islands-diving.co.uk). For a local
wildlife guide operating trips offshore, try Northern Experience
Pelagics (① 01670 827465 Ⓦ www.northernexperiencepelagics.co.uk;
see advert, page 219).

 RSPB Coquet Island (⊙ NU293045 ① 0191 233 4300 Ⓦ www.
rspb.org.uk/coquetisland) lies offshore from Amble (⊙ NU267047).
Dave Gray runs boats (① 01665 711975 Ⓦ www.puffincruises.co.uk).
Alternatively, phone Amble Tourist Information Centre (① 01665
712313) for sailing times. **Holy Island/Lindisfarne** (⊙ NU098435 for
The Snook ① 01289 381470 Ⓦ www.lindisfarne.org.uk) is linked to
the mainland at Beal by a 5km-long tidal causeway that is accessible
for limited periods each day. Safe crossing times are published:
Ⓦ http://tinyurl.comholytide.

Suggested bases: Amble (Ⓦ www.visitnorthumberland.com/amble),
Bamburgh (Ⓦ www.bamburgh.org.uk) and Seahouses
(Ⓦ www.seahouses.org). Inland in Chatton, **The Old Manse** (① 01668
215343 Ⓦ www.oldmansechatton.co.uk) is a spacious country house,
set in its own gardens, with three well-equipped bedrooms.

Flexibility: Boat trips largely coincide with the seabird breeding
season (May to July) but run at other seasons (eg: to see grey seal).
Optimum diving is between June and July. Marsh orchids flower June
and into July; helleborines from end June to mid-July. The wrasse and
seal are resident.

Accessibility: ③ (⑤ for the diving element)

27 Butterfly high season

Cumbria for high brown fritillary, mountain ringlet, large heath, dune helleborine, dark-red helleborine

After a half-hour, fat-burning yomp uphill from the pass, you reach a grassy plateau. With low cloud cover caressing the mountainside, catching breath by taking in the view is pointless. Abruptly, a chink of sunlight appears. Then a full window. Within 15 minutes, the sun has fried away enough of the morning vapour that you can enjoy the magnificent Lake District panorama. And enough that the plateau now dances with butterflies of a very special kind: mountain ringlet.

> **The grassy plateau dances with very special butterflies: mountain ringlet**

Fleetwith, above Honister Pass, is the most accessible site for England's most high-maintenance butterfly. Mountain ringlet is Britain's sole 'Alpine' butterfly, inhabiting remote northern hillsides mostly above 550m altitude. Cumbria is its sole English outpost. Adults fly only in bright sunshine and temperatures above 15°C, otherwise huddling inside dense tussocks. They live but a few days, and the entire emergence is usually over within a fortnight.

A late June visit to Honister Pass (or, alternatively, Langdale Pikes and Cold Pike, near Ambleside) offers the best prospect of these chocolate-coloured insects. With a backdrop of Buttermere north to Scotland, there may be no more scenic butterfly hotspot. As long as the sun emerges...

▶ High brown fritillary (RP-J)

Once you succeed (or rain stops play), your afternoon destination depends on what you want to see. For red squirrel and osprey head north to Dodd Wood, east of Bassenthwaite Lake. Russet rodents cavort around the raptor observation point; scan the lake below for England's most famous breeding ospreys (although they can be distant). Alternatively venture just outside the Lake District to Cliburn Moss near Penrith to try for creeping lady's-tress (a petite northern orchid) and possibly late-flowering lesser twayblade (a waspish northern orchid) at the reserve's eastern tip. Or head coastwards.

The ridges of Sandscale Haws' wonderful dune slacks are flecked with the lilac and lime of Britain's largest population of dune helleborine, a subtly beautiful orchid. The *coccinea* subspecies of early marsh orchid glows crimson and round-leaved wintergreen gleams white. The odd coralroot orchid might still be on show (see *May, 4* pages 83–6). Amidst creeping willow in damper terrain, green-flowered helleborine may be budding alongside yellow bird's-nest, a remarkable, orchid-like plant that 'feeds' by parasitising fungi. Finally, check out the shallow dune pools that nudge boardwalks for newly emerged natterjack toadlets readily identifiable by a yellow stripe along their backs.

Next day, enjoy butterflies and orchids in one of northern England's hottest habitats: limestone pavement. Start at Whitbarrow Scar where 100ha of plateau offer wraparound views. So big is the vista and so distant the horizon that you may need to jolt yourself into focusing on the small and close.

Whitbarrow is excellent for high brown fritillary, a large, burnt-orange butterfly suffering a disconcerting population slump; Cumbria

▲ Mountain ringlet: a subtle delight more than worth the climb (os)

is now its British bastion. To see it, walk from The Howe around Township Plantation or from Witherslack Hall School northeast through the juniper-rich Hervey Nature Reserve onto the scar. An early start offers the best chance of photography: once warmed up, fritillaries are hyperactive. As you wander, look for northern brown argus, a delightfully diminutive butterfly.

Intersperse your limestone forays by calling at an upland peat bog 5km south. Meathop Moss is a stronghold for large heath (a scarce, northern butterfly), and day-flying moths such as northern eggar. Black darter and the surprisingly large bog bush cricket should be starting to emerge. To explore, walk west to the bog, strewn with bog asphodel and hare's-tail cottongrass.

Then go further south for more limestone. At the cusp of Cumbria and Lancashire lie two prime pavements: Gait Barrows (see *May, 4 pages 83–6*) and Arnside Knott – the latter a small limestone hill with grassy glades. If time permits, visit both. If you only manage one, fret not: the specialities are similar – although the Barrows edges the Knott on the grounds of easier target orchids.

Gait Barrows is better for high brown fritillary, particularly around posts 5–6 on the purple-marked Yew Trail; here, dark green is the scarcer of the fritillary pair. Northern brown argus is rarer still. In the 'grikes' (or fissures) between the pavement 'clints' (blocks), dark-red helleborine flowers. The best area for this scarce northern orchid is between posts 3–5 on the white-marked Limestone Trail.

At Arnside Knott's pavement, check out common juniper and limestone fern. Look closer for smaller secrets. Mounds made by southern wood ants can be seen between the trig point and the Knott's limestone spine. But, above all, enjoy the butterflies. Dark green fritillaries are ten times commoner than high brown: both occur over much of the area, particularly in wooded glades, feeding on bramble, thistles and knapweed. There are the added attractions of other butterflies such as small pearl-bordered fritillary, northern brown argus (between Heathwaite and Hollins Farm) and grayling (along the scree path between car park and viewpoint). Brilliant butterflies and awesome orchids: the joys of a Cumbrian summer.

▶ The beautiful dark-red helleborine (MW)

Practicalities

Where to go: For **Fleetwith**, park at Honister Pass Slate Mine (☀ NY225135), 8km southeast of Buttermere on the B5289. Walk west for 500m, then south for 200m to the cairn (☀ NY216135); check boggy areas immediately west. Alternatively, check sheltered coombes towards Grey Knotts (such as ☀ NY213125). **Dodd Wood** car park (☀ NY234283 ① 01768 778469 Ⓦ www.visitcumbria.com/kes/osprey-watch.htm) is on the A591 from Keswick–Bothel.

For **Cliburn Moss National Nature Reserve** (☀ NY574255 Ⓦ http://tinyurl.com/cliburnmoss), take the A66 east from M6 junction 40, then the A6 south to Eamont Bridge. After 1km, turn left to

▼ Dark-red helleborines love limestone. (MW)

Cliburn; after 5km, turn left towards South Whinfell Farm. Park after 500m. **Sandscale Haws** (⊙ SD189750 ① 01229 462855 Ⓦ www.nationaltrust.org.uk/sandscale-haws) is 5km north of Barrow-in-Furness. Leave the A590 following signs for Roanhead, then take minor roads northwest to the car park (⊙ SD200756). Walk west to the dunes; asking National Trust rangers for directions. Disturbing natterjacks (a 'Schedule 1 species') is a criminal offence.

Whitbarrow Scar lies north of the A590 west of M6 junction 36. Park by The Howe quarry (⊙ SD454884), west of the A5074. Follow yellow arrows west, via Township plantation, for 2km. Or, park by Witherslack Hall School (⊙ SD437860), then walk northeast for 500m via Hervey Nature Reserve (⊙ SD439866 Ⓦ http://tinyurl.com/whitbarrow1). For Howe Ridding Wood (Ⓦ http://tinyurl.com/whitbarrow2), continue beyond the school for 1.5km. Park and follow the footpath northeast. For **Meathop Moss** (Ⓦ www.cumbriawildlifetrust.org.uk/meathop-moss.html), leave Witherslack and rejoin the A590 towards Barrow. Immediately turn south towards Ulpha. After 900m, park near High Stock Bridge (⊙ SD447821), then walk 500m west.

For **Gait Barrows** (⊙ SD478776 ① 07747 852905 Ⓦ http://tinyurl.com/gaitbarrows, http://tinyurl.com/d6y47ft), return to Arnside: head south from the railway station on a minor road, then follow the road east under the railway for 2km. Take the first right and park after 300m. Walk southeast on the footpath and follow marked trails. Permit needed for other areas (Ⓔ rob.petley-jones@naturalengland.org.uk). For **Arnside Knott** (⊙ SD450774 ① 01524 702815 Ⓦ www.nationaltrust.org.uk/arnside-and-silverdale), leave M6 at junction 36, following the A65 north. At Crooklands, follow the B5282 west to Arnside, then follow signs.

Suggested bases: Ambleside (Ⓦ www.amblesideonline.co.uk), Ulverston (Ⓦ www.ulverston.net) and Windermere (Ⓦ www.visitwindermere.co.uk). **Cote How** (① 01539 432765 Ⓦ www.cotehow.co.uk) is grade II-listed and a delightful 16th-century property.

Flexibility: Late June to early July is optimum for seeing all four butterflies. Dune helleborine is best from mid-July; dark-red helleborine in early July.

Accessibility: ⑤ 🚶

There's no need to travel abroad to enjoy leaping dolphins. Various sites in Britain offer opportunities to watch energetic, playful bottle-nosed dolphins, among them Cromarty Firth in Inverness-shire (see *July 3* pages 117–20). (JM/A)

28
The purple empire

Hampshire for purple emperor, bog orchid, southern damselfly, scarce blue-tailed damselfly, nightjar

Early morning in a wood straddling Hampshire and Wiltshire. The air is dry, the sun smiling, the audience fidgeting with anticipation. Ten pairs of eyes bore through canopy foliage. All crave sight of an enormous underwing, resplendent in chestnut and ivory. An underwing belonging to His Imperial Majesty the purple emperor. Acknowledging the adulation of his people, Britain's joint-biggest butterfly takes to the wing with glides of breathtaking power, then swoops elegantly to the ground. And promptly undermines its stateliness by feasting on fresh canine faeces. Such is the paradox of the purple empire.

> ❝ Britain's biggest butterfly takes to the wing with glides of breathtaking power ❞

Bentley Wood is a Premiership site for purple emperor; the second weekend of July is peak season. Arrive early: although emperors rarely stretch wings until the air is warm, their feeding forays to ground level usually cease by 10.00, whence they return to canopy concealment. Their Houdini act cues your move from Bentley's eastern car park to enjoy the rest of the wood's winged bonanza.

White admirals – a mini-emperor in looks – proliferate. Luxuriously large and outrageously orange, silver-washed fritillaries applaud in abundance. Small pearl-bordered fritillaries favour damp parts of the

A male southern damselfly, one of Britain's rarest dragonflies. (IL)

eastern clearing. Purple hairstreaks favour oaks and brambles. White-letter hairstreaks (rarer, fussier) need more tracking: try around the Ralph Whitlock memorial. From the car park, head west, then turn right at the crossroads. Continue over the next crossroads until the track bears right: check elms here.

Around lunchtime relocate southwest to the nearest fringes of the New Forest. Visit Ogdens, one of the national park's least-disturbed sites. Because ponies greatly outnumber humans, Ogdens is a prime place for perhaps Europe's rarest mushroom. In Britain, nail fungus occurs exclusively on pony poo in the New Forest, Purbeck and Brecks. If scatology doesn't appeal, fear not: you have other objectives at Ogdens. Stroll eastwards along Latchmore Brook for a dragonfly treat.

Beautiful demoiselles bounce above streamside vegetation like iridescent yo-yos. Golden-ringed dragonflies patrol; marauding missiles seeking inattentive insects. Keeled skimmers buzz over muddy banks. Southern damselfly, a localised species that frequents dense vegetation beside slow-moving water, and the waif-like small red damselfly can both be common – yet are threatened nationwide. Best of all, seepages north of the brook are a haven for scarce blue-tailed damselfly and purple-bordered gold, a sumptuous moth, both of which love boggy mires where surface water dribbles.

Pursuing the boggy theme, head southeast to Stoney Cross for a most special plant. From the car park walk east to Long Beech Inclosure then follow the wood boundary south. Where you encounter mires with running water, descend to ground level. Keeping eyes low, look across (but absolutely do not enter) the mire. You should pick out the lime-green form of Britain's tiniest orchid – bog orchid – flirting with the carnivorous round-leaved sundew, itself a food plant for sundew plume moth larvae.

After dinner, make a dusk sally to heathland deep in the New Forest – south of Beaulieu Road station, say – for 'goatsuckers'. At twilight, nightjars (their proper name) demarcate territories by 'churring'. Even if you do not glimpse this nocturnal bird, its call is enough to characterise heathland evenings. On the way to bed, you may bump into light crimson underwing (a large moth favouring old oaks), badger, red or fallow deer. Bonus!

Start the following day on the north border of Wilverley Inclosure. Walking eastwards towards 'Naked Man' (an oak stump, before you ask), search pathside bracken for two stunning, rare flowers. The sublime lesser butterfly orchid can be abundant, but you will need luck to find wild gladiolus which, in Britain, occurs only in the New Forest. Silver-studded blues – daintily attractive butterflies – adore and adorn the adjacent heather.

As the day warms, have another stab at yesterday's star dragonflies. From Puttles Bridge car park, a few kilometres northeast, walk south along Silver Stream and/or northwest along Ober Water. The former is particularly good for southern damselfly. Ober Water can be great for scarce blue-tailed damselfly (check tiny channels and seepages, particularly north of the copse 600m east of Markway Bridge), white-legged damselfly (at its New Forest stronghold) and small red damselfly. Keeled skimmers should be numerous, along with a range of commoner fare including golden-ringed dragonfly, the odd silver-studded blue, dotted border wave (a moth) and numerous heath spotted orchids in the heather, plus birds such as common redstart. Bliss.

Finish the weekend by wandering amidst heathland at Pig Bush, near Beaulieu Road station. Your bird list should be topped by wood lark, Dartford warbler and stonechat, butterflies by grayling. All Britain's native reptiles occur, offering you a good chance of adder (but smooth snake or sand lizard only for the amazingly lucky). A fabulous suite of plants – marsh gentian, bog asphodel, heath fragrant orchid, lesser butterfly orchid and heath spotted orchid – occurs along the ridge leading southwest to the railway line and beyond to Denny Lodge Inclosure (where you have a shout of finding wild gladiolus). Best of all, mooch in the lilac of summertime heather and muse fondly about the sovereign star of your weekend in the purple empire.

▶ Search mires carefully for the appropriately named bog orchid. (JL)

Practicalities

Bentley Wood is 10km east of Salisbury.
Leave Winchester northwest on the B3049 to
Stockbridge, then continue west on the A30. Just after
the A343 junction, turn south to East Winterslow then
West Dean along Tytherley Road. Bentley Wood eastern
car park (☀ SU256293) is signposted west of the road.

The **New Forest National Park** (Ⓦ www.newforest
npa.gov.uk) lies between Southampton, Fordingbridge and
Christchurch. From the A338/B3078 junction in Fordingbridge, take
the minor road southeast through Stuckton to Hyde, then follow
signs for **Ogdens** car park (☀ SU181123). Walk east along the north
bank of Latchmore Brook to where Lay Gutter Valley joins the brook
(☀ SU190126). Return to the B3078 and head east; 2.5km after the
B3080 junction turn south for 3.5km to **Stoney Cross** (☀ SU248126).

For **Wilverley Inclosure**, park on the A35 at the Inclosure's
northern apex (☀ SU241020); walk southeast towards Naked Man,
woodland to your right. Access **Ober Water** from two points. Either
take the A35 4km north towards Lyndhurst; at Markway Bridge, park
on the verge (☀ SU250038). Or continue 3km further north on the
A35, turning southeast along Rhinefield Ornamental Drive. After
4km, park at Puttles Bridge (☀ SU270029). **Beaulieu Road station**
(☀ SU347065) and **Pig Bush** car parks (☀ SU364050) lie between
Lyndhurst and Beaulieu on the B3056. Walk southwest to the railway
line and Denny Lodge Inclosure.

Suggested bases: Fordingbridge (Ⓦ www.visitfordingbridge.
co.uk), Brockenhurst (Ⓦ www.brockenhurst-newforest.org.uk) and
Lyndhurst (Ⓦ www.newforest-online.co.uk/lyndhurst.asp). South
of Fordingbridge, **Furze Hill Cottage** (Ⓣ 01425 650581 Ⓦ http://
bedandbreakfastnewforest.org.uk) is a delightful guesthouse, with
breakfast eggs from the owners' chickens.

Flexibility: Purple emperor flies late June–mid-July, but are most
reliable in the week after emergence. Bog orchid flowers early July
to mid-August. The rare damselflies fly early June–early August. Wild
gladiolus and lesser butterfly orchid flower June–mid-July (best in
June). Nightjars occur mid-May–mid-August.

Accessibility: ③ 🚶

29

There be dragons... and dolphins

Inverness-shire for white-faced darter, northern damselfly, creeping lady's-tress, bumblebee robberfly, bottle-nosed dolphin

From delicate damselflies to demonstrative dolphins, via rare breeding birds and tantalisingly scarce flowers, this Highland weekend offers great variety. To see it all, however, you need some Speyside sun (a typically scarce commodity). Cross fingers for a favourable forecast – and plan carefully. Devote sunny periods to searching for invertebrates, specifically three dragonflies and a single butterfly, beetle and robberfly. Keep birding and botany in reserve for if (when?) rainclouds loom.

> **"The world's most northerly bottle-nosed dolphins perform acrobatically just offshore"**

Abernethy Forest holds the core subset of target critters. As you approach Loch Garten's Osprey Centre from the B970, pause at the small pool south of the road. Using the short boardwalk, check semi-submerged sedge until you find northern damselfly, a nationally threatened species restricted to the Highlands, at its most reliable site. Nearer the Centre, call at Loch Mallachie car park. Between vehicles and road and along the path to the loch, look for creeping lady's-tress, delicate white-flowered orchids that caress the ground beneath Caledonian pines.

▲ Bottle-nosed dolphin leaping. (PM)

At the Centre, enjoy ospreys at their best-known location (see *April,* *2* pages 57–60); the incumbent pair should have fledged young by now. RSPB staff may help you track down further clumps of creeping lady's-tress and suggest good spots to find a red squirrel or crested tit to bouncing through the pines. Seeing Caledonian bird specialities in July can be tricky, however, so don't harbour strong hopes of the punky tit, crossbills or capercaillie. Instead, if the sun shines, head 1.2km southeast for another star dragonfly. The classy-looking, multicoloured white-faced darter frequents a boggy pool tucked off the road just shy of the turnoff to Tulloch.

While wandering Abernethy, keep an attentive eye on both ground and prostrate deadwood. Fallen trees are the domain of timberman beetle, a remarkable creature with huge antennae, and bumblebee robberfly, a fiercesome predator of insects that disguises itself as an unthreatening bee. Groundwise, you may bump into more creeping lady's-tress, common and serrated wintergreen, or the delicate twinflower. A relict of the last ice age now confined to 50 sites in native Scottish pinewoods, this Arctic-Alpine plant has two pink bell-like flowers topping a slender stem.

If the weather remains fair (what luck!), take advantage of long northern days to explore mountain tops at Cairn Gorm. During the summer, you must walk two hours from Coire Cas car park to the plateau to look for rare montane birds and plants. But the trek is worth it. Birdwise, ptarmigan allows close approach although its summertime camouflage may make it 'disappear' amidst lichen-covered rocks. The odd snow bunting, males smartly attired, frequents corrie rims. Best of all is dotterel, a confiding plover with an inquisitive eyestripe, which climate change threatens to force to ever higher latitudes.

Plantwise, the rough path into Coire an t-Sneachda offers congregations of globeflower and roseroot. The northern corries host rare cliff flora, including Alpine saxifrage, Highland saxifrage and curved wood-rush. On the plateau look for trailing azalea, crowberry and cloudberry. With sharp eyes and a considerable amount of luck, you may even bump into a rare and localised moth, the scarlet-and-black Scotch burnet.

As darkness falls, two options stand out. Try for pine marten (as well as badger, red deer and wood mouse) in Rothiemurchus Forest

▶ White-faced darter is a striking northern dragonfly. (DE)

(see *April, 2* pages 57–60). Or, at RSPB Insh Marshes, listen for the 'whiplash' call of one of Britain's rarest birds, spotted crake. The ambitious or insomniac could even coast forest roads into the night on the off-chance of wildcat.

Next day, start by walking the circumference of Loch an Eilean, famed for its island castle and voted Britain's best picnic site. This scenic site is good for creeping lady's-tress and crested tit. As the day warms, day-flying moths such as chimney sweeper and pretty pinion, and a subtle butterfly, Scotch argus, should wake up. The latter is one of the tardiest butterflies to emerge each summer. As you think of departing, a flash of orange alerts you to a fritillary: size will determine whether it is dark green or small pearl-bordered.

If butterflies are flying, use the fine weather to seek out your final boreal dragonfly. Northern emerald is a scarce Scottish species that helicopters low above water, eyes sparkling metallic green atop a largely sooty body. To see it, focus on tiny bog pools, a habitat shunned by the similar-looking brilliant emerald and downy emerald. A convenient site is Uath Lochans in Inshriach Forest.

Once sated with dragons, it's north to the 'Black Isle' for exhibitionist dolphins! The Moray Firth hosts the world's most northerly population of bottle-nosed dolphin. For landlubbers, Chanonry Point offers the best views, particularly on an incoming tide when the cetaceans perform acrobatically close offshore. For a more intimate encounter, join a licensed boat trip from Cromarty. With the light at your back, late afternoon offers the best photographic opportunities, so your Highland weekend culminates here on – appropriately – a high.

Where to go: The focal point of **RSPB Abernethy Forest** is Loch Garten Osprey Centre, (see *April, 2* pages 57–60). The 'northern damselfly pool' (☀ NH966193) is 900m east of the B970. Loch Mallachie (☀ NH972185) is halfway between pool and Centre. Another damselfly pool (☀ NH954192) is by the B970, 700m southwest of the Loch Garten road. The white-faced darter pool (☀ NH982175) is 1.2km southeast of the Centre, 100m before the turn to Tulloch.

For **Cairn Gorm** see *April, 2* page 60. Use the ski-lift car park (☀ NH990061) and walk two hours to the plateau (May–November, there is no access from ski-lift to plateau). **RSPB Insh Marshes** (☀ NN775998 ① 01540 661518 ⓦ www.rspb.org.uk/inshmarshes) is along the B9152 northeast of Kingussie. For **Loch an Eilein**, follow the B970 south from Aviemore, turn right to Insh and the car park (☀ NH897084). Book the Rothiemurchus Hide through Speyside Wildlife (① 01479 812498 ⓦ www.speysidewildlife.co.uk). **Uath Lochans** (☀ NH835023 ⓦ http://tinyurl.com/uathlochans) is signposted 2.5km south along a minor road off the B970 at Insh House. The **Black Isle/Moray Firth** lie north of Inverness off the A9/ A832. Watch from Chanonry Point lighthouse (☀ NH749557), 2.5km southeast of Fortrose, or by boat from Cromarty (① 01381 600323 ⓦ www.ecoventures.co.uk). For a local wildlife guide, try ScotNature (① 07718 255265 ⓦ www.scotnature.co.uk; see advert, page 219).

Suggested bases: Cairngorms towns (ⓦ http://visitcairngorms. com) include Aviemore (ⓦ www.visitaviemore.co.uk), Grantown-on-Spey (ⓦ www.visitgrantown.co.uk), Nethybridge (ⓦ www.nethy bridge.com) and Boat of Garten (ⓦ www.boatofgarten.com). Near Grantown-on-Spey, **Tigh Na Sgiath Hotel** (① 01479 851345 ⓦ www. tigh-na-sgiath.co.uk) is an elegant Victorian mansion in spacious grounds.

Flexibility: June–July is best for dragonflies. Late June to early July is best for Alpine flowers. Creeping lady's-tress flowers end June to August. Dotterel departs end July. Dolphins are best April–September. Bumblebee robberflies are active May–September.

Accessibility: ② (⑤ for Cairn Gorm element) 🚶

30
Snorkelling and skippers

Dorset for shiny spider crab, Lulworth skipper, small red damselfly, heath tiger beetle, Dorset heath

> **"Multicoloured fish such as ballan and corkwing wrasse bring to mind tropical reefs "**

Legs kicking languidly, your eyes scan submerged seaweed forests, unlocking their underwater secrets. Later, back on dry land, you inspect coastal turf for noteworthy butterflies and heathland mires for carnivorous plants. In this weekend of two halves, enjoy brilliant marine and terrestrial life along Purbeck's Jurassic Coast (see *April, 4* pages 65–8).

On your marine day, swim a snorkelling trail and rummage among rocky pools. Kimmeridge Bay is a sheltered cove backed by soft shale cliffs. Dorset Wildlife Trust provides a self-guided route for wetsuit-clad naturalists, enabling appreciation of seabed diversity: from sandy bottoms through rocky reefs to seaweed gardens. The 400m-long trail in warm, shallow water is best on falling neap tides in calm conditions; visibility is poor after wind or rain. Buoys mark different habitats.

A turf of small red seaweeds, interspersed with snakelocks anemones (beware their sting!), lines much of the bay. On swirling patches of kelp, look for the neon striplights of blue-rayed limpet. Dense seaweeds harbour inshore fish such as rock and twin-spot goby, tompot blenny (replete with punky horns), worm pipefish and various clingfish.

▲ Look for the stunning corkwing wrasse amongst seaweed and rocks in shallow water. (ST/FLPA)

Seaweeds are worth enjoying in their own right: tamarisk seaweed is stunning, and Japanese seaweed is sumptuously golden.

Check overhanging ledges for crabs, including velvet swimming (fiery of eyes and temper: keep fingers clear!), broad-clawed porcelain and shiny spider. Starfish such as brittlestars and cushion stars are common, and colourful sponges layer purple algae-encrusted rocks. Dark mini-caves are the domain of black-faced blenny, an otherwise rare fish that thrives here. Most exciting are the larger fish. Multicoloured wrasse such as ballan and corkwing evoke tropical reefs. Schools of baitfish – sandeels or sand smelt – flash silver as they shoal, enticing into the cove predators such as bass and mackerel. Manna from marine heaven!

A Bay day is incomplete without a landlubbing stint: rockpooling on the wave-cut platform called Washing Ledge, the air tangy with the scent of seaweed and sponges. Kimmeridge has an extended low-water period of four hours, enabling leisurely ferreting. In unhelpful contrast to snorkelling, however, rockpooling is impossible on neap tides (and best on spring tides). Regrettably, you can never have the best of both worlds. Nevertheless, you should find invertebrates such as beadlet anemone, barnacles, limpets and common periwinkles (often predated by dog whelks).

When the incoming tide beats your retreat or you are done with peering into pools, forsake marine wildlife to spend the remainder of the weekend tracking down terrestrial fare. The Jurassic Coast's star butterfly is Lulworth skipper. In Britain, this tiny golden insect flies

▲ A vibrant abundance of gorse and heather on Hartland Moor (BG/A)

only along a 50km stretch of chalk downland between Swanage and Weymouth, and for just six weeks each year.

A good place to search is around the chalk quarry at Winspit (see *April, 4* pages 65–8. The slopes are alive with skippers and marbled white. You may strike lucky with an early Adonis blue: the intensity of colour beggars belief. Search inside the quarry for ivy broomrape and wild cabbage, the slopes for sunbathing adder, and just east for common wall lizard. A second prime site – indeed, the original home of the eponymous skipper – is the steep Bindon Hill east of Lulworth Cove. Chalkhill blue and marbled white should flutter by as well.

Inland, grassy slopes surrounding Corfe Castle offer a good chance of Lulworth skipper. If you indulge in a tourist trip around the fortress, look for common wall lizard guarding its ramparts. Immediately south of Corfe Castle village is a great site for the nationally threatened southern damselfly. Some 200m east of the A351/B3069 junction, look for copulating pairs in streamside vegetation south of the footpath.

Then explore several sites strewn across Hartland Moor. Just south of New Mills Heath a small roadside pond backed by steep, sandy slopes is a good place to find sand lizard and adder. Carry on north a further 2km to boggy heathland west of the road, which holds keeled skimmer, black darter, the impressive wasp spider and the lilac-flowered marsh gentian. Smooth snake inhabits higher, drier land on Middlebere Heath, but you will need luck to spot one basking semi-concealed in the heather. You may have more luck with a smaller predator: heath tiger beetle hunts hyperactively on bare terrain. Continuing north to a T-junction, turn west towards Stoborough: stout spikes of marsh helleborine – a sublime mid-summer orchid – may still decorate the southern roadside.

Taking the next left (Soldier's Road), park after 1.5km. This area, covered pink with blooming Dorset heath, is good for wood lark, Dartford warbler, grass wave, silver-studded blue and grayling. On Stoborough Heath's mires west of the road, the tiny bog orchid hides demurely but small red damselfly, bog asphodel and three species of carnivorous sundew – round-leaved, oblong-leaved and great – are more easily seen. If you consider plants to be passive and unthreatening, sundews force a re-examination of your prejudices. Woe betide any insect that ventures onto these scary-looking plants.

Where to go: For **Kimmeridge Bay** (☀ SY909789
☎ 01929 481044), leave the A351 at Corfe Castle,
heading west for 6km, through Church Knowle, then
turn south to Kimmeridge. Drive through the village to
the Bay car park. Dorset Wildlife Trust run the Fine
Foundation Marine Centre, which offers guidance and
hires masks/snorkels. For **Winspit**, use the car park in
Worth Matravers (☀ SY974776), then take the footpath south to the
coastal quarry (☀ SY977761). For **Bindon Hill** (☀ SY821801), 15km
southwest of Wareham, follow the B3070 to its southernmost point
at West Lulworth. Park near the Heritage Centre and walk east uphill.

   Corfe Castle car park (☀ SY959824) is immediately north of
the village at the B3351/A351 junction. Some 500m northwest of
here, turn north to access **Hartland Moor**. After 1.1km you reach the
small pond west of the road near New Mills Heath (☀ SY956838).
Further north, park around ☀ SY962855, then walk west for marsh
gentian, etc. Marsh helleborines occupy the south side of the Arne–
Stoborough road (centered on ☀ SY950864). On Soldier's Road,
heading back south to the A351, park after 1.5km (☀ SY942852) where
a track heads north over a hillock and across **Stoborough Heath**.

Suggested bases: Wareham (Ⓦ www.purbeck.org.uk), Swanage
(Ⓦ www.virtual-swanage.co.uk) and Poole (Ⓦ www.pooletourism.
com). Between Kingston and Langton Matravers is **Kingston Country
Courtyard** (☎ 01929 481066 Ⓦ www.kingstoncountrycourtyard.com),
a new development with a large range of tastefully attired farmstead
accommodation, many with bare stone walls.

Flexibility: The Kimmeridge Bay snorkelling trail is open May to
September. Falling neap tides on calm days are best. The lowest tides
(a few days after the new moon) create the greatest expanse of rocky
reefs and residual pools. Lulworth skipper flies June to early August,
small red damselfly June–August. Heath tiger beetle ia active
April–July.

Accessibility: ⑤ 🚶

▶ Heath tiger beetle (JL)

31 Shark!

Cornwall & Devon for blue shark, basking shark, greater horseshoe bat, southern damselfly, silver-studded blue

> **When the blue shark detects the bait and approaches, you slip into the cage**

A triangular fin scythes through the sea surface then slips under the boat. At a sign from the Cornish skipper, you make the final micro-adjustment to your mask, then slip through a hatch into salty water. Beyond the sturdy steel bars that now surround you, a blue shark rushes your way before turning parallel a metre or so from your saucer-like eyes.

Cage-diving in Cornwall? With sharks? This has to be a joke, right? Not in the slightest. In 2005, seeking to convert shark-based tourism from fishing to watching, the Shark Conservation Society pioneered offshore excursions to look for blue shark. Applying techniques familiar to anyone who has sought great white sharks in South Africa, a purpose-built cage is lowered beneath the waves, and snorkelers slip into it. Scent is trailed in the water, sharks approach, and thrilling (yet safe) encounters unfold.

Between June and September blue sharks hunt off the north coast of England's westernmost county. This striking shark is a couple of metres long, deep blue in colour and disarmingly large eyed. July's calm waters offer the best chance of connecting, with seven trips in ten succeeding. To see sharks in their element, take an all-day cage-diving boat trip from Newquay or Bude. Once 25km into deep water, the crew churns out the bait (or

▶ Cute brute?
Blue shark (JP)

'chum': usually mashed fish). A shark may be distant, but its highly attuned sense of smell detects the offering. Initially nervous, the shark approaches... then vanishes. Eventually, it trusts that the boat's occupants do not intend to snare it and approaches the boat closely. At this point you slip into the cage.

Should you fail, the typical supporting cast would constitute a 'red letter day' in its own right. Most trips come across basking shark, another summer speciality of southwestern waters. Britain's largest fish is a gentle giant: many exceed five metres in length. You may get the chance to enter the water and truly appreciate this serene shark's might. There is also a decent chance of marine mammals: pods of short-beaked common dolphin bow-riding breathtakingly, while harbour porpoise or grey seal swim more sedately. Whenever you chum, check your wake for seabirds such as British storm-petrel or even Sabine's gull, enticed by the free lunch.

Once back on *terra firma*, head 90 minutes southeast to the fringes of Dartmoor for a magnificent mammal experience. The mass emergence of bats at dusk from subterranean slumber is a common component of wildlife documentaries from far-flung places. Yet, like the shark trip, you can witness this wonder close to home.

Arriving in Buckfast before dusk, take a terrace table at the Abbey Inn, sundowner in hand. Unwind by scanning the River Dart for dipper, grey wagtail and otter. A few minutes after sunset greater horseshoe bats emerge from nearby caves that hold Europe's biggest gathering of the species. Hundreds (some say thousands) of bats stream past and (appropriately) dart over the river, before gradually dispersing. Thereafter, try the footpath by Buckfast Church, where the bats hunt.

Greater horseshoe is not Buckfast's only bat. Daubenton's bat is strongly associated with waterbodies, routinely skimming the River Dart surface for insects. You should see pipistrelles and, if armed with a bat detector to determine the frequency of echolocatory clicks, can differentiate between soprano and common pipistrelle.

After such a mammoth day, treat yourself to a lie-in and a leisurely breakfast: there's only one site on today's itinerary, and it does not require an early start. Your destination is the East Devon pebble-beds, specifically the hilly heathland at RSPB Aylesbeare Common. Flora

▲ Greater horseshoe bat preparing to emerge from its roost to feed (DC)

here is dominated by three heathers (ling, bell and, in damper terrain, cross-leaved heath) and two species of gorse (counterintuitively, western is more abundant than common), often parasitised by the red-stemmed, white-flowered dodder.

Dartford warbler and stonechat scold from the prickly bushes, and the heathers are embellished with silver-studded blue, a refined butterfly that repays close examination. On open, sandy tracks, look for grayling (a master of camouflage). In wooded areas, prepare for a hefty silver-washed fritillary to fly past at any moment.

In the mires, you should see the tall, yellow-flowered spikes of bog asphodel. Hugging the ground, look for the glutinous sap of round-leaved sundew and the pin-striped pink flowers of bog pimpernel. Keeled skimmers pose on the marshy margins and the gargantuan golden-ringed dragonfly hangs still on gorse bushes, but you need to look carefully for small red damselfly and the globally threatened southern damselfly. Try sedge-fringed seepages around Five Ponds in the west of the Common.

Alert to the abundance of insect prey, the odd hobby may power overhead. Down on the ground, there's a good chance of finding a sunbathing adder or common lizard (the latter often basks on fenceposts). But, above all, after yesterday's exertion and exhilaration, relax amidst the wildlife of a southern heathland, one of England's most treasured, picturesque and biologically valuable habitats.

In their element:
blue shark (NW/FLPA)

Practicalities

For **blue shark trips**, travel with a
member of the Cornwall Cage Diving Operators
Association, which operates a code of conduct designed
to minimise disturbance to sharks. Most trips depart
Bude or Newquay. Try Atlantic Diver in Newquay
(☎ 07860 927833 ⓦ www.atlanticdiver.co.uk). There are
fixed departures and charters. Alternatively, Shark
Cornwall (☎ 07799 490552 ⓦ www.peirceshark.com/shark.cornwall)
operates trips for members of the Shark Conservation Society or
Shark Trust. Trips are subject to suitable weather (calm seas).

Buckfastleigh bats are best watched from The Abbey Inn on
Buckfast Road (⌖ SX743667 ⓦ www.theabbeyinn-buckfast.co.uk).
Leave the A38 at the B3380 junction, following signs to Buckfast
Abbey; turn right after the bridge to find the pub on the right.
Alternatively, try the top of the footpath at Buckfast Church
(⌖ SX742665), 200m southwest. **RSPB Aylesbeare Common**
 (⌖ SY058896 ☎ 01395 233655 ⓦ www.rspb.org.uk/
aylesbearecommon) lies 13km east of Exeter. From M5 junction 30
take the A3052 east; 800m after the B3180, use the car park at the
junction with the minor road to Hawkerland. Explore heathland north
of the A3052. Five Ponds lies on the footpath towards Halfway Inn on
the west of the Common.

In Cornwall, the nearest towns include Newquay
(ⓦ www.visitnewquay.org) and Bude (ⓦ www.visitbude.info). In
Devon, a good base is Buckfastleigh (ⓦ www.buckfastleigh.org); see
April, 1, pages 53–6. **The Beach at Bude** (☎ 01288 389800 ⓦ www.
thebeachatbude.co.uk) is a boutique hotel offering spacious, modern
rooms decorated in New England seaside style.

Blue sharks frequent Cornish waters from June
to September, basking sharks from May–October. Greatest
numbers of greater horseshoe bats are on warm evenings,
June–September. Heathland dragonflies are best
early June to early August. Silver-studded blue flies
from the end of June to late August.

⑤

◄ A male silver-studded blue feeding on bell heather. (JL)

32 Basking on the Lizard

Cornwall for Cornish heath, yellow centaury, bog asphodel, chough, basking shark

A carpet of lilac spreads across the foreground: Cornish heath, our rarest heather in full bloom. As a backdrop, double fins punctuate the waters of an arresting rock-shouldered cove: basking sharks, the biggest fish in Britain's sea. In this weekend, drop to your hands

> ❝ **The telltale twin sails of basking sharks sprinkle an arresting rock-shouldered cove** ❞

and knees (to examine the botany of arguably Britain's most important plant area), don wet suit and snorkel (to swim with sharks), scan cobalt-blue skies (for chough and peregrine) and rummage in tidal pools (for crabs and anemones). Welcome to the Lizard Peninsula, Britain's southernmost spot.

Botanically, the Lizard is in a class of its own. Overlaid with maritime heathland, wet woodland, moorland plateau and clifftop grassland, the peninsula harbours more than half of Britain's native flora *and* a greater density of nationally scarce plants than any other area. The Lizard's secret is a combination of climate (frost-free winters) and geology (rocks include serpentine and schists, gabbro and gneiss).

Plant enthusiasts debate whether May or August is the best month. For rarities, spring probably wins. But for a floral spectacle, with the added bonus of near-guaranteed basking shark, visit during late summer. In this season, the

◀ Red-billed and red-legged, the chough (PH/FLPA)

heather glows. Each of the four species of heath lends a particular shade of pink or purple to the composite display. Ling, bell heather and cross-leaved heath are widespread in Britain, but the nationally rare Cornish heath is exclusive not just to the eponymous county but to the Lizard Peninsula itself.

Top spots for the Cornish heath spectacle are Goonhilly Downs, Predannack Downs and Kynance. These largely inland heaths are also decorated with dayflying moths such as the aptly named beautiful yellow underwing, and less ostentatious but similarly special plants. Remarkably, several are associated with ancient cart-tracks that traverse the heathland. So dependent are species such as pygmy rush and yellow centaury on ephemeral pools that saturate the wheel-rutted terrain that they have become radically rarer since the demise of horse-drawn transport. In redress, Cornish conservationists have been working frantically to recreate this micro-habitat and have been rewarded by the resurgence of plants feared doomed. Scrutinise any rutted tracks you come across, particularly around the Ruan Pool at Windmill Farm reserve.

Windmill Farm is gaining a reputation for a host of dragonflies. Notably, the farm is Britain's most regular site for red-veined darter, a scarce migrant and occasional breeder. On boggy heaths such as at Goonhilly, look for keeled skimmer amidst the golden glaze of bog asphodel, and keep your eye trained for basking common lizard or adder on bare terrain.

Then wander coastwards. Clifftop grassland, particularly on the west coast south of Kynance Cove, offers rich botanical treats. Search for autumn squill, a relative of the bluebell and a local speciality. Two valleys running inland from the cove hold bloody crane's-bill, spotted cat's-ear, hairy greenweed and thyme broomrape amidst the rocky outcrops and boulder scree. Peruse rocks themselves for rare lower plants such as ciliate strap and golden hair lichens. On the cliffs, look for wild asparagus lying prostrate; it is abundant on the inaccessible Asparagus Island, just offshore.

The valley leading east from Caerthillian Cove is famous for a sackful of clovers, and marks the site where a 19th-century botanist managed to cover ten species of clover with his straw boater (an innovative 'hat-trick'). Regrettably, the clovers will have ceased flowering so you need

◀ Bog asphodel: a striking, ankle-high plant of heathland mires (JL)

superlative identification skills to differentiate long-headed clover from twin-headed, or knotted from upright. Kneeling on the ground, keep eyes peeled for hairy bird's-foot trefoil and fringed rupturewort.

Casting your eyes upwards into the coastal skies, you may spy a peregrine cruising, looking for an inattentive pigeon. Territorial stonechats top coast-loving gorse bushes, demanding attention with their clacking call. But the most significant vocalisation you should hear is the piercing *chiaa* of a chough. This curve-billed crow returned to breed on the Lizard, Cornwall and England in 2002, after a half-century of silent absence.

As you amble the tops, peer down into the turquoise coves. Those on the east of the Peninsula – notably Coverack and Porthkerris – are particularly favoured by basking sharks. Seeing these gargantuan plankton-eaters from a height is impressive enough, enabling appreciation of the beast's stature. More intimate is to watch these *überfish* with their telltale twin sails at sea level. Best of all is to snorkel with the gentle giants, your head underwater as the fish feast, both its massive mouth and your incredulous eyes wide open. Boat trips from Porthkerris are designed for you to do so, tracking the fish and dropping you into their paths.

For more marine wildlife, try rockpooling at low tide. Search Kennack Sands' numerous seaweed-strewn shallows for common blenny, shore crab, velvet swimming crab and snakelocks anemone. As its name suggests, Kennack also hosts a sandy beach, so after a weekend at the toe of Britain enjoying basking sharks and watching lizards bask, why not soak up some Cornish sun yourself?

▲ Is there anywhere better than the Lizard Peninsula to snorkel with basking sharks? (DP/A)

Where to go: Access the **Lizard Peninsula** (Lizard Point
☀ SW701116 ⓦ http://tinyurl.com/lizardpeninsula,
ⓦ www.wildlifetrust.org.uk/nature_reserves) via the
A3083 and B3293 south of Helston. For **North Predannack
Downs** (☀ SW692180), park in Penhale (A3083/B3293
junction); take the bridleway southwest. **Windmill Farm**
(☀ SW693152) is 1km west of the A3083, 3.5km south of
Penhale. Turn southwest at Mount Hermon, following the lane to the
windmill; footpaths run by Ruan Pool (☀ SW696158). For **Goonhilly
Downs** park at Traboe Cross (☀ SW735206) on the B3293, 1.5km
southeast of Goonhilly Earth Station; explore south either side of
the minor road. For **Kynance Cove** (☀ SW688132 ⓣ 01326 561407
ⓦ www.nationaltrust.org.uk/lizard-and-kynance-cove), take the
minor road west immediately north of Lizard village to the car park.
Walk southwards along the coast and explore valleys leading inland.
Valleys leading to **Caerthillian Cove** (☀ SW694125) harbour fine flora.

The east coast is best for basking shark. Try **Coverack Cove** (use
the village car park off the B3294; ☀ SW782185). Snorkelling trips
depart **Porthkerris** (Porthkerris Divers ⓣ 01326 280620 ⓦ www.
porthkerris.com). From St Keverne on the B3293, drive northeast
towards Porthallow, then follow signs to Porthkerris car park
(☀ SW806228). **Kennack Sands** car park (☀ SW734165) lies at the end
of the minor road, northeast of Ruan Minor, Poltesco and Kuggar.

Suggested bases: Various villages offer accommodation on the Lizard
Peninsula (ⓦ www.lizard-peninsula.co.uk, www.visitlizardcornwall.
co.uk). Between Lizard and Caerthillian, **Atlantic House** (ⓣ 01326
290399 ⓦ www.atlantichouselizard.co.uk) is a luxury B&B offering
sunny, spacious rooms with elegant décor.

Flexibility: Cornish heath blooms July–September, peaking in August.
Most other plants mentioned cease flowering end August. Basking
sharks occur May–August (peaking end July to mid-August), but
timing is erratic and partly dependent on plankton blooms. Go
rockpooling at low tides, particularly a few days after the new moon.
Chough is resident.

Accessibility: ④ 🚶

33

Pelagic paradise

Isles of Scilly for Wilson's storm-petrel,
great shearwater, blue shark,
grey seal, lesser white-
toothed shrew

> **"** Boat trips off
> Scilly provide the
> easiest way to
> encounter Wilson's
> storm-petrel, a
> maritime marvel **"**

The sky is blue; the sea too. The boat swells gently above the Poll Bank reef. To the east, a few kilometres distant, lies England's westernmost land: the Isles of Scilly. To the west, for thousands of kilometres, lies nothing but ocean until you hit the New World. Where better to await maritime wanderers? The 'chum' (diced mackerel and cod liver-soaked bread, buoyed by popcorn) floats on the surface. You bait... and wait.

Whirring wee wings announce the arrival of the first dinner guest: a British storm-petrel. This starling-sized seabird dances over the water, snatching fishy snacks. This is a local breeder: England's sole population nests among Scilly's 140 uninhabited rocky islets. A handful more petrels join the advance guard. Cue a breathless cry: 'Wilson's!'

Born and bred in Antarctica, Wilson's storm-petrels switch hemispheres during the southern winter, some even congregating in Britain's southwestern approaches during our summer. Boat trips off Scilly provide the easiest way to encounter this maritime marvel. Pelagic birding has boomed this century, offering opportunities to see an array of seabirds at close range. Gannet, fulmar, puffin and terns are common.

▲ Wilson's storm-petrel, bouncing along the sea surface. (JL) 133

A graceful Sabine's gull may bounce by or a pomarine skua harry past. You could see five species of shearwater: local-breeding Manx, Cory's and (the critically endangered) Balearic from the Mediterranean, plus great and sooty from the Southern Hemisphere.

It's not just birds that are on display. You may spot the distinctive double fin of a basking shark breaking the surface. Many trips come across blue shark. Fret not if this agile, attractive fish is caught and landed on the boat: it is simply being fitted with a satellite transmitter so marine biologists can track its movements. Short-beaked common dolphin pods as hefty as 50 animals frequently bow-ride within touching distance. You may glimpse the odd minke whale, but it will be too timid to interact with the boat. Nearer to land, you should see harbour porpoise or one of the archipelago's grey seal population.

There are four options for seeing Scilly seabirds. On at least one August weekend (usually the second), all-day pelagics explore distant waters. On Fridays and Mondays in August (an excuse for a long weekend?), evening birding trips foray offshore. On other days, you could join a fishing trip to reach the same waters. Finally, one way of reaching Scilly is by ship from Penzance. Traversing 40km of open sea may help you see basking shark, common dolphin, ocean sunfish and shearwaters. Try this for at least one leg of your journey.

It is insufficient to experience Scilly sealife from above water. To max out, explore beneath the waves (or rockpool if you prefer to get only

A grey seal as you've never experienced it before. (B/GS/FLPA)

your feet wet). With 150 dive sites at wrecks, reefs and walls, Scilly is renowned among divers, but can also be enjoyed by snorkellers. Between June and September, visibility may exceed 15m: a fantasy for most British dive sites.

Underwater meadows of sea grass drift in the current above gleaming white sands. Rocky reefs are caked in vibrantly coloured jewel anemones, sponges and fan corals. Look closer for ross coral, dead man's fingers and plumrose anemones. On underwater rocks, search for edible crab, hermit crabs and common squat lobster – or for crevice sea cucumbers and featherstars. Fish include corkwing wrasse, rock goby, worm pipefish and tompot blenny.

Best of all, grey seals are routinely seen underwater, particularly on dedicated seal-snorkelling excursions. The best areas are Eastern Isles, Western Rocks and Norrad Rocks: the boats know where to head. Watching seals in their marine element is *so* different to watching them lubbing on land: the intimate, playful contact is as uplifting an experience as any.

Back on dry land (most likely the main island, St Mary's), there is much to find. Scilly's star land mammal is Britain's only population of lesser white-toothed shrew. Although not rare, seeing one takes planning... and luck. Try ivy-clad stone walls around Old Town Church or, particularly, the adjacent upper beach on a rising tide. For a mammalian oddity – melanistic rabbit – wander to the Garrison, a 16th-century fortification. Along its walls, the tops are good for autumn lady's-tress – a delicate swirl of an orchid that may just be venturing above ground – and the crevices for four-leaved allseed, a petite annual herb that is otherwise rare in Britain.

Indeed, if marine activities are not your kettle of fish, you could easily spend your weekend botanising on sun-drenched, species-rich St Mary's. On the Garrison, compare common and western gorse side by side, likewise bell heather and ling. At Holy Vale, contrast water cress and fool's water cress, and enjoy the regal splendour of royal fern. At Higher Moors, gasp at greater tussock-sedge. All that said, should you elect not to hop on at least one boat and tour Scilly's pelagic paradise, you really are missing out.

▲ Great shearwater: the black cap and white collar are diagnostic. (RCh/FLPA)

Practicalities

Where to go: Travel to **Scilly** is by sea or air (to St Mary's ℡ 0845 710 5555 Ⓦ www.islesofscilly-travel.co.uk). Several planes per day depart Lands End and Newquay, with single flights from Exeter, Bristol and Southampton. The MV *Scillonian* sails once daily from Penzance. There is no transport of any kind on/off Scilly on Sundays, meaning a long weekend is essential. Shame!

Members of St Mary's Boatmen's Association (℡ 01720 423999 Ⓦ www.scillyboating.co.uk) run boats between and around the islands. All-day and evening pelagic birding trips are provided aboard the *Sapphire* (℡ 07776 204631 Ⓦ www.scillypelagics.com) and *Kingfisher* (℡ 07768 662229). Companies offering diving and snorkelling trips include Dive Scilly (℡ 01720 423162 Ⓦ www.divescilly.com) and Scilly Diving (which also has a base on St Martin's ℡ 01720 423420 Ⓦ www.scillydiving.com). Hiring a bike enables you to cover more of St Mary's (St Mary's Bike Hire ℡ 0796 638506 Ⓦ www.stmarysbikehire.co.uk).

Suggested bases: St Mary's has the widest range of accommodation (Ⓦ www.simplyscilly.co.uk, www.scillyonline.co.uk) and is the departure point for most day-trips. It is the logical base for a short visit but that should not prevent you from exploring other islands if time allows. **Pelistry Cottage** (℡ 01720 422506 Ⓦ www.scillyholidays.com) is a pleasant Grade II-listed guesthouse in the centre of Hughtown, Scilly's main settlement.

Flexibility: Diving/snorkelling is best between June and September. Dedicated birding pelagics are best July through to August, though are sometimes offered June and September–October. July is arguably the best month for the shrew. Autumn lady's-tress flowers early August to mid-September. grey seal is resident.

Accessibility: ④

▲ Short-beaked common dolphins often ride the bow. (DP)

34 Mad Manx and mountains

Ceredigion & Snowdonia for Manx shearwater, osprey, soprano pipistrelle, feral goat, Alpine saw-wort

The morning tide is high, the sea calm. Wind and sun are both at your back. Conditions are perfect for Britain's top seabird spectacle, and the numbers of participants challenge credulity. Just a couple of score metres off the Ceredigion beach, a feeding frenzy is underway.

> **Arguably Snowdonia's wildlife highlight, shaggy ungulates are in their element on rugged mountain inclines**

Wherever you look, there is feathered commotion: a seething mass of famished birds with long wings and sharp bills.

Manx shearwaters dominate the action. Tens of thousands of these black-and-white tubenoses stream along the surf. At the typical rate of four birds per second, your eyes can barely keep up. The sea beyond is black with dense rafts of these pelagic wanderers, congregating to feast on whitebait, clupeid and sandeel. Perhaps one-tenth of the world's breeding population assembles in Borth Bay between the end of July and mid-August, fattening up to fuel their autumn migration south of the Equator.

'Manxies' are not the show's sole star. Search carefully through the teeming masses to discern a sooty shearwater, dusky-brown with shining white wing-linings.

◄ One of Snowdonia's feral goats (MH)

Or perhaps a Balearic shearwater, a mud-coloured Mediterranean cousin of the Manx. Gannets from Welsh breeding colonies throng, spearing sea then seizing fish with their dagger of a bill. Sandwich, Arctic and common terns add grace to the proceedings, plunging into the sea to grab smaller fry.

The retreating tide dissipates activity. Catch your breath then head north to Cors Dyfi reserve. Here Montgomeryshire Wildlife Trust has facilitated the return to Wales of breeding ospreys by constructing an artificial nesting platform. In mid-August, the brood should be honing fishing skills before flying south for the winter.

Finish off your day of Manx madness with a batty bash in Snowdonia, Britain's second-largest national park. Mixed woodland at Coed y Brenin hums with nocturnal flying mammals. Your best chance of success is to coincide with a guided bat walk. Equipped with bat detectors, experts help you differentiate the echolocatory clicks of various species. Failing that, site yourself with a view over the River Mawddach and wait for dusk to cloak the environs. Typical species are common and soprano pipistrelles, and noctule bat, but there are also scarcities such as brown long-eared, lesser horseshoe and whiskered bats. Alternatively, head to Capel Curig. At dusk, more than 1,000 soprano pipistrelles – probably Britain's largest gathering – stream out of gaps between the gutters topping Cobden's Hotel. Stunning!

The following day, explore the environs of Mt Snowdon. The raw majesty of Wales' highest peak needs little introduction, and there is no beating the combination of stony summits and magical moorland. A croaking call, echoing against bare rock, draws your attention to a raven: this coal-black carrion-eater is our heftiest crow. Red grouse, peregrine and common buzzard are frequently seen, the odd chough occurs, and typical songbirds include skylark and meadow pipit.

Snowdonia is revered by botanists, but specialities tend to be rare and localised. Rarities that need quite some finding, but for which Snowdonia is a stronghold, include Alpine saw-wort (a stately burdock with purple flowers) and Alpine saxifrage. More familiar plants are headed by a yellow-bloomed duo (globeflower and Welsh poppy), the cushion-forming moss campion plus wild angelica in marshy areas. Should you walk past a montane flush with scree topped by grasses and wild thyme, it would be rude not to search for rainbow leaf beetle – but

don't expect to find it! Both rare and beautiful, this insect is decorated in red, gold, green and blue. Snowdonia encompasses its entire British range and there have been few records in recent decades.

Arguably Snowdonia's wildlife highlight is an ostensibly surprising mammal. Unquestionably non-native but unequivocally wild in feel, feral goat is in its element on rugged mountain inclines. Introduced by Neolithic man 5,000 years ago, feral goats ascended the hills 3,500 years later. Their descendants, unshackled from herders' clutches, have never left. Now a thousand or so shaggy ungulates with backswept horns inhabit Snowdonia.

Snowdonia's feral goats are best seen from the A-roads that intersect Llanberis, Capel Curig and Beddgelert. There are several particularly good sites. The best is mountain slopes around the old slate quarry above Padarn Country Park near Llanberis. Near Beddgelert, try Craflwyn just west of Llyn Dinas on the scenic A498. The best for all-round wildlife interest (particularly plants) is Llyn Idwal, northwest of Capel Curig. If all else fails, the Snowdon viewpoint, 1.6km south of the A498/A4086 junction, can be good. To locate the herbivores, scan the rocky slopes. If you spot (or hear) a foraging group, approach quietly: these goats' domesticated past is many generations behind them.

The males may even provide ample evidence of their wildness by rutting. While September normally marks the onset of the breeding season, particularly hormone-charged males may start challenging one another in August, initiating spectacular headbutting and posturing that will culminate in the right to breed. Eat your heart out, ibex.

▲ Borth's feeding frenzy of Manx shearwaters and gannets (JB)

Where to go: Watch Ceredigion's seabird feeding frenzy from **Borth** (☀ SN607890) north along the B4353 to Ynyslas Beach (☀ SN606925). **Cors Dyfi** (☀ SN701985 ℗ 01938 555654 ⓦ www.montwt.co.uk/ cors_dyfi.html) is 5.5km southwest of Machynlleth on the A487 Abersytwyth road. Some 4km south of Derwenlas, turn right after Morben Isaf caravan park and use the reserve car park.

For an overview of **Snowdonia** see ⓦ www.snowdonia-npa. gov.uk) or ⓦ www.snowdonia-society.org.uk (the latter sometimes offers walks to see feral goat). **Coed y Brenin Forest** is 12km north of Dolgellau. Leave the A470 at Aber Eden, continuing east 1km to a riverside car park (☀ SH733251). **Capel Curig** lies at the A5/A490 junction. Cobden's Hotel (☀ SH732574 ℗ 01690 720243 ⓦ www. cobdens.co.uk) is 2km southeast along the A5.

Localities for **feral goat** are above Padarn Country Park (☀ SH591611); Craflwyn (☀ SH604490), Llyn Idwal (1km south from Llyn Ogwen car park; ☀ SH648605) and the Snowdon viewpoint (☀ SH658542). Footpaths up **Mount Snowdon** lead from several car parks: Pen y Pass (☀ SH647555) on the A4058, 9.5km southeast of Llanberis; Bethania (☀ SH628507) on the A498, 5km northeast of Beddgelert; Rhyd-Ddu (☀ SH572526) on the A4085 11km north of Beddgelert; and Snowdon Ranger (☀ SH564551), 4.5km north. Dress appropriately and respect conditions. Alternatively, take the steam train from Llanberis station (℗ 0844 493 8120 ⓦ www. snowdonrailway.co.uk), then walk back down.

Suggested bases: In Snowdonia (ⓦ www.visitsnowdonia.info, www. staysnowdonia.co.uk) include Betws-y-Coed (ⓦ www.betws-y-coed. co.uk), Llanberis (ⓦ www.llanberis.org) and Beddgelert (ⓦ www. beddgelerttourism.com). **Pengwern Country House** (℗ 01690 710480 ⓦ www.snowdoniaaccommodation.co.uk) has pretty rooms in a beautiful slate-and-stone house with wooded grounds.

Flexibility: Borth seabirds occur late July to late August; best on high tides. Osprey occurs April to September. Plants flower July–August at least. Bats are best May–September. Feral goat is resident.

Accessibility: ⑤

35
The magnificent seven

Essex & Kent for southern migrant hawker, southern emerald damselfly, water vole, wasp spider, shrill carder bee

> **❝ Pause on bridges to see whether a water vole emerges from reedmace ❞**

This millennium, Britain's dragonfly contingent has been in the throes of revolution. Several sparkling species have crossed the sea to start colonising Britain, particularly southeast England. Excitingly, most of the neophytes appear to be here to stay. In this ambitious weekend, chance your arm at finding up to seven magnificent dragonflies unknown in Britain two decades previously.

Wat Tyler Country Park in Essex is the most reliable site for southern migrant hawker. This large, inquisitive dragonfly with electric-blue eyes first bred in Britain in 2010 and has the merest toe-hold in the country. Look for it above ponds or ditches along the entrance road, particularly immediately south of the refurbished toilet block.

While you search, check for scarce emerald damselfly in sedges lining the pools. While no newcomer, this metallic-green damsel is nationally threatened: its distribution centres on the Thames Estuary so it is a local speciality. Commoner dragonflies include migrant hawker and ruddy and common darters.

Check flower banks for two nationally threatened bumblebees: shrill carder bee and brown-banded carder bee. The former occurs at fewer than ten localities in Britain, including three involved this weekend.

▲ August is a great month to enjoy prolonged views of water voles. (TW/FLPA)

Finally, scan the margins of pools along the boardwalk southeast of the toilet block and behind the RSPB South Essex Marshes visitor centre. These are good for great crested newt: you should see frilly-gilled youngsters and possibly black-and-orange adults.

Then head west under the M25 to RSPB Rainham Marshes (see *March, 1* pages 37–40). In late summer, the reserve is excellent for both rare carder bees. To find them, make a beeline (ahem) for pathside flowers around the visitor centre or along the inner river wall. Shrill carder bee reveals its presence with high-pitched, mosquito-like buzzing.

Rainham is fabulous for common dragonflies, with darters zipping, hawkers hovering, and damselflies dipping. Of rarer species, small red-eyed damselfly abounds at the westernmost pool along the northern boardwalk. This waspish damsel is arguably the most spectacular colonist of them all. After first breeding in Britain in 2002, its range expansion has been dramatic, being recorded from north to Yorkshire and west to Devon. From vagrant to widespread in a decade!

En route, check grassland by the Ken Barrett Hide for the striking (and sizeable) wasp spider. Webs of this recent arrival from the continent are often helpfully waymarked. And pause on bridges to see whether a water vole emerges from reedmace fringing channels – or listen for one chomping on vegetation. August can be great for prolonged views of family groups.

Then drive south, crossing the Thames, and head along the A2 into north Kent. Pass the afternoon at RSPB Cliffe Pools. A high-tide visit could produce the amazing sight of 800 avocet and black-tailed godwit on Radar or Flamingo Pool. Cliffe is a stronghold for shrill and brown-banded carder bees, so check flowers. Wall butterflies are rare in Kent, but common along Cliffe's seawall.

Common dragonflies abound at Cliffe, but a trio of rarities share top billing. Cliffe is a stronghold for scarce emerald damselfly, which particularly inhabits sedge-lined ditches north of 'pipe pool

◀ Shrill carder bee is a speciality of the Thames Estuary. (JL)

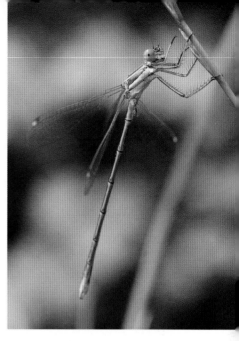

viewing mound', north of the 'black barn pools'. More remarkably, these ditches have become Britain's most reliable site for southern emerald damselfly, a verdant species that colonised in 2010. Amazingly, the vicinity sometimes also hosts southern migrant hawker (as does the southern side of Flamingo Pool), and you should keep an eye out for both wasp spider and water vole.

Start the next morning on the Isle of Sheppey for undoubtedly the rarest (and thus least likely) of the magnificent seven. After an assumed absence from Britain of nearly 60 years, dainty damselfly was rediscovered here in 2010, frequenting dense grassland by pools west of the old road bridge. This tiny, feeble-flying damselfly has the most precarious grasp on British terrain. Search hard but keep expectations low.

More reliable is willow emerald damselfly south of Reculver. With only three records in Britain prior to 2009, an amazing 400 were found that year at 35 sites in East Anglia. This confiding green dragonfly has subsequently been found in Kent, including at Marshside where it allows close approach in channel-side vegetation. Look on the channels themselves for small red-eyed damselfly.

Hence to Sandwich Bay on the Isle of Thanet. Restharrow Scrape, 1km south of the bird observatory, is one of the most reliable British sites for red-veined darter. From the hide, check muddy islands or look for a territorial male hovering like a red helicopter over warm, shallow waters. Also here should be brown hawker, black-tailed skimmer and red-eyed damselfly.

For your final dragonfly rarity, journey south to Dungeness. First recorded in Britain in 1996, lesser emperor breeds now each year at the Long Pits, inland from the bird observatory. Seeing this imperial immigrant would provide a remarkable finale to a weekend searching for the magnificent seven – with a supporting cast of a further dozen dragonfly species.

▲ Southern emerald damselfly: one of the 'magnificent seven' recent dragonfly colonists (JL)

Where to go: Wat Tyler Country Park is 2km south of the A13 at Pitsea (⚬ TQ738864 ① 01268 550088 Ⓦ www.wattylercountrypark.org.uk). Follow the A13 west then A1306 southeast to **RSPB Rainham Marshes** (⚬ TQ552792 ① 01708 899840 Ⓦ www.rspb.org.uk/ rainhammarshes).

RSPB Cliffe Pools is on the Isle of Grain (⚬ TQ722757 ① 01634 222480 Ⓦ www.rspb.org.uk/cliffepools). In Cliffe, turn down Pond Hill, a stony track leading to Radar Pool. Park then walk north to Black Barn Pools and Pipe Pool viewing mound. Take the path north to view the dykes.

From M2 junction 5, head north on the A249. Just before the **Isle of Sheppey** bridge, switch onto the B2231 and park near Swale station. Cross the 'old' bridge and search grassy terrain around pools below the flyover (⚬ TR915695). Leave the A299 3km east of Herne Bay, follow signs for **Marshside**. Check channel-side vegetation 50m south of Little Grays Farm.

For **Sandwich Bay** (① 01304 617341 Ⓦ www.sbbot.co.uk), leave Sandwich east on Sandown Road. Entering the Sandwich Estate, park at the bird observatory (⚬ TR356575). Walk 1km southeast to Restharrow Scrape (⚬ TR362582). From Lydd, follows signs to **Dungeness** (Ⓦ www.dungeness-nnr.co.uk). Park at the old lighthouse (⚬ TR089170); walk northwest 1.3km to Long Pits (⚬ TR084184).

Suggested bases: Rochester (Ⓦ www.cometorochester.co.uk), and Canterbury (Ⓦ www.canterbury.co.uk/accommodation). **Hartlip Place** (① 01795 842323 Ⓦ www.hartlipplace.co.uk) oozes grandeur, offering quirky rooms and candlelit dinners.

Flexibility: Mid-July to end August should work for the 'magnificent seven'. Dainty damselfly (if present) flies from early June, southern emerald damselfly from late June and red-veined darter from late May. Lesser emperor, southern migrant hawker and red-veined darter may still be flying in September, and willow emerald damselfly in October. Wasp spider is best from early August–early September. Water vole can be seen February–October, but abounds August– September. Shrill carder bee flies June–September.

Accessibility: ②

36
Chiltern challenge

Oxfordshire & Buckinghamshire for brown hairstreak, silver-spotted skipper, glowworm, edible dormouse, Chiltern gentian

> **" A Chiltern speciality, the seal-eyed silver-spotted skipper is incessantly active "**

The Chiltern evening is balmy, windless and expectant. As the gloaming retreats into night, a hoarse grunting erupts from the twiggy yews. As you wait, the guttural calls jump an octave and become excited squeaking. You position yourself carefully, check that the red filter adequately shields your torch and illuminate the area. Two huge eyes plead back at you from the branches, bushy tail dangling below. Incomparable cuteness in mammalian form: an edible dormouse.

Introduced to England in 1902, Europe's cuddliest rodent thrives in forests around Tring. Wendover Woods is a splendid location to spot these nocturnal creatures, and warm nights in late summer present primetime viewing. Arrive shortly before dusk, and wait for the mammals to start calling and clambering, before flicking the switch on your lamp. A neat opening to a trip packed with Chiltern creatures.

The weekend proper commences next day beside the M40 at Aston Rowant. Spectacular in their own right, the steep chalk escarpments are perfect for photographing red kites, which coast on the updrafts, forked tails twisting and rufous tones glowing in the morning sun. The kite reintroduction scheme has met with such success that 300 pairs now breed locally. Ravens also reside here, croaking their way across the sky.

▶ Natural lighting: a female glow worm (PS/SD)

Aston is brilliant for smaller flying creatures as well: a bevy of chalk-loving butterflies. You should have few problems spying the silvery-blue hue of chalkhill blue. But you'll need sharper eyes to discern the smaller duo of brown argus and silver-spotted skipper. A seal-eyed Chiltern speciality, the skipper is incessantly active and invariably fast-flying. Photographing it on the short turf requires swift footwork and patience. The best area lies south of the M40, along the bridleway leading northwest from Upper Vicar's Farm.

Aston offers plenty for those with a botanical bent, notably a recovery programme for common juniper, abundant dwarf thistle and harebell, plus a dapper display of the nationally scarce Chiltern gentian. Beneath the lilac carpet of flowers, large grassy mounds house citadels of yellow meadow ants: some 500 million reside here. Passage migrant birds may include common redstart and tree pipit. And watch out for deer: roe, fallow and muntjac are frequently seen.

If your luck was out with silver-spotted skipper (or if you crave more of this teddy bear-faced cutie), nearby Watlington Hill offers another shot. From the car park, walk west, parallel with Hill Road, and search north-facing slopes after 500m. Then follow the path south up, over and down Watlington Hill to search south-facing terrain for both the skipper and brown argus. Further west, on west-facing slopes, chalkhill blue occurs, so Watlington provides a second bash at all three downland butterflies – plus Chiltern gentian, which often grows by rabbit burrows.

From here to Warburg reserve, where flower-rich grassland decorates the dry valley at Bix Bottom, ceding to stately woodland on valley

▲ Bright-eyed and bushy-tailed: edible dormouse (DM/FLPA)

slopes. The orchids for which Warburg is famed are, regrettably, over for another year, so focus on locating autumn gentian, an erect plant with purple stars for flowers, and its close relative Chiltern gentian.

Have an early dinner and, if you still have some energy left, return to Aston Rowant for dusk. Unlike the previous night's walk, keep torchlight to a minimum since your target generates its own illumination. Particularly around the base of Beacon Hill, female glowworms ascend grass stems and signal their readiness to mate by emitting a vibrant green incandescence from their abdomen. The living light show from these beetles is simply remarkable.

The next day, visit three sites northwest along the M40. RSPB Otmoor bestows a decent start. Migrant waders – perhaps greenshank, green sandpiper and black-tailed godwit – lope or saunter around the scrape as they break their journey to southern wintering grounds. Hobbies glide overhead, catching dragonflies such as ruddy darter. If the morning is dewy, you may find great crested newtlets crossing paths as they move between desiccating pools. Young common lizards lounge on the purpose-built log pile near the first reedbed viewing screen. And a 'master' ash tree on the Roman road offers your first shot at brown hairstreak.

This beautiful butterfly, tail-like protrusions trailing from its bronze hindwing, is the last to emerge each year. It is scarce, localised and elusive, usually remaining concealed in the canopy. Stands of blackthorn, however, entice females down to eye-level, where they deposit tiny white eggs. One of the best sites to see egg-laying in action is along blackthorn-lined rides through ancient forest at Whitecross Green Wood. Follow the waymarked wildlife walk and keep your eyes peeled. Should you fail here, but fancy another roll of the hairstreak dice, finish the weekend nearby at Bernwood Meadows. Search blackthorns along the meadow perimeter, and be patient. This will be your only chance to see Britain's classiest butterfly: the Chiltern challenge is yours for the taking.

▶ Arguably Britain's cutest butterfly: silver-spotted skipper (DM/FLPA)

Practicalities

Where to go: Midway along the B4009 Tring–Wendover road, use **Wendover Woods** car park (✷ SP884099) on Mansion Hill. Walk 100m southeast. **Aston Rowant National Nature Reserve** (☎ http://tinyurl.com/astonrowant) traverses the M40 between junctions 5 and 6. There are car parks at Beacon Hill (✷ SU731965) and Cowleaze Wood (✷ SU726958; walk 500m northeast along the road to Upper Vicar's Farm where bridleways lead northwest onto downland). **Watlington Hill** is 500m west of Christmas Common (✷ SU710935 ☎ 01494 755573 Ⓦ http://tinyurl.com/watlingtonhill). **Warburg** (✷ SU721879 ☎ 01491 642001 Ⓦ http://tinyurl.com/warburgreserve), a Berkshire Buckinghamshire and Oxfordshire Wildlife Trust (BBOWT) reserve, lies 6km northwest of Henley-on-Thames. Leave the A4130 at Bix Hall, taking the minor road north past Bix into Rectory Lane for 2km.

   RSPB Otmoor (✷ SP570126 ☎ 01865 351163 Ⓦ www.rspb.org.uk/otmoor) lies near Beckley, northeast of Oxford. From Beckley High Street, drive east past Abingdon Arms pub, then left along Otmoor Lane for 1.5km. **Whitecross Green Wood** BBOWT reserve is 8km south of Bicester (✷ SP602144 ☎ 01442 826774 Ⓦ http://tinyurl.com/wgwood) and 3km south of Upper Arncott. For **Bernwood Meadows/Forest** (☎ 01442 826774 Ⓦ http://tinyurl.com/bernwoodmeadows) BBOWT reserve, take the minor road southeast from Horton-cum-Studley for 1.8km. At the T-junction, turn left (Forest:✷ SP610116) or right (Meadows: ✷ SP606111).

 Suggested bases: Thame (Ⓦ www.thame.net) and Princes Risborough (Ⓦ www.princesrisborough.com). Near Stone, **Badgers Cottage** (☎ 01296 749085 Ⓦ www.badgerscottage.com) offers bedrooms in a delightful Grade II-listed thatched cottage.

Flexibility: Edible Dormouse is best on warm, dry, calm evenings July–end September. The butterflies fly mid-July–mid-September. The gentians flower August–September. Glow worms are active late May–early September.

Accessibility: ③

▲ Look for Chiltern gentian at Aston Rowant. (IB/FLPA)

37

Webs, willows and waders

Suffolk for fen raft spider, willow emerald damselfly, migrant waders, bittern, otter

> **"One of Europe's scarcest and most striking spiders, dashing in its 'go faster' stripes "**

You perch sedately on a wooden platform half-a-metre above a tiny peaty pool fringed by tussocky sedges. The dawn wind has abated; the Indian summer sun cossets the Suffolk air. You bask and watch. In the pool margins, one of Britain's rarest and most remarkable predators is doing likewise.

The fen raft spider is poised, rear legs on a stem emerging from the water and front appendages caressing its surface, tiny hairs producing the tension needed to walk on water. Among Europe's largest arachnids, 7cm from toe to toe, this is also one of the most striking, with broad white 'go faster' stripes directing body towards prey. This is also one of Europe's scarcest spiders, categorised as globally threatened.

In the late 1950s, Britain's first-ever fen raft spider was discovered at Suffolk's Redgrave and Lopham Fen. It has subsequently been found at single sites in Sussex and South Wales (see *June, 2* pages 95–8). Start this weekend at the 'Ur-site'. From the car park, enter the picnic area then head right along 'Spider Trail' to the viewing platform on Middle Fen.

▲ Keep alert for a bittern flypast. (SL/FLPA)

September weekend 2

To find the spider, scan pool edges for hunting arachnids and surrounding vegetation for nursery webs. In early September, you may find juveniles, or even a maternal female guarding her second brood.

After enjoying the spiders, or perhaps in the cooler hours before you try for them, wander the trails of this attractive reserve. Amidst England's largest remaining river-valley fen, there are tracts of wet heathland, open water, scrub and woodland. Check the shallows of small pools near the visitor centre for great crested newtlets, which will be preparing to hibernate. Listen for the metallic message of a bearded tit, which breeds in Little Fen's reedbeds. As you walk the marshy areas, you may flush common snipe.

Adjacent to the River Waveney in particular, you may spy a water vole munching at the foot of the lesser pond sedge. Special plants include greater bird's foot trefoil, hemp agrimony and devil's-bit scabious. Among the dragonflies, migrant hawker and southern hawker remain on the wing, patrolling dykes with fierce possessiveness. These attract hobbies, Britain's sexiest falcon, which speeds past in pursuit of flying insects.

One particularly special dragonfly provides your next port of call. Willow emerald damselfly was almost unheard of in Britain before 2009. That year, this sturdy lime and olive 'dragon' arrived with a bang. Several hundred were seen, particularly in Suffolk, which has remained the epicentre of the emerald's rapidly spreading distribution. The damselfly favours grassy vegetation and overhanging trees (often, you guessed it, willows) flanking lazy rivers. This new arrival has swiftly

Fen raft spider, walking on water (ST)

become a photographer's favourite, posing fearlessly for macro lenses.

To welcome this new arrival to British shores, visit one of three sites along the A14 heading coastwards. Just downstream of Needham Market, search the bramble-strewn banks of the River Gipping, east of Alderson Lake. Or look at Alton Water, southeast of Ipswich, specifically along the footpaths leading east and west from Lemons Hill car park, and the trail leading northwest from the south of Lemons Hill Bridge. Alternatively, visit Candlet Farm, northeast of Trimley St Mary, examining nettles along the public footpath east of the farm pond. Whichever site you try, walk slowly and check vegetation.

Spend the whole of the next day at RSPB Minsmere (see *March, 2* pages 37–40, and *October, 1* pages 163–6). This gives you time to explore fully the wealth of habitats at the charity's most famous reserve. September is slap-bang in the middle of wader migration, and the 'Scrape' and North Levels Wader Trail (the latter peppered with marsh mallow and tansy) should be humming with scurrying and striding shorebirds.

Among larger waders, ruff, black-tailed godwit and greenshank predominate. Smaller fry present in numbers include dunlin, ringed plover and common sandpiper. Amongst these, look carefully to pick out spotted redshank, little stint, curlew sandpiper and wood sandpiper. Amidst the flock of teal, sullenly huddling as they moult their flight feathers, there may be a clandestine garganey or two.

The dunes are worth a look: the odd wasp spider may still hang at the nucleus of its frizzy orb, and passage passerines may include wheatear, yellow wagtail and whinchat. For migrant warblers such as lesser whitethroat and – if the wind is easterly – something rarer like a wryneck (a ground-loving woodpecker with a reptilian demeanour), mooch around bushes near the sluice or stroll the North Bushes Trail. Save some time for the Reedbed Trail to look for family parties of bearded tit, and drop into Bittern Hide for a chance of the eponymous brown heron and perhaps an otter.

It is a little early for rutting red deer and you can come back later for these (see *October, 1* pages 163–6), but that might not be enough to dissuade you from finishing the weekend with a wander over nearby Westleton Heath. If you locate a herd, enjoy their calm before October's tempest...

▲ Hobby: aerial athlete specialising in plucking dragonflies from the skies. (JL)

Practicalities

Septemberweekend 2

Where to go: Redgrave and Lopham Fen is a Suffolk
Wildlife Trust reserve, 8km west of Diss (⊙ TM052802
ⓣ 01379 687618 ⓦ www.suffolkwildlifetrust.org/
reserve/redgrave-lopham-fen). Leave the A1066 at
Pooley Street, following Low Common Road 1km to the
reserve. Intentionally disturbing fen raft spiders is illegal.

The three willow emerald damselfly sites are
Alderson Lake, Alton Water and Candlet Farm. **Alderson Lake**
(⊙ TM099544) is 1km east of Needham Market. Leave the A14 on
the B1078 towards Needham Market. After 500m park by the River
Gipping (⊙ TM096546). Follow the footpath southeast. Search
riverside vegetation beyond the lake. **Alton Water** is 8km south of
Ipswich. From the A14 junction 56, head south on the A137. After 2km
bear left towards Tattingstone and use Lemon Hill car park on the
reservoir's northern shore (⊙ TM137376). Follow shoreline footpaths
west and east. Or cross the bridge, then explore the southern shore
along the footpath leading northwest (⊙ TM133376). **Candlet Farm**
is northeast of Trimley St Mary. From the A14/A154 roundabout, take
the A154 southeast for 800m, then turn north on Gulpher Road. Park
safely near the entrance to Hill House Farm (⊙ TM298365), then walk
west for 500m to Candlet Farm (⊙ TM293367).

RSPB Minsmere (⊙ TM473672 ⓣ 01728 648281 ⓦ www.rspb.org.
uk/minsmere) is signposted from the A12 northeast of Yoxford. Leave
Westleton village east on minor roads and follow signs. The Reedbed,
North Levels and North Bushes trails are open seasonally, usually
from early September.

Suggested bases: Felixstowe, Woodbridge (ⓦ http://woodbridge
suffolk.info) and Saxmundham (ⓦ www.saxmundham.org). **Melton
Hall** (ⓣ 01394 388138 ⓦ http://meltonhall.co.uk) near Woodbridge is
a Regency villa with splendid rooms and extensive grounds.

Flexibility: Any weekend August to end September should work;
August additionally offers antlion and silver-studded blue on
Dunwich Heath. Fen raft spider occurs from April to early October.
Willow emerald damselfly flies July to October. Waders are best early
August to end September. Otter is resident.

Accessibility: ②

38 The Flamborough front

East Yorkshire for gannet, sooty shearwater, pomarine skua, rockpool life, migrant songbirds

> " As in all seafaring stories, a swarthy pirate sears into frame "

Half-a-dozen nautical miles offshore, Britain's largest seabird pierces the North Sea surface in pursuit of fishy fare. Gannet! Another plunges, a gleaming white arrow with golden head. Another follows. And another. From your ringseat on a gently cradling boat, you watch the gannets plunder the shoal. Then, as in all exciting seafaring stories, a swarthy pirate sears into frame. A great skua or 'bonxie' hassles a gannet or harries a gull, forcing the victim to sacrifice its catch.

You are aboard a RSPB 'shearwaters and skuas' cruise off the Yorkshire coast. Departing Bridlington, you spend a half-day exploring the 'Flamborough front', a marine upwelling rich in nutrients that serves as a supermarket for the thousands of migrating seabirds that traverse the North Sea in early autumn. Most passage takes place far offshore. 'Seawatching' from a promontory such as 130m-high Flamborough Head, which protrudes 13km into marine waters, can uncover these magical movements. But to see the seabirds at close range, join them in their element offshore. Hence the genius of the long-running RSPB trip.

▲ Great skua, a North Sea pirate (BC/FLPA)

September weekend 3

Standard feathered fare is provided by local breeders from the chalk cliffs at Flamborough and Bempton. You should see good numbers of fulmar, kittiwake, razorbill, guillemot and puffin. But you are really after *migrating* seabirds. In addition to bonxies, bodybuilding brutes with white wing blazes, you should encounter Arctic skua, a more modest but equally piratical adversary that bullies kittiwakes and terns. And be alert to the possibility of two rarer brethren: pomarine and long-tailed skuas, the latter a svelte seabird with the flight of a tern.

Manx shearwaters surround the boat, flashing alternately black then white. A notch up in size and several in scarcity is sooty shearwater, which breeds no closer than Tristan da Cunha, 3,000km southwest of South Africa. Silvery underwings glinting on dark brown body, 'sooties' pitch down to chomp on the 'chum' (diced fish bait) floating behind the boat. Keep your eyes peeled for oddities. Perhaps a Sabine's gull, a waif-like Arctic breeder, or a 'blue fulmar', the dusky phase of 'our' fulmar, which breeds similarly far north. And watch out for marine mammals: grey seal and harbour porpoise are likely.

Back on land, further the maritime theme by getting your feet wet on the rocky shores of Flamborough Head's South Landing. An afternoon here exploring life exposed by the low tide can be fascinating and fun. Even without children in tow, rockpooling brings out the kid in you. Wildlife rewards abound: beadlet anemones resembling purple jelly; sea hares, a sort of marine slug; common shore crab and common blenny, a saucer-eyed fish secluded beneath seaweed. Before departing, contextualise your explorations at Yorkshire Wildlife Trust's Living Sea Centre, conveniently sited nearby.

The next day, explore Flamborough Head's terrestrial birdlife. Flamborough is renowned among birders as one of Britain's prime migration hotspots. Clear skies over Scandinavia prompt mass departures of breeding birds, seduced into thinking that their passage southwards is straightforward. Should the North Sea be shrouded in rain-bearing cloud, those same migrants take refuge on the first *terra firma* they encounter. Thrusting seaward, Flamborough's headland is often that landmass, and the sudden invasion of weary birds is called a 'fall'. There is arguably no more exciting birding experience.

▲ A beadlet anemone at low tide (JL)

During a fall, willow warblers and blackcaps may drip from trees. Common redstarts and pied flycatchers may festoon bushes. Wheatears and wagtails may flock in the fields. And scarce birds may pitch up in the strangest habitats: wryneck on a wall, red-backed shrike on a fence or barred warbler in a bramble bush.

The huge Head can seem a daunting place to birdwatch. Focusing your day on a trio of areas is more productive than aimlessly wandering clifftop paths (scenic though that may be). Start at South Landing, but this time forego the tideline. Instead, walk slowly coastwards along the small wooded ravine, scanning tall trees, high hedges and dense undergrowth for movement, then circumvent the eastern side of the wood past Highcliffe Manor back to the car park.

Then make for the Outer Head, using the lighthouse car park. Start immediately north by checking the 'Bay Brambles' and bushes in Selwick Bay. Then search the 'Gorse Field' east of the car park. Following the hedge-lined footpath forming the field's eastern perimeter brings you to Head Farm and eventually to the cliff path. Follow this west, then cut north inland along Old Fall Hedge, past a small wood to the road. Follow this back to the car park.

Finally, go north, to North Landing. Yorkshire Wildlife Trust's reserve is great for breeding seabirds in summer, but in autumn the scrubby valley leading inland often harbours migrant landbirds. Suddenly there is an insistent call from an elusive sprite: a flicker of bright green, a flash of white stripes. Have you just found the autumn's first yellow-browed warbler, freshly arrived after a 3,000km flight from the Urals?

▶ A woodpecker, but not as you know it: wryneck. (KD)

Practicalities September weekend 3

Where to go: RSPB 'skuas and shearwaters' cruises depart Bridlington North Pier, exploring offshore for a half-day. Check the RSPB website for details (Ⓦ www.rspb.org.uk/datewithnature) and booking instructions. Bridlington North Pier lies immediately south of the A1034/B1254 junction. There is a seafront car park at Langdale Wharf.

For **Flamborough Head** (Ⓦ http://flamborough birdobs.org: includes useful map and birding site details), leave Bridlington on the B1255 northeast to Flamborough village. Then take the B1259 east towards the Head. Turn right immediately after the village to reach **South Landing** car park (⊙ TA231695); walk south to the bay and do a circuit anti-clockwise. Alternatively, continue to the lighthouse car park (⊙ TA253708) at the eastern end of the B1259, which gives access to named sites around the **Outer Head**. Please stick to footpaths. From Flamborough village, follow the B1255 northeast to **North Landing** car park (⊙ TA240720). Explore the gully inland from the Yorkshire Wildlife Trust reserve (⊙ http://tinyurl.com/flamborough).

Suggested bases: Flamborough, Bridlington (Ⓦ www.bridlington.net) and Filey (Ⓦ www.fileytourism.co.uk). A few kilometres inland, **Wold Cottage** (Ⓣ 01262 470696 Ⓦ www.woldcottage.co.uk) is an award-winning Georgian country retreat with six individually designed suites amidst landscaped gardens.

Flexibility: Cruises run once each weekend from early September to early October. Migrating landbirds can be seen any time from mid-August to late October, although the composition of any 'fall' varies during that period. Weather conditions are critical: winds with an easterly element, ideally originating from high pressure over Scandinavia or further east, combined with poor visibility (rain, cloud, fog) over the North Sea, are key. For rockpooling, the lowest tides (a few days after the new moon) are optimal.

Accessibility: ③ 🚶

Sooty shearwater: at close range, birds are distinctly brown, not black. (JL) ▲

39

Blubber and bucks

Norfolk for grey seal, harbour seal, rutting fallow deer, migrant songbirds, fungi

As the boat throttles round the shingle spit, you encounter a beach packed with sunbathers. Bikini-clad holidaymakers they are not. Instead, the lounging

> **" Young bucks, hormones throbbing, take each other on "**

sun-worshippers are harbour and grey seals. Several hundred blubbery marine mammals reside here on sandy flats. There may be no better way to watch both species rub haunches than from aboard a small vessel in Blakeney Harbour.

Boats depart neighbouring Norfolk villages of Blakeney and Morston for Blakeney Point. Excitement mounts as you approach the shoreline, but seals appear blasé about engine noise and human gabble. Enjoy stunning views of these wonderful creatures, scrutinising them to differentiate the two species. While it is a little early for breeding grey seals (November and December are best; see also *December, 3* pages 207–10) there may still be some harbour youngsters around.

▼ Fallow deer stags in full rut (DP/FLPA)

Boat trips are short, so there is plenty of daylight left to explore the coast. Head first to nearby Cley, one of Britain's most famous Wildlife Trust reserves. After a restorative cuppa in the visitor centre, which looks out over the reserve's jigsaw of reedbeds and marshes, trek the trails.

The *ping* of an old-style cash register alerts you to a party of bearded tits, energetically climbing reed stems before bumbling into cover. Another reedbed resident, marsh harrier, will be prominent: you should see several of these stately raptors cruise past. On the various muddy scrapes, your focus is the freshwater waders for which Cley holds magnetic allure. Examine scurrying flocks of dunlin for little stint and curlew sandpiper. Enjoy loose groups of ruff stuttering through the shallows. Witness hordes of black-tailed godwit and stately greenshanks striding in deeper water. And double-check any shorebird you do not immediately recognise: September is the prime period for oddities from distant climes, such as pectoral sandpiper.

Finish the day at Sculthorpe Moor, a splendid wooded fen bordering the River Wensum near Fakenham. Protected for its great fen-sedge, the reserve is developing a reputation for mammal-watching. Bank voles commonly pilfer grain spilt below the bird table at Fen Hide, allowing splendid views of an often secretive mammal. Harvest mouse and short-tailed field vole are sometimes seen, and the allure of feeding rodents may entice weasel and stoat into the open. Dykes and drains are the domain of water vole, and the lucky few even occasionally encounter water shrew. Definitely worth a patient wait.

Spend the next morning at Holkham Meals. Park on Lady Anne's Drive, then walk west along the footpath bisecting wood and grazing marsh. Your prime target is migrant landbirds, pausing to refuel on their

▲ The colony of grey seal breeding on Blakeney Point. (JL)

post-breeding journey. Particularly if the wind has been blowing from the east, you have decent prospects of scarcities amidst large numbers of common songbirds.

Holkham's resident robins and blackbirds will be joined by individuals hailing from the continent. A common redstart shivers its russet tail, while – if your luck's in – a red-breasted flycatcher sallies from an aged ivy-garbed tree. Search flocks of tits and goldcrests for yellow-browed warbler, a delightful Siberian waif that zips through trees. With migration under way, who knows what else might lurk in the woods today?

As you wander beneath or beside the pines, look for fabulously named fungi. This is peak season for bonnets and brackets, tufts and toughshanks – and Holkham is a hotspot. Orange milkcap is numerous, saffron milkcap frequent. There are also waxcaps, the orchids of the fungal kingdom: look for blackening and glutinous waxcaps. Enjoy primrose brittlegill and, in damper areas, red swamp brittlegill. Lilac bonnet, yellow stagshorn, yellow fieldcap, plums and custard, common puffball and russet toughshank are all present and correct. Search hard for death cap, common stinkhorn and collared earthstar. The longer you look, the more variety you discern. Finally, make time to regale in the marvellous, massive expanse of beach at Holkham Gap, supine beneath Norfolk's big blue sky.

Once your walk is complete, drive inland to Holkham Hall. Strolling the grounds of this quintessential English country estate, usually beneath the veteran oak trees between gate and hall, are feral herds of fallow deer (and a small group of red deer). September is the most important month in the fallow deer calendar: the rut. The prize for dominant males: a harem through which to secure a succession.

These feral deer live constrained within the walls of the estate, so you are sure to see them. Even if the animals themselves are not *truly* wild, the rutting scene certainly is. Adult males groan at each other, posture in parallel, then interlock palmate antlers, neck muscles rigid, legs tense, and thrust against each other, dust billowing around them. Young bucks, hormones throbbing, take each other on – but with no prize for the victor. On the sidelines, a doe with a fawn barks a warning when the bucks, blinded by vitality, career too close. You should also stay alert to wheeling sparrers; no inattentive lounging in the sun like the seals that started your weekend.

Practicalities

Where to go: Seal trips to Blakeney Point (1–2hours) depart from Morston (✹ TG005433) or Blakeney (✹ TG028442) quays; try Bishop's Boats (Ⓣ 0800 0740754 Ⓦ www.norfolksealtrips.co.uk) or Temples (Ⓣ 01263 740791 Ⓦ www.sealtrips.co.uk). **Cley Marshes** (✹ TG054440 Ⓣ 01263 740008 Ⓦ www.norfolkwildlifetrust.org.uk/cley.aspx), the Norfolk Wildlife Trust's flagship reserve, is 1km east of Cley-next-the-Sea on the A149.

Sculthorpe Moor Community Reserve (✹ TF900305 Ⓣ 01328 856788 Ⓦ www.hawkandowl.org/SculthorpeHome) lies just south of the A148 2km west of Fakenham. About 1.2km west of the A148/A149 roundabout, opposite Sculthorpe village, turn south along Turf Moor Road to the reserve.

For **Holkham Meals**, leave the A149 at the Victoria Hotel in Holkham, 3km west of Wells-next-the-Sea, following Lady Anne's Drive 1km to the car park (✹ TG891448). Footpaths lead west (to the hides) and east through the Meals. Alternatively, walk north onto the

▲ A fallow deer stag enjoying a brief rest between rutting. (JL)

▲ Fungi repay close examination. (DC)

marvellous beach at Holkham Gap. For **Holkham Hall** (☀ TF891437 ⓣ 01328 710227 Ⓦ www.holkham.co.uk), drive back south and cross the A149. Fallow deer normally favour the trees between the entrance gate and hall. There is information on Norfolk birding sites at Ⓦ www.norfolkbirds.com/SitesMap.aspx.

Suggested bases: Wells-next-the-Sea (Ⓦ www.wells-guide.co.uk), Burnham Market (Ⓦ www.burnhammarket.co.uk) and Holt, but most north Norfolk accommodation is in or near villages.

Flexibility: Seal trips depart daily February to November: harbour seal breeds June to August, grey October to December. Passage waders are best mid-August to mid-October. Falls of migrant songbirds may happen late August to late October, providing the weather conditions are right. Fallow deer start rutting end September, peaking mid-October. Fungi are best mid-September to end October.

Accessibility: ③

Bedding down

Cley Windmill (ⓣ 01263 740209 Ⓦ www. cleywindmill.co.uk) is a marvellous one-off in Cley-next-the-sea. Converted from an 18th-century windmill, stables and boathouses, beamed rooms enjoy stunning views over marshes. Excellent candlelit dinners feature unabashedly old-fashioned, homemade English country cooking.

They may have been introduced, but the Kashmir goats of Great Orme (see *October, 3* pages 171–4) feel very wild indeed with their shaggy coats and scythe-shaped horns. (CR)

40
Winner takes all

Suffolk for red deer rut, otter, bearded tit, bittern, curlew sandpiper

> **❝ Witness an 'eruption' of the charming bearded tit with parties flying up into the sky, gaining height and circling ❞**

The throaty, far-carrying groan is as primal as a lion's roar, and its message as unequivocal: "I am here! And here is mine! And she is too!". The bellow thunders from Britain's largest land mammal, the red deer stag, and signals the fulcrum of the deer year: the rut.

For a month from late September, but peaking in the first half of October, the most visceral competition in Britain's wildlife calendar is unmissable. Opinion is divided as to where best to gasp at the intensely physical, testosterone-charged duels. Exmoor, the Scottish Highlands, New Forest and 'deer parks' such as Richmond Park each have advocates. But Suffolk's coastal heaths more than hold their own against such competition.

Organise your weekend around the rut schedule, spending the opening and closing three hours of both days deer-watching. Red deer range between the approach to RSPB Minsmere (along Vault Road), northwards across Westleton Walks, through Westleton Heath National Nature Reserve and into Dunwich Forest. Driving tracks late afternoon or walking footpaths anywhere in the whole area could bring you within earshot of a vocal stag.

▲ A male bearded tit (JL)

October weekend 1

Start at the RSPB viewpoint south of Westleton Heath between the car parks on Dunwich Road. At weekends in season, RSPB volunteers offer views of the deer through telescopes. As the need for such optics implies, however, animals can be rather distant. For intimate views, you could pay a moderate fee to join a RSPB vehicular safari. Alternatively, proceed by foot, for example along the west–east footpath that starts near King's Farm, 500m south of Dunwich Road. Be wary, however, of approaching *too* close: hormonal stags will readily charge any mammalian intruder.

Whatever your preferred viewing strategy (and you have time to test several), the rut should not fail to astound. Little wonder really, given the prize: access to a harem, and thus to descendents. The winner really does take it all.

Preparation takes all year. Mature stags shed antlers in late winter, and grow a new set during spring and summer. In mid-August, the 'velvet' covering to the antlers withers, then the stag shreds the remnants against a tree. The resulting armoury is ready for deployment.

Combat, however, is the last resort, only required when all other methods of dispute resolution have failed. The first tactic is vocal: the guttural bellowing. The bigger the stag, the more resonant and further-carrying the bellow. The fitter the stag, the longer he can holler. The further the sound carries and the longer it lasts, the less likely a young pretender is to risk confrontation.

Should voice not deter a challenger, the rivals proceed to stage two. Walking in parallel, they literally size each other up. Should a physical discrepancy be clear, the smaller or weaker male retreats. But should the strutting not reveal any tangible difference in stature, one male will lower his head in declaration of war.

The opponents then charge at each other and interlock antlers with an audible *clack*. As each stag seeks to surmount the other's guard, musclebound necks thrust and twist while hind legs tense and turn. Combat frequently turns brutal until one male acknowledges that his time is up, and retires. The victor pauses for breath, and either resumes or assumes command of his troop of females.

Take a break from deer voyeurism by looking for another charismatic mammal at nearby RSPB Minsmere. The reserve has become East Anglia's most reliable location for otter. Check the noticeboard for

A deep bellow from a red deer stag serves as the call to rut. (CD)

details of favoured sites or simply spend a few patient hours in Bittern or Island Mere hides. Quietly stake out reedy borders and open waters for a lone male fishing or a female and cub cavorting.

Conveniently, the same hides also overlook prime real estate for another shy, brown resident: bittern. Minsmere is one of Britain's most significant sites for this rare heron, and it is here that the RSPB tested and perfected many of its reedbed-management techniques. The reeds through which bittern may stride or over which it may fly are equally the domain of bearded tit. If the day is windless and the sun bright, you may witness an 'eruption' of this charming bird. Parties fly up into the sky, gain height, circle and then disperse westwards or southwards to spend the winter elsewhere in Britain.

If time remains, sift through the waders and wildfowl on the 'Scrape'. You may find scarce shorebirds such as curlew sandpiper, and pintail amongst the teal. When you spot a little egret, take a moment to remember that this now widespread heron was a national rarity as recently as 1989.

Yet while you revel in the reserve, you will not resist keeping half an eye on your watch. As mid-afternoon draws near, your anticipation starts to soar: the energy and spectacle of the rut is utterly addictive.

Practicalities

Where to go: Leave the A12 northeast of Yoxford, heading towards Westleton. From the village depart east on Dunwich Road and use the Natural England car parks at **Westleton Heath** (☀ TM459696). When operational, the RSPB viewpoint is signposted, 800m distant. Heading back west towards Westleton, take the first left and continue south for 500m. Park near the entrance track to King's Farm (☀ TM450690) and take the public footpath east. For **RSPB Minsmere** (☀ TM473672 ☎ 01728 648281 Ⓦ www.rspb.org.uk/minsmere), leave Westleton village east on Mill Road, which leads into Vault Road, and follow signs. No dogs. Explore the wider area, including **Westleton Walks** and **Dunwich Forest** on minor roads, footpaths and bridleways. Take great care when venturing close to rutting stags: there is a real risk of injury.

An alternative nearby site for rutting red deer is near **Walpole**, northwest of Yoxford. Drive southwest along the B1117 from Walpole. Park opposite Heveningham Hall (☀ TM355740) and look north onto cultivated fields that slope up away from the road. Deer emerge from Broomgreen Covert (a copse) to rut.

Suggested bases: Yoxford and Saxmundham (Ⓦ www.saxmundham.org), with villages including Eastbridge and Westleton. **Westleton Crown** (☎ 01726 648777 Ⓦ www.westletoncrown.co.uk) in Westleton is a traditional Suffolk coaching inn offering 34 stylish, comfortable rooms with luxurious linen, and excellent food.

Flexibility: Red deer rut late September to late October, peaking in the first fortnight of October. Otters, bittern and bearded tit are resident, but bearded tits 'erupt' only on calm days in September through to October. Passage waders are best July to mid-October.

Accessibility: ②

▼ A gang of little egrets (JL)

41 Scilly season

Isles of Scilly for vagrant birds, lesser white-toothed shrew, grey seal, prickly stick-insect, rockpool life

In a copse on an isolated archipelago, east meets west. From Asia hails a Pallas's warbler; from North America, a grey-cheeked thrush. The delicate eastern sprite hovers above the head of the demure, ground-feeding thrush. Such an exceptional avian juxtaposition, both protagonists being thousands of kilometres from home, would be a sure sign that we have entered 'Scilly season'.

> **"Scilly's magic means that any weather conditions can conjure up something special"**

The Isles of Scilly, plonked in the North Atlantic some 40km off the Cornish coast, are a magnet for lost birds. The reason is simple: location, location, location. The 140 islands form the first British landfall for New World vagrants that have been carried east by strong winds – and the last *terra firme* for those oriental oddities that have overshot the English mainland.

Mid-October is prime time to see migrant birds from all points of the compass – and birdwatchers from all parts of Britain. Fortunately for the claustrophobic, the days of thousand-strong crowds of Barbour-clad birders are largely over; feathered visitors now once again outnumber their admirers.

If you depart mainland Cornwall by water rather than air, your journey unlocks the adventure. Crossing open ocean gives you a chance of seeing seabirds such as shearwaters and grey phalarope (a remarkable marine wader), plus short-beaked common dolphin and basking shark.

▲ Yellow-browed warbler, a striped sprite fresh in from Siberia (RN)

Once you land on the largest island of St Mary's almost anything is possible – and the unpredictability is the essence of the attraction. For peak action, onshore winds are a must: ideally southwesterlies tracking an Atlantic depression or easterlies emanating from a bank of high pressure over Asia. But Scilly's magic is such that any weather conditions can conjure up something special.

To optimise your visit, two approaches stand out. Stay on one island and check every ounce of interesting habitat to find your own birds. Or profit from the inter-island boat service that connects St Mary's, St Agnes, St Martin's, Tresco and Bryher, and trail after others' finds. Or a bit of both, if time permits!

To find rare birds, think in terms of the habitats that provide a weary vagabond with sustenance and shelter. Look on beaches for shorebirds: might a spotted sandpiper lurk amongst the common sandpipers? Scan expanses of cropped turf (cricket pitches, airfields) for Richard's pipit and dotterel. Wait by bushes for a firecrest to emerge or a little bunting to start feeding.

Crick your neck in copses, straining for a flash of yellow-browed warbler or, if you're really lucky, the bumble of a red-eyed vireo, hailing from across 'the Pond'. Talking of ponds, freshwater bodies such as Porth Hellick and Lower Moors (St Mary's) and Abbey Pool (Tresco) are a magnet for jack snipe – a bouncing yo-yo of a wader – but could just as well harbour spotted crake or pectoral sandpiper. The possibilities are endless.

Should you crave a change from birding, fear not: a flock of alternatives are on offer. Monarch is the non-avian winged rarity that everyone hopes to see, and nowhere is better in Britain to see it than Scilly. This giant of the butterfly world frequently gets caught up in the same fast-moving Atlantic depressions as North American birds. Its safe arrival on British shores is all the more remarkable, given its fragility. If you see a dragonfly, give it a second glance. In October, any such four-winged insect could have far-flung origins:

▲ Lesser white-toothed shrew (DH/FLPA)

perhaps red-veined darter from southern Europe or, the nirvana of Odonata, green darner from North America.

That mammals are somewhat less prone to vagrancy than winged wonders does not mean that Scilly is bereft of furry favourites. October is early in the breeding season for grey seal (see *August, 2* pages 133–6), so a boat trip to the Eastern Islands could conceivably produce pups as well as adults. And it would be rude not to try for lesser white-toothed shrew, a species unknown elsewhere in Britain. On St Mary's, favoured spots include Old Town beach and churchyard, and the path towards Peninnis Head. But check rocky beaches anywhere – and, while there, go rockpooling at low tide (see *August, 2* pages 133–6).

If bryophytes tickle your fancy, track down lichens for which Scilly's clean, Gulf Stream-moistened air is famous. Peninnis Head holds ciliate strap lichen (among grass) and golden hair lichen (on bare rock), among others. Worth looking for if there are no migrant birds.

For something completely different, search for stick-insects! In the 1940s, prickly and smooth stick-insects arrived in plant shipments from New Zealand, survived and have thrived. These camouflage champions breed without need for fertilisation by males; indeed, no males have ever been seen. Recently, an additional species from closer to home – Mediterranean stick-insect – has been discovered, so there's now a trio to try for. Key sites include Old Town cemetery on St Mary's and Abbey Gardens on Tresco. But wherever you tread, keep your eye on suitable foodplants (bramble and privet) and sunny, south-facing walls (perfect for basking before winter sets in). As with birds, the unexpected is never far away during Scilly season.

Practicalities

Where to go: Travel to **Scilly** is by sea or air (to St Mary's: ① 0845 710 5555 Ⓦ www.islesofscilly-travel.co.uk). Several planes per day depart Lands End and Newquay, with single flights from Exeter, Bristol and Southampton. The MV *Scillonian* sails once daily, departing Penzance. There is no transport of any kind on/off Scilly on Sundays, meaning a long weekend is essential. Shame!

Members of St Mary's Boatmen's Association (① 01720 423999 Ⓦ www.scillyboating.co.uk) run boats between and around the islands. Hiring a bike enables you to cover more of St Mary's (St Mary's Bike Hire ① 07796 638506 Ⓦ www.stmarysbikehire.co.uk).

Suggested bases: Accommodation is scattered across the main islands (Ⓦ www.simplyscilly.co.uk, www.scillyonline.co.uk). St Mary's has the widest range and is the centrifugal point for day-trips. It is the logical base for a short trip but that should not prevent you from exploring other islands if time allows. **The Belmont** (① 01720 Ⓦ www.the-belmont.co.uk) is on the edge of Hugh Town and is a double-fronted property with six spacious bedrooms.

Flexibility: Any time mid-September to the end of October can be excellent for vagrant birds. Grey seal is resident but breeds October to December. Stick insects are best August to October. Lesser white-toothed shrew and rockpool creatures are resident.

Accessibility: ② 🏃

▼ Birders travelling by boat between the islands (RT/FLPA)

42

Estuarine exodus

Cheshire & Conwy for pygmy shrew, harvest mouse, Kashmir goat, short-eared owl, chough

> " Such profusion of the displaced and disoriented attracts a predatory throng "

Time and tide wait for no man. Nor, indeed, for *any* mammal. Nowhere is the impact of tidewater more apparent on mammals than the Dee Estuary. Shared by Wales and England, the Dee has long been cherished as one of Europe's most bird-rich estuaries. But only recently has an additional attraction spread beyond the binoculars of local wildlife-watchers: the spring-tide mass exodus of small mammals with attendant throng of predators.

For all but a few score hours of the year, the saltmarshes protecting the town of Neston from marine waters are a fabulous place to live... for shrews, voles, mice and rats. There is ample seed- and invertebrate-rich terrain to scurry across and plenty of dense sea aster to hide beneath, safe from the attention of predators. But particularly high tides, with a following wind, cause chaos for the inhabitants, a feast for carnivores and a thrilling visit for you.

To see the spectacle, head to Old Bath House car park in RSPB Dee Estuary–Parkgate on the Wirral, and peer over the seawall.

▲ Short-eared owl (PM)

October weekend 3

Schedule your visit for the autumn's highest tides (whether or not on the third weekend of October): waters of 10m or more are a must. Just as importantly, pray for low pressure and a west-based wind, ideally northwesterly. This combination of elements pushes the tide higher so that it reaches the seawall and literally flushes out mammals.

The show starts benevolently with classic high-tide fare of wildfowl and waders. As the encroaching waters flood favoured roosting spots, flocks of shelduck, teal, pintail and wigeon take to the air. Clouds of waders – oystercatcher, dunlin, knot, common redshank, curlew – wheel into the air as their preferred dry spots are swamped. All have no option but to approach the seawall. As water penetrates the marsh – trickling through furrows, inundating tussocks – landbirds such as meadow pipit, skylark and linnet flock and flee.

As flood nudges coastal defence, propelled by wind and intensified by rain, it prompts a mass evacuation of landlubbing mammals. Any creature ill-adapted for aquatic life must beat a retreat landwards. Common and pygmy shrews depart *en masse*. Bank and short-tailed field voles scarper. Wood mouse and brown rat skedaddle. A harvest mouse scrambles up a reed, clinging on for dear life. A mole (rarely seen above ground) swims for safety. Even those small mammals accustomed to a watery life find conditions overbearing, so you could see water vole and perhaps water shrew.

Harvest mice are one of several mammal species flushed out by Parkgate's rising tide. (DC)

The furry morass finds transport and shelter wherever it can: a wood mouse coasts past on driftwood, a bank vole squats on the seawall, a pygmy shrew shivers in the car park. Such profusion of the displaced and disoriented is gold dust for the predatory troupe. Avian opportunists such as grey heron, carrion crow and gulls jostle to seize the fugitives. Red fox, weasel and stoat hunt the marshes until they too are forced to exit. Raptors abound: kestrel, marsh harrier and sparrowhawk for sure, and probably peregrine and merlin too. The prize avian hunters are short-eared and barn owls, butterflying over the marsh at close range. Exhilarating!

For day two, drive along the north Wales coast to the limestone protrusion of Great Orme. Here heathland, limestone grassland and seacliffs nestle on a towering peninsula that divides Conwy and Llandudno bays. The star bird is chough, an energetic ragamuffin of a crow often seen around the lighthouse. This is also a good spot for peregrine, attracted by the plethora of cliff-dwelling pigeons. Mid-October is peak bird migration season, and the Orme is a migrant hotspot. Check any cover for warblers, thrushes and goldcrests. St Tudno's Cemetery often holds black redstart, the male a sumptuous smoky-black peppered silver on its crown sides. The country park's limestone plateau, particularly near the cairn, can be good for buntings including snow and Lapland.

The birds are decent enough, but Orme is most famous for its hundred-strong population of feral goat, resident here for 100 years. Formally named Kashmir goat – the mammalian supplier of cashmere – Orme's shaggy, white billies are distinct from those in Snowdonia, toting spectacular horns that arc napewards. Goats range across the headland, but, in autumn, often frequent grassy slopes southwest of the country park (nearer the town in a northerly wind). October is rutting season, so you may even encounter some male-on-male aggression.

Finish the weekend with a relaxing trip to nearby RSPB Conwy. Flanking the estuary, the reserve's pools, rough grassland and scrub hold a fair variety of birdlife. Star among wildfowl is red-breasted merganser, a shaggy-naped, saw-billed diving duck. Waders include black-tailed godwit and the odd greenshank, while a water rail often flirts with visitors watching from within the cosy coffee shop. Best of all, up to 10,000 starlings roost here some evenings. After a weekend focused on mass *emigration*, it is heartening to watch plentiful *immigration*.

Where to go: RSPB Dee Estuary–Parkgate (℡ 0151
3367681 Ⓦ www.rspb.org.uk/dee-parkgate) is on the
west shore of the Wirral, 2.5km northwest of Neston.
Access is from the B5135 off the A540 Neston–Heswall
road. View from Old Bath House car park (☀ SJ273789)
north of The Boathouse pub in Parkgate. Alternatively,
try the less-visited car park on Riverbank Road in Lower
Heswall (☀ SJ263795). Location details, maps and high-tide times
are at Ⓦ www.deeestuary.co.uk. Tide heights are as for Liverpool;
peak water is 20 minutes later (Ⓦ www.pol.ac.uk/appl/liverpool.
html). Tide times are often given as GMT even during British Summer
Time. Arrive two hours before high water.

    For **Great Orme** (Ⓦ www.greatorme.org.uk), leave the A55
northwest on the A470. Drive through Llandudno until you reach
the toll house. Follow Marine Drive anti-clockwise around the Orme,
parking at St Tudno's Church (☀ SH770839). Other car parks are
northwest of the Head, near the café and lighthouse (☀ SH756844),
and on the plateau (☀ SH766833). You can reach the plateau by cable
car (Ⓦ www.greatorme.org.uk/cablecar.html) and tram
(℡ 01492 879306 Ⓦ www.greatormetramway.com). **RSPB Conwy**
(☀ SH797773 ℡ 01492 584091 Ⓦ www.rspb.org.uk/conwy) is on the
northeast shore of Conwy Estuary. Just south of Llandudno Junction,
at the A55/A546 roundabout, follow reserve signs southwards. For a
local wildlife guide, try The Biggest Twitch (℡ 01492 872407 Ⓦ www.
thebiggesttwitch.com; see advert, page 220).

Suggested bases: Chester (Ⓦ www.visitchester.co.uk), Connah's Quay
and Flint (Ⓦ www.flintshire.org). In Colwyn Bay, **Ellingham House**
(℡ 01492 533345 Ⓦ www.ellinghamhouse.com) is an elegant,
recently refurbished Victorian villa with spacious, opulent rooms.

Flexibility: For Parkgate, the key variables are a spring tide over
10m, low pressure and a westerly based wind during September–
November and February–March. Given successive tides, the first will
force the departure of the most mammals. Chough and Kashmir goat
are resident.

Accessibility: ②

43
Don't spurn the chance

East Yorkshire for migrant songbirds, estuary waders, little auk, long-eared owl, woodcock

> **" Birds raindrop from the sky before cascading into cover "**

Seeeep! The exasperated sigh of a flock of redwings exploding from a coastal bush is audible above the shushing of the easterly wind. In the half-light of pre-dawn, this is a good sign. It means that songbird migration is happening – right here, right now. As visibility improves, you realise that the hawthorn hedgerow is swarming with thrushes: not just redwing, but fieldfare, song thrush and blackbird too. All freshly arrived from the continent, all hungry, all tired. This is a *very* good sign. You should be in for a day of magical, miraculous migration.

Perhaps no site is better to appreciate such bird bedlam than Spurn Point in East Yorkshire. Spurn's location – jutting across the mouth of the Humber Estuary, and one of the most easterly points in northern England – is one reason for its pre-eminence. The other is its geography: a 6km-long sandy spit, in places no wider than 20m, covered in dense sea buckthorn, and subject to cycles of seaborne destruction and reconstruction.

▲ A hungry redwing, one of many brought in by easterly winds. (GF/FLPA)

October weekend 4

Clear skies over Russia or Scandinavia coax birds into starting their migration to winter climes. Easterly winds blow them over the North Sea, where fog, rain or cloud confuses them into dropping onto the British coast. There are four categories of migrant birds to look for: nocturnal migrants stranded by day, day-flying migrants passing overhead, seabirds and shorebirds. You need different strategies to maximise your opportunities with each grouping.

Nocturnal migrants – warblers, chats, flycatchers and thrushes in particular – will have plonked down on the Yorkshire coast under the cover of darkness and sought solace and shelter in any dense vegetation. At Spurn, this largely means hedgerows from the bird observatory north towards Easington, extensive and often impenetrable sea buckthorn (from the observatory southwards along the Point), gardens (including at Kew Villa and along Beacon Lane, Kilnsea) and bushy terrain (at Sammy's Point, for example). Walk such areas, eyes alert to a flicker of movement and ears pricked for a contact call.

In perfect 'fall' conditions, birds raindrop from the sky before cascading into cover. Vegetation bristles with birds. Carpets of thrushes fly away when you approach, ring ouzels betraying their presence with a stony *chakk*. Goldcrests forage amidst seaweed rather than their normal arboreal domain. Woodcocks explode from under a bush, in the depths of which a long-eared owl snoozes. Bramblings wheeze from every furrow; pipits teem in each tussock. Black redstarts shiver their tail at the foot of the slumping clay cliffs. Robins treat people as trees, feeding beneath legs or even perching on shoulders. You turn from observer to participant, and the adrenalin is coursing through your veins. The keener your attention, the greater your chances of finding a rarity: red-breasted flycatcher or Pallas's warbler, say.

For diurnal travellers, headwinds are ideal, and the basic technique is to look up. Flocks of birds – finches, buntings, hirundines, larks, pipits and starlings – fly overhead, often quite high. Ideally, park yourself where geography funnels the passage (above the Warren near the Yorkshire Wildlife Trust visitor centre). Over a couple of hours scanning the skies, your roll call may number thousands of birds. Over the years, 1.5 million meadow pipits have been counted overflying Spurn.

If the wind has an element of northerly in it, park yourself at the seawatching hide to watch the waves for passing seabirds. At its worst,

▶ If conditions are right, thrushes flood in by the thousand. (JH)

seawatching can be just that; watching the sea. At its best, the flask of tea remains unopened as your eye and telescope are glued together. Ducks pile past in tightly packed groups: wigeon, scoters and eider. You should see skuas (notably pomarine), little gull and divers. Amongst the guillemots and razorbills, look for the buzzing balls that are of little auks. And keep an eye out for marine mammals: harbour porpoise and both seals (harbour and grey) are regular.

As for shorebirds, you have plenty of choice. You could check saline lagoons north of Kilnsea (Beacon Ponds and Easington Lagoons) or freshwater scrapes near Long Bank (Kilnsea wetlands). There is always the chance of something unusual amongst the dunlin and ringed plover. Spurn's position at the mouth of the Humber Estuary means that the muddy expanse west of the peninsula is alive with dark-bellied brent geese, shelduck and waders. Dunlin and knot are joined by curlew and common redshank. As the tide rises, the waders congregate, with the smaller birds swarming onto dry land on which to roost.

If you can drag yourself away from the birdlife – no mean feat – check out the maritime plant communities. Sea buckthorn covers much of the peninsula, grey-green vegetation offset by orange berries. Amongst the marram grass binding the dunes, look for sea-holly. And keep your eyes open for terrestrial mammals. Spurn and surroundings are a good spot for roe deer, brown hare and red fox. But, above all, enjoy the seething mass of migrating birds.

Where to go: Spurn National Nature Reserve
(⊙ TA410159 ① 01904 659570 Ⓦ www.ywt.org.uk/
reserves/spurn-national-nature-reserve) is run by
the Yorkshire Wildlife Trust. Take the A1033 east of
Kingston-upon-Hull. At Patrington, head southwest
on the B1445. From Easington, follow minor roads
southeast to Kilnsea and Spurn. There are several car
parks: Sammy's Point, Easington (⊙ TA394174), Kilnsea village by the
Crown and Anchor pub (⊙ TA410158), Kilnsea Bluebell café
(⊙ TA418159), Spurn Canal Zone (⊙TA417154), the Warren
(⊙ TA419150) and Spurn Head (⊙ TA402112). A fee is payable to
drive south of the Warren/Spurn Bird Observatory. To help you
explore the area, download the map of birding sites at Ⓦ www.
spurnbirdobservatory.co.uk/map.

Suggested bases: Easington, Patrington and Withernsea, although
little accommodation is available. Spurn Bird Observatory offers
simple self-catering accommodation (Ⓦ www.spurnbirdobservatory.
co.uk). **Westmere Farm** (① 01964 650258 Ⓦ www.westmerefarm.
co.uk) in Kilnsea offers five comfortable rooms overlooking either the
Humber Estuary or fields towards the North Sea.

Flexibility: Migrating landbirds can be seen any time from mid-
August to early November, although the composition varies between
months. Weather conditions are critical. For October falls, winds
with an easterly element, ideally originating from high pressure over
Russia or further east, combined with poor visibility (rain, cloud, fog)
over the North Sea. For visible migration a southerly or southwesterly
headwind is favoured. For seabird passage, northerly winds are best.
For visible migration ('vis mig'), a headwind is best, so southwesterly
winds are ideal.

Accessibility: ③ 𝕜

▶ Long-eared owl (JW)

44 **Leap of faith**

**North Yorkshire, Cumbria & Lancashire for the
salmon run, red deer, otter, dipper, fungi**

> **❝Salmon leap
> four times their
> body length
> to ascend the
> Falls❞**

This weekend is unashamedly orchestrated around a single event that marks the near-culmination of one of the most remarkable journeys in the natural world. A journey that epitomises perseverance, demands supreme fitness and requires exceptional navigational ability. A voyage that is all about life, yet ends in the protagonists' deaths. The salmon run.

Many people associate the spectacle of leaping salmon with nature documentaries on grizzly bears in North America. Yet the selfsame sight – hirsute orsines apart – can be enjoyed along unpolluted rivers across Britain. So head to Stainforth Force on the River Ribble in the Yorkshire Dales National Park.

Atlantic salmon season usually lasts for three to four weeks during mid-October to mid-November, and is contingent on autumn's first heavy rains. These raise river levels to a height that facilitates fishy leaps into the unknown. Arrive at Stainforth Force early morning or late afternoon to coincide with peak activity.

Walk 100m southeast from the road bridge along the wooded river then seat yourself beside an obvious cascade of 2m height. Crouch low, to better appreciate the scale of the challenge for the Atlantic salmon. Shuffle right to the river edge, to really *feel* the rush of water. Surrounded by the burnt tones of autumn and half-hypnotised by the torrents, wait.

▶ Yellowleg bonnet, a petite and delicate fungus (JL)

October weekend 5

You may need to linger for barely half a minute until the action starts. Or it may be half an hour. Or perhaps the morning will be quiet, with kick-off late afternoon. But if conditions are right, the fish will come. The intervals between each individual leap could be a few seconds or a few minutes. Stay alert: blinking could mean missing.

With a flash of silver and a muscular wriggle of tail, salmon leap four times their length to ascend the falls. Usually only larger fish make it first time, others crashing and burning. After recovering and refuelling, they venture once more into the fray. Many endure several failures before succeeding.

Look closely to differentiate the darker females with a rainbow glimmer on their sides from the red-bellied, streaky-flanked males. That both sexes are simultaneously heading in the same direction makes their purpose as crystal clear as the Ribble waters: to spawn. And herein lies what is extraordinary about the salmon story.

The salmon you see hatched in this very river up to four years previously. They left as youngsters ('smolt'), spending the intervening time fattening up in deep waters offshore and running the gauntlet of innumerable predators. Eventually, when the urge to breed proves irrepressible, salmon expertly navigate their way back to their birthplace by dint of stars, magnetic field, an understanding of oceanic currents and 'chemical memory'. A miraculous migration against improbable odds: just one in every thousand fertilised eggs develops into a successfully breeding adult. Remarkable.

And ultimately tragic. From the moment adults enter the freshwater system, they cease to eat. Surviving on reserves, their days are numbered. Indeed, procreation is the final act for nine of every ten salmon that returns to spawn.

In downtime between fishy flurries, look for dipper. While not famed for migratory feats, this bird is no less special than salmon. The only British songbird to feed underwater, dippers are as adapted for aquatic life as a duck. An extra eyelid enables vision when submerged, scales close nostrils in the currents, and feathers are coated in oil.

For another bash at salmon – if Stainforth didn't produce or if you simply crave more – try Force Falls in the Lake District, a touch over an hour's drive west. Watch the River Kent rapids from the cottage overlooking the falls.

For what remains of your trip, visit RSPB Leighton Moss. October is *the* month for red deer and while Halloween week is late on in the rut (see *October, 1* pages 163–6), an opportunity to view Britain's largest land mammal is hard to pass up. Males should still be roaring, and you should see the odd harem-flanked stag from Griesdale hide.

Late October is prime time for fungi. Scan the ground and tree trunks for numerous species. While ostensibly amorphous in appearance, fungi repay close examination, with their different sizes, shapes, colours, textures and patterns. Among common species, look for blackfoot polypore, tawny funnel cap and lemon disco. Along the causeway, an abundance of lichens adorns the trees, notably oakmoss lichen.

Before the weekend expires, check out three Moss specialities. The Cetti's warblers here are the most northerly in Britain – and regularly erupt into uncompromising serenade near Public Hide. Bearded tits are often easy to see in autumn: grit trays interpolating the causeway are favoured. Best of all, watch quietly for otter from Lower or Public hides – even if there is something rather unnerving about ending a fish-watching weekend by watching a fish-eater.

▲ The Atlantic salmon's leap of faith (JB)

Where to go: For **Stainforth Force** in North Yorkshire,
leave Settle north on the B6479. After 3.5km, park at
Stainforth village 'pay and display'. Walk west along
a minor road (Dog Hill Brow), crossing the railway line,
until you reach the river bridge. Then walk 100m southeast
along the river to view the falls (☀ SD818671). **Force Falls**
(☀ SD340911) is at Force Mills in Grizedale Forest Park,
8km northwest of Newby Bridge in southern Cumbria.
From the A590 at Newby Bridge, drive north on minor roads to
Thwaite Head, then north then west to Force Mills. Park northeast of
the hamlet at the Forestry Commission picnic site, then walk back to
watch from the cottage overlooking the falls. The entrance to **RSPB
Leighton Moss** (☀ SD478750 ① 01524 701601 ⓦ www.rspb.org.uk/
leightonmoss) is off Storrs Lane in Silverdale, 10km north of Carnforth.
Suggested bases: Settle (ⓦ www.settle.org.uk), Kirkby Lonsdale
(ⓦ www.kirkbylonsdale.co.uk) and Kendal (ⓦ www.visitcumbria.
com/sl/kendal). **Littlebank Country House** (① 01729 822330 ⓦ www.
littlebankcountryhouse.co.uk) is a secluded 17th-century manor set in
wooded grounds southwest of Giggleswick.
Flexibility: The first substantial rains during mid-October to mid-
November prompt the upstream rush of salmon, which should then
last three to four weeks. Insufficient rain and the river flow will be
inadequate; excessive rain and the salmon will not have a fighting
chance of successfully leaping. Fungi season is September to
November. Red deer rut late September to late October. Dipper
is resident.
Accessibility: ③

Otters are regular at RSPB Leighton Moss. (JL)

45
Yew and yours

Sussex for huge yews, fungi, water shrew, estuary
waders, brent goose

In a weekend showcasing the big (skies, trees and flocks), start with a shot at the small. Officially, Woods Mill is the Sussex Wildlife

> **❝Let your imagination be buffeted by the contorted shapes and flayed forms❞**

Trust HQ: the organisational hub of a conservation charity. Unofficially, it is one of Britain's more reliable sites for our only venomous mammal: water shrew.

Although neither rare nor restricted in range, this aquatic carnivore is seldom seen – a consequence of life largely spent underwater and underground, and a hyperactive demeanour which sees it racing here, there, everywhere in pursuit of prey. Enquire at the visitor centre for the whereabouts of recent sightings. Your chances are highest (or, rather, less slender) on unvegetated water channels with unencumbered views. Good spots have included the leat supplying the mill wheel and footbridges along the upper path. Watch for movement in or by the water, or for air bubbling up to the water surface as it escapes from the shrew's velvety fur.

Call time after an hour or two. Go west to RSPB Pulborough Brooks, a reserve with a variety of wildlife-rich landscapes. First, check with the wardens whether they trapped any moths overnight.

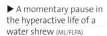

▶ A momentary pause in the hyperactive life of a water shrew (ML/FLPA)

If so, take a look. Autumn is a fine season for seeing merveille du jour, red-green carpet, sallow and feathered thorn, among others. The visitor centre is also a good place to look for water rail, so linger some to see this usually reclusive bird.

Then head out. On the Wetland Trail, the 'brooks' (flooded lowlands) hold a thousand or so ducks, principally wigeon, teal and pintail. A couple of hundred lapwing may be joined by a few score black-tailed godwit. A peregrine typically lurks near Hanger viewpoint. On the Heathland Trail, look along rides for fallow deer and up into trees for common crossbill and siskin… but down to the ground for fungi. Although somewhat past their peak, you could still see a couple of dozen species. Look for clumps of sulphur tuft and common rustgill, a sprinkling of amethyst deceiver, rosy bonnet, a handful of boletes and colourful ochre and blackening brittlegills. Not forgetting, of course, the fairytale toadstool: the scarlet and white fly agaric. Splendid.

Finish the day revering some of Britain's most gargantuan trees. Lying low in a steep-sided coombe, the yews of Kingley Vale figure among the country's oldest life-forms. Twisted and mystical, several trees surpass 5m in girth and 500 years in age. The yew forest shrouds the dissipating light, and encases you with wooden pillars and arches. As the gloom broods below the thickening canopy, let your imagination be buffeted by the contorted shapes, flayed forms, gnarled boughs, sinewy trunks, severed limbs, shadowy hollows and the layering of serpentine root systems. You may be distracted by roe or fallow deer (the latter may even still be rutting), red kite or common buzzard, green woodpecker or yew berry-chomping fieldfare, but keep bringing your eye and mind back to the trees: yew and yours. There is nowhere quite like Kingley Vale.

After a night in the clutches of Morpheus, experience a day in the life of an estuary. A full day on Pagham Harbour's seawall and paths enables you to appreciate what tide and time mean for wildlife (and their watchers).

If arriving at low tide, you are greeted by a vast sweep of muddy channels and moraines, ravines and hummocks. In greatest evidence are ducks. Whistling wigeon upend alongside piping teal. Refined pintail resemble wildfowl

▲ Fly agaric (JL)

supermodels when juxtaposed with stocky, thuggish-looking shoveler. There are waders too. Grey plover and curlew feed quietly and solitarily; common redshank less so. Lapwings – with their dodgy quiffs, oversized head and spindly legs – bring to mind gawky teenagers. A nervous, fidgeting huddle of golden plover suddenly explodes to the air as one, glinting white then spangling ochre as they evade a famished peregrine.

As the tide turns, walk back from Spitend Hide to North Wall keeping the marsh to your left. Stay alert for the shuffling of a harvest mouse. Use your ears to track down the thousand-strong flock of brent goose that winters around the harbour. More often than not they will be grazing in nearby stubble fields. Scrutinise the flock to possibly unveil a black brant, the brent's North American relative.

As you walk west along North Wall, check the sluice for kingfisher and the autumn's final water vole. Cetti's warblers and bearded tits may call to reveal their presence in the reeds. Cormorants wheel overhead, a blend of stork and pterodactyl. Black-tailed godwits lope across the pool, a common snipe imitates a sewing machine and a water rail scurries along reedy fringes. Overhead a Mediterranean gull circles with commoner cousins, and dozens of little egrets file roostwards. A barn owl emerges to hunt. Look southwards to the estuary to find that the rising tide has entirely concealed the earlier mudscape and now mirrors the molten autumnal sunset. Take your cue, and depart.

Dark-bellied brent geese lining an estuary creek. (KD)

Where to go: Woods Mill (☀ TQ218138 ☎ 01273
492630 ⓦ http://tinyurl.com/woodsmillhq), the
Sussex Wildlife Trust HQ is 2km south of Henfield;
access to the car park is from Horn Lane off the A2037.
RSPB Pulborough Brooks (☀ TQ058164 ☎ 01798 875851
ⓦ www.rspb.org.uk/pulboroughbrooks) lies immediately
south of Pulborough. Access is by footpaths south of
Pulborough or from the car park/visitor centre/café west of the A283
at Wiggonholt, 3km south of Pulborough. There are three trails. For
Kingley Vale National Nature Reserve (☀ SU822105 ☎ 0300 0602681
ⓦ http://tinyurl.com/kingleyvale), 5km north of Chichester, leave the
A286 at Mid Lavant and head 3km west to the car park just beyond
West Stoke. Take the footpath 1km north to the reserve.

    Parts of **Pagham Harbour** (☀ SZ857966), immediately southwest
of Bognor Regis, are managed by RSPB (☎ 01243 641508 ⓦ www.
rspb.org.uk/paghamharbour) and Sussex Wildlife Trust (☎ 01243
641508 ⓦ http://tinyurl.com/paghamreserve). The main access
points are from Pagham village (park sensibly near the church at ☀
SZ883975, and walk west to the North Wall or south to Spitend Hide),
and, off the B2145 west of the tidal flats, from Sidlesham Ferry (car
park and visitor centre at ☀ SZ856965) or Church Norton (car park at
☀ SZ872956). Footpaths circumnavigate the harbour.

Suggested bases: Chichester (ⓦ www.visitchichester.org), Arundel
(ⓦ www.arundel.org.uk) and Bognor Regis (ⓦ www.sussexbythesea.
com). An overview is at ⓦ www.westsussex.info. A stone's throw
from Arundel Castle, **Arundel House** (☎ 01903 882136 ⓦ www.
arundelhousearundel.co.uk) is a boutique B&B and restaurant, with
sumptuous rooms including walk-in rainfall showers.

Flexibility: Estuary wildfowl and waders occur mid-October to March.
Fungi are best mid-September to late October, but any time until
the end of November works. Water shrew is arguably best August to
September.

Accessibility: ③

▼ Sulphur tuft form in dense clusters. (RB/FLPA)

46

Wildcat!

Argyll & Bute for wildcat, pine marten, otter, harbour seal, white-tailed eagle

> **"A near-mythical and increasingly rare beast saunters into the night"**

In the youthful darkness, you drive remote roads deep in the Scottish Highlands. Slowly, eyes fixed on the carriageway ahead. Your companion swings a spotlight along scree slopes and vegetated hillsides flanking the tarmac. All is quiet. Then... there! In mid-carriageway, a cat! A stocky feline with flared jowls directs a disdainful look your way, then saunters on striped haunches into the roadside and the night beyond. The thick furred, banded and black-tipped tail provides your parting glimpse of a near-mythical and increasingly rare beast. Wildcat!

An isolated protrusion on Scotland's west coast that peers southwards towards Mull, Ardnamurchan Peninsula is the best area to see Scottish wildcat. Indeed, Ardnamurchan arguably offers Britain's finest mammal-watching. Your target list comprises pine marten, otter, harbour porpoise, two seals and three deer. All amidst rugged scenery with craggy hillsides, rocky coastlines, sandy beaches and autumn's burnt tones.

Such wildlife-watching paradise does not come easy so plan for a long weekend. The drive from Glasgow alone is four hours. Once on Ardnamurchan, some mammals (deer, seals) give themselves up easily but others

▶ A view of wildcat we all dream of; this one is captive... (JMB)

(otter, pine marten and, of course, wildcat) take time, sharp eyes and luck. But the end more than justifies the effort.

At the eastern base of Ardnamurchan, the A861 sinews beside Loch Sunart. Between Strontian and Salen, pause several times to scan. You should find harbour and grey seals bobbing in the water or lounging on the shoreline. The strand also holds the invasive American mink (unfortunately), water shrew (reportedly, east of Salen) and otter (delightfully). For the latter, two sites stand out: Garbh Eilean Hide at Ard Airigh and the stretch of water leading 500m west from Resipole Farm. Resipole is also the first of several sites for pine marten, which is attracted to food after dark put out by wannabee watchers. (A midnight feast of jam sandwiches, cut into small squares, is optimum!)

In Salen, decant onto B8007 to continue westwards. Checking Loch Sunart should reveal harbour porpoise plus further seals. The road traverses Glenborrodale, another pine marten site; it formerly bred in the hotel roof. Immediately west, halt at RSPB Glenborrodale. Scan for marine mammals from the car park then wander the umber oak-clad hillside. There's a chance of red squirrel, and you should see various fungi.

Heading 3km west, call at Glenmore's natural history centre, Nàdurra. This is a good place to exchange information on sightings over a cuppa – and to see mammals! Scan slopes northwards for red deer, and southwards for red and roe deer on the islet of Eilean Mòr. Pine marten occurs nearby and brown long-eared bat inhabits the centre itself. Even better, the bay 300m west, Port na Croisg, is a well-known haunt of otter and both seals. A falling tide is best for twisting and diving otters, especially at either end of the day. What a fabulous place to while away an hour or two!

Continue 2km further west and stop at Cladh Chiarain car park. Look down into Camas nan Geall bay for possible harbour porpoise, eider and red-throated diver. And look up for golden and white-tailed eagles. The latter deserves its reputation as a 'flying barn door', while the former is no small fry either.

From Clad Chiarain, the B8007 swings inland. After 5.5km a conifer plantation nuzzles

◀ Pine marten: often curious, particularly if jam butties are involved. (DG)

the road, with Loch Mudle lying to your right. Late afternoon, you might bump into pine marten running with rocking-horse gait amidst prostrate pines, a hedgehog or barn owl. You should see the odd roe deer, nervously huddling the wooded fringes, and the recently introduced fallow deer. On the moorland northwest, red deer can be common: as the light dwindles, you should see several herds. For more, continue to the T-junction, then head north on the minor road through Branault and Kilmory to Ockle. Perhaps pop down to the coast just northwest of Kilmory, which can be good for otter.

Once darkness falls (blessedly early in autumn), shift up a gear. Wildcat prospects are highest in the first hours of night, as famished felines hunt voles, but you still need great fortune. Prime terrain is the B8007 from the Kilchoan–Kilmory junction south to Port na Croisg; drive this stretch slowly and repeatedly. The ultimate areas are Doire Darach where the road forges between conifers and Loch Mudle, and the 3km sweep north of Cladh Chiarain (particularly the basin of rush fields northwest of Allt Tòrr na Mòine River and scree slopes 500m further on).

In addition to the car's beam, train a spotlight perpendicular to the car. Your search image is the 'twin headlights' that denote a predator's forward-facing eyes. To be sure the cat is genetically pure (and only 1% of Scotland's 'wildcats' are thought untainted by tabby), clock the clublike, ringed tail and striped legs, and confirm the absence of telltale hybrid characteristics of white patches or spots. Result!

Where to go: Ardnamurchan Peninsula (Ⓦ www. ardnamurchan.com) is west of Fort William. From the A82, use the Corran Ferry to reach the A861. Follow this west through Glen Tarbet then along Loch Sunart. For the hide at **Garbh Eilean**, 12km west of Strontian, use Ard Airigh car park (☀ NM745619 Ⓣ 01397 702184 Ⓦ http://tinyurl.com/garbheilean). **Resipole Farm** (☀ NM722640) is 3km before Salen (☀ NM690648), where you switch onto the B8007. Where the road flanks Loch Sunart, good locations comprise: **RSPB Glenborrodale** (☀ NM595615 Ⓣ 01463 715000 Ⓦ www.rspb.org.uk/glenborrodale); **Nàdurra Natural History Centre** (☀ NM586624 Ⓣ 01972 500209 Ⓦ www.nadurracentre. co.uk) plus adjacent Port na Croisg (☀ NM583620) and Cala Darach (☀ NM578618); and **Cladh Chiarain** car park above Camas nan Geall (☀ NM563617).

The B8007 between Cladh Chiarain and **Loch Mudle** is best for wildcat, particularly the scree slopes (☀ NM560623), the 'basin' rush fields (☀ NM553630) north of Allt Tòrr na Mòine River, and Doire Darach (☀ NM545651). At the T-junction with the Kilchoan–Kilmory road (☀ NM526665), the right turn ends at **Ockle** (☀ NM556705). Find good information on wildcats at Ⓦ www.scottishwildcats.co.uk. **Suggested bases:** Villages include Salen, Kilchoan and Glenborrodale (Ⓦ www.ardnamurchan.com); additional accommodation is scattered around the peninsula. With a view over Loch Shiel, **Ardshealach Lodge** (Ⓣ 01967 431399 Ⓦ www.ardshealach-lodge. co.uk) offers four traditionally styled rooms and an on-site restaurant. **Flexibility:** Wildcat and pine marten are resident; in autumn, populations of predator and prey should be at their peak, and night draws in early making it easier to see these nocturnal mammals. Weather is important for cats: don't bother searching during rain, but the first dry night thereafter is optimum. Other mammal targets are resident. In spring/summer you should also see minke whale and perhaps other cetaceans. White-tailed eagle is resident. **Accessibility:** ②

47

A pup is for life

Lincolnshire for pupping grey seal, brent goose, knot, twite, Lapland bunting

From a secluded hollow in coastal sand dunes, disproportionately large and endearingly liquid black eyes smoulder atop the creamiest and fluffiest of marine mammals. 'Love me! Don't leave me!', the eyes seem to plead. Not 50m distant,

> **" Black eyes smoulder atop the fluffiest of marine mammals "**

different individuals of the same species engage in a visceral, hormone-fuelled duel. It is hard to imagine two more contrasting dimensions to a single creature in such proximity. Such is the charming paradox of a grey seal colony.

Britain hosts half of the world's grey seal population, so it is fitting that intimate encounters with this species feature prominently in several weekends (*January, 4* pages 13–16, *June, 4* pages 103–6, *August, 2* pages 133–6, *September, 4* pages 157–60, *December, 3* pages 207–10). But arguably none is more breathtaking than at Britain's second-largest breeding colony, at Donna Nook. Here Lincolnshire Wildlife Trust works with the Royal Air Force to manage coastal sand dunes and mudflats for the benefit of all coastal wildlife. Year-on-year there has been an increase in seal numbers... and an explosion in seal-watchers. Some 3,000 seals

◀ Maternal moment: a female grey seal and her pup (SB)

now breed here, with pups tipping the 1,000 mark. On some weekends, however, there can be even more people visiting!

This mass of mammal creates potential tension between watchers and the watched. Clearly, wildlife welfare must come first. Accordingly, the Trust provides a wardened viewing area in the dunes that enables superb views of seals without disturbing them. To improve prospects of a memorable trip and display consideration to seals and land managers, consider two tactics. First arrive early in the morning before the crowds descend and while the light is at its purest. Second – notwithstanding this being a book about weekends – visit on weekdays.

Whenever you go, sit down, take your time and imbibe. Focus on a small number of individuals and observe their lives for several hours. Females arrive ashore a day or so before they give birth. The first sign that a newborn has emerged is usually a squabble of gulls scavenging the afterbirth. The pup's shockingly clotted cream-coloured coat hints at a throwback to the species's ice-breeding heritage. Youngsters suckle every few hours; the mother's milk is so rich that newborns double their weight within a week.

Sweep the beach for the hefty, hormonal males. Each has carved out a stretch of the maternity ward along which it reigns as 'beachmaster'. Cows that pup within a bull's territory form his harem: mating happens as soon as the females come into season. While neighbourhood relationships are usually placid, evenly matched rivals sometimes spar – and the brutality may turn bloody.

Once you have had your fill of the seal soap opera (or, indeed, the human throng), make for adjacent Saltfleetby–Theddlethorpe. This mouthful of a National Nature Reserve offers several trails along which to explore an 8km tract of coast. Sand dunes form, drift and reform in the wind, with only stabilised structures hosting dense vegetation such as sea buckthorn, hawthorn and elder. November is often characterised by influxes of thrushes from the continent. The orange berries of sea buckthorn refuel blackbirds, fieldfares, redwings and the odd ring ouzel.

▶ As their name suggests, Lapland buntings are boreal breeders that arrive in Britain from October onwards.
(B/FD/FLPA)

Coastwards, saltmarsh cedes to muddy foreshore. Lapland buntings could be anywhere. At Brickyard Lane, tight flocks of twite, sometimes a hundred strong, buzz amongst the samphire beds. Further out, brent goose, curlew and shelduck forage. At Rimac, the trail crossing maritime fen proffers an outside chance of water shrew. Short-tailed field vole abounds at Churchill Lane, attracting barn owls as dusk whispers its imminence. Finally, check Sea View Washland: who knows what might turn up at these youthful Wildlife Trust scrapes?

Spend the following day wandering leisurely at Gibraltar Point, a National Nature Reserve one hour south at the stand-off between Wolds and Wash. After a cuppa in the visitor centre café, walk south along Rock Ridge to the Wash Estuary viewpoint for harriers, brent geese and, if the tide is high, thousands of roosting knot. As the shorebirds arrive two hours before peak water, they smoke across the sky before eventually pitching down to huddle as a single mass. Movement is kept to a minimum, but every so often, sometimes in response to a peregrine real or imaginary, flock members lift into the air, wings frantically flapping, before eventually returning to their prostrate repose.

For passage migrants, try east along South Beach Road to the bird observatory in the East Dunes. Thrushes scoff sea-buckthorn berries, and you may flush a woodcock or long-eared owl from the dense cover. A black redstart flicks up onto a fence, body bobbing and tail quivering. After lunch, visit poolside hides either side of the beach car park. A jack snipe, water rail or water pipit may skulk on the margins: not to be sniffed it, even if somewhat less showy than the seals with which you started the weekend.

▲ Knot: birds of a feather flock together. (JL)

Where to go: Donna Nook, Saltfleetby–Theddlethorpe
Dunes and **Gibraltar Point** are National Nature
Reserves (Ⓦ http://tinyurl.com/donnanook) managed
in whole or part by Lincolnshire Wildlife Trust
(Ⓣ 01507 526667 Ⓦ www.lincstrust.org.uk/reserves/nr/
reserves-list.php): access details and site maps are on
both websites. For **Donna Nook**, leave the A1031 at
North Somercotes, driving 4km to Stonebridge (✹ TF422998). Park
sensibly in the small car park; sometimes a local farmer opens a field
for overflow parking. From the car park, go the beach and turn right
following the dune path to the viewing area. Check the Trust website
for current viewing arrangements.

   Saltfleetby–Theddlethorpe lies immediately southeast along the
coast. Access is via a series of car parks off the A1031. From north to
south: Howden's Pullover (✹ TF449952); Sea Lane, Saltfleet
(✹ TF456944); Saltfleet Haven (aka Paradise, ✹ TF467935); Seaview
(✹ TF465925); Rimac (✹ TF468918); Churchill Lane (✹ TF477901) and
Brickyard Lane in Theddlethorpe St Helen (✹ TF484892). There are
nature trails at Seaview, Rimac and Churchill Lane. **Gibraltar Point**
(Ⓦ www.gibraltarpointbirdobservatory.blogspot.co.uk) is c6km south
of Skegness, along Gibraltar Road. Park at the visitor centre
(✹ TF556581) or beach car park (✹ TF559590), 1km nearer Skegness.
Suggested bases: North Somercotes (Ⓦ www.somercotes.clara.
net), Theddlethorpe (Ⓦ www.theddlethorpe.org.uk), Mablethorpe
(Ⓦ www.mablethorpe.info) and Skegness (Ⓦ www.visitskegness.
co.uk). A good regional website is Ⓦ www.visitlincolnshire.com.
Inland off the A18, **The Old Farmhouse** (Ⓣ 01472 824455 Ⓦ www.
oldfarmhousebandbgrimsby.com) offers large, stately rooms and a
beamed communal lounge in an 18th-century manor.
Flexibility: Grey seals are present late October to January, but peak
November–December. Check the Lincolnshire Wildlife Trust website
(Ⓦ www.lincstrust.org.uk/wildlife/index.php) for updates on
numbers. The first half of November is best for passage migrants.
Accessibility: ③

48 Murmuration

Somerset, Avon & Gloucestershire for Cheddar whitebeam, starling roost, Eurasian white-fronted goose, Bewick's swan, Eurasian crane

As the evening sky turns fiery and the clouds start to burn, a column of birds smokes upwards and outwards. The funnel of feather wisps through the air, expands into a hot-air balloon then seethes into a spiral that twists

> **" A million itchy wings ascend into the rosy dusk, shape-shifting afresh "**

into a tornado before slumping into its reedbed roost. Slumber may beckon but the chattering and fidgeting persists, until a million itchy wings again ascend into the rosy dusk, and the shape-shifting starts afresh. A tennis ball, a spinning top, an undulation – but above all, a murmuration. Somerset's starlings, at their best.

It is ironic that as breeding starlings have declined dramatically in recent years, so the spectacle of their winter roosts has garnered public appreciation. Metaphorically if not geographically, starlings have been everywhere the past few years. Gasping at their silhouetted communal forms is in vogue: black has become the new black. So much so that one wildlife broadcaster has described them, tongue-in-cheek, as 'so last year'. Yet starlings can never be passé: each night's display is unique in size and shape.

Hosting Britain's second-largest starling gathering, the wetland reserves collectively known as Avalon Marshes slosh across the Somerset Levels. Shapwick Heath, Shapwick Moor, Ham Wall and

▶ Cranes are subject to considerable conservation attention in Britain. (DT)

Westhay Moor may be under different management, but this 'landscape partnership', an increasingly frequent and welcome approach, shares a purpose: conserving and celebrating nature.

Avalon is in flux. Old peat workings are being given a new lease of life, so the area will only get richer in wildlife. Under the nose of Glastonbury Tor, these damp lowlands demand exploratory footfall along trails, on viewing platforms and in hides.

Perhaps prioritise RSPB Ham Wall. In carr fenland, you might encounter roe deer, barn owl and hen harrier. Follow lines of hawthorn scrub for redwing and fieldfare flocks, and bullfinch families. Along channels ('rhynes' in Somerset-speak) you might glimpse a tardy, hardy water vole. At lakes and scrapes, look for otter, wildfowl such as pintail and wigeon, and snipe. Remarkably, great white egret (a Mediterranean species that first bred in Britain – here! – in 2012) is starting to call the Levels home. Best of all are reedbeds, where specialities include bittern, bearded tit and marsh harrier. Plus, of course, half-a-million starlings.

Split day two in three. Start with 'The Great Crane Project', an ambitious initiative to reintroduce cranes to Somerset and beyond. Each year, 20 young cranes are hand-reared and released into the wild. In late autumn, the resultant flock ranges widely but often frequents Aller Moor or the southern edge of Stan Moor, near Stathe.

Next, ascend the steep slopes of Cheddar Gorge for some special trees. Cheddar was long known to host a quintet of whitebeams, relatives of pears, including rarities like English whitebeam. Yet revelations in 2009 astounded botanists. The discovery in the gorge of three new whitebeams – new not merely for Cheddar or Britain, but new *to science* – suggested that Cheddar had become a centrifuge for whitebeam evolution.

Do not be disappointed if you fail to find the three new species – named Cheddar, Gough's Rock and twin cliffs whitebeams. Fewer than a score of each exist and, being deciduous, they will be shedding the leaves that form the basis of the subtle identification features. But failing to discern the different species should not matter one jot: what counts is experiencing an evolutionary hotspot, beneath towering limestone cliffs, crags and pinnacles. You can always console yourself with dipper and, possibly, a belated water vole on the river near the gift shops.

Moving north, lunch at Slimbridge. Straddling the east bank of the River Severn, this is the Wildfowl and Wetlands Trust HQ and a

reserve imbued with the foresight and achievements of Sir Peter Scott. Conservationist, broadcaster and artist, it was Scott who realised that every single Bewick's swan wintering at Slimbridge had a unique pattern of yellow and black on its bill (a feature as distinct as a human thumbprint but less fiddly to discern). This discovery kickstarted the world's longest-running single-species study – a decades-long soap opera featuring the life histories of thousands of individual swans.

And thus Bewick's swans form the highlight of today's visit. Up to 300 winter; at least 100 should have arrived by now. They favour Rushy Pen, and can be enjoyed from Peng Observatory, particularly during afternoon feeds. Every bird is known to Trust researchers, so watch family interactions then cross-refer bill patterns to individual stories.

Slimbridge simply heaves with birds. Britain's largest wintering flock of Eurasian white-fronted goose grazes the New Grounds; a few score may have already arrived. There are ducks in abundance, and hundreds each of golden plover, lapwing and dunlin. Cetti's warblers scold from scrub. Water rail and the occasional bittern skulk in the reeds. As afternoon quickens, barn and short-eared owl hunt in terrifying silence. As night draws close, guess what? Another ribbon of 50,000 starlings – and another murmuration.

▲ The magic of a murmuration: thousands of starlings perform a ballet. (DD/FLPA)

Practicalities   November weekend 4

Where to go: Avalon Marshes (Ⓦ www.somerset
wildlife.org/avalon.html) are 4km west of Glastonbury,
off the A39 east of M5 junction 23. Park at Avalon
Marshes Visitor Centre (signposted north of the A39
between Shapwick and Westhay ☀ ST423411) or Ashcott
Corner (3km further east, at Ashcott, turn north towards
Meare and continue to the metal bridge ☀ ST449397).
Starlings may roost at any of the reserves; an automated 'starling
hotline' shares the roost's whereabouts (Ⓣ 07866 554142 Ⓔ
starlings@rspb.org.uk). **RSPB Ham Wall** (☀ ST449397 Ⓣ 01458
860494 Ⓦ www.rspb.org.uk/hamwall; park at Ashcott Corner) and
Shapwick Heath ☀ ST435405 Ⓦhttp://tinyurl.com/shapwickheath)
are favoured. **Westhay Moor** (☀] ST456437 Ⓦ www.somersetwildlife.
org/westhay_moor. html) is along a minor road east of the B3151, 1km
north of Westhay. **Shapwick Moor** lies between the visitor centre and
Shapwick (☀ ST417401 Ⓦ www.hawkandowl.org/shapwickhome).

'The Great Crane Project' (Ⓦ www.thegreatcraneproject.org.uk)
is centered on Somerset Moors/Levels. Favoured areas include Stan
Moor (☀ ST364283) and Aller Moor (view from the River Parrett Trail
between Oath Lock and Staithe; ☀ ST378283). The B3135 runs through
Cheddar (☀ ST468543 Ⓣ 01643 862452 Ⓦ www.cheddargorge.
co.uk). Park at ☀ ST475545. For **WWT Slimbridge Wetland Centre** (☀
SO723048 Ⓣ 01453 891900 Ⓦ www.wwt.org.uk/visit/slimbridge),
follow signs from the M5 junction 13.

Suggested bases: Glastonbury (Ⓦ www.glastonbury.co.uk), Wells
(Ⓦ www.wellssomerset.com) and Cheddar (Ⓦwww.cheddarvillage.
co.uk). In Chewton Mendip, **The Post House** (Ⓣ 01761 241704
Ⓦ www.theposthousebandb.co.uk) is an elegant Grade II-listed
cottage offering rustic French-style bedrooms.

Flexibility: Starlings roost November–March; numbers are highest
December–January. Calm, dry conditions prompt the best spectacles.
Bewick's swan and white-fronted goose arrive late October; numbers
accelerate from late November. Crane is resident but is best seen
in winter.

Accessibility: ③

49

Hundreds and thousands

Norfolk for whooper swan, pink-footed goose, wader roost, grey seal, muntjac

As the eastern sky exceeds a mere glimmer, and the winter sun struggles above the horizon, so starts the weekend's first show. With that feeble light at your back, you turn eyes and ears westwards. A muffled chorus metamorphoses into a cacophony of cackling as the first skein of pink-footed geese departs its estuarine roost and wings overhead to graze inland. Another skein follows, this one bigger. Then a flock of a thousand birds. And so successive 'v's continue to take up to the air until some 30,000 geese have awoken and absented themselves. A procession both remarkable in itself *and* for being merely the entrée to your Snettisham morning.

> **❝A muffled chorus metamorphoses into a cacophony of cackling as the first pink-footed geese depart ❞**

Sited on the northern side of Norfolk's share of the Wash Estuary, Snettisham is justifiably famous for its high-tide shorebird spectacle. Particularly on a spring tide, incoming waters smother muddy feeding grounds before inundating all dry land, depriving tens of thousands of waders of safe, dry terrain on which to roost.

So the air fills with birds and their cries. Oystercatchers take to the skies, straggling piebald flocks with carrots for bills, bleating hysterically. Searing overhead, curlews bubble away, turnstones quip, dunlins wheeze and redshanks yelp. Best of all, knot fly up *en masse* and cloud through

▲ Pink-footed goose (ML/FLPA)

the air, billowing and alternately flashing silver and white to bewilder would-be predators such as peregrine. Knot rarely call, but nor are they silent. Their wings do the talking as they whoosh astonishingly low over your head.

The feathered throng whirls over the adjacent gravel pit, confirming the coast to be clear before pitching down. Each species keeps to its own: knot here, oystercatcher there. The knot cram so close together that 50,000 birds merge into one. After a few nervy flits and the odd commuter-like surge, the gathering settles down for some shut-eye. After an hour or so, the tide starts to retreat and the waders return to their salty restaurant. The curtain has fallen on Snettisham's show.

For the remains of the day, wander to Welney in Norfolk's watery southwestern reaches. At the northern tip of the Ouse Washes (see *January*, 2 pages 5–8), luxuriate in the centrally heated observatory: respite from any whipping wind. This and other hides enable you to get up close and personal with hundreds of ducks as diverse as wigeon and pochard. The afternoon feeding time attracts huge numbers of whooper swan, family groups bugling to announce their wingborne arrival. As the setting sun closes the day, ever more swans – Bewick's as well as whooper – materialise to seek nocturnal solace on 'swan lake'.

On day two, try an early morning drive around the scissor-roads of the 'Wolferton triangle', on the fringes of the royal estate of Sandringham. Your quarry is some of Britain's last few golden pheasants, a species introduced from China in the 1870s but rapidly declining. Shortly after dawn, regal males and subtly resplendent females exit dense rhododendrons to scrabble on the roadsides. If you fail and fancy stretching your legs, meander around Dersingham bog, where you may see lesser redpoll and common crossbill.

Spend the remainder of the day on the north Norfolk coast for whatever combination you desire of seals, saltmarshes and sand dunes. Should tide times permit, take a boat to Blakeney Point. The grey seal colony (see *September*, 4 pages 157–60) should be at capacity, and the beach may be littered with furry white pups.

For raw-feeling marshes, try Thornham. Gilted hordes of golden plover hunker down or float around like a glittering shower. Dark-bellied brent geese graze pastures and shore. Tiptoe up to the creeks for close views of both godwits, spotted redshank and grey plover. And scan

open terrain for marsh and hen harriers, tacking low in pursuit of voles.

For sand dunes, nowhere eclipses Holkham Gap. Park at Lady Anne's Drive and walk north onto the spartina. This is the winter home of pipits, larks and finches. Shore lark is a speciality: a lemon face topped with black horn-rimmed spectacles makes this Arctic breeder worth the patient search. Amongst the flocks of linnet, you might discover the closely related and superficially similar twite, distinguished by its tawny face and gingery bill. In the dunes themselves, look for trilling, fluttering snow buntings: remarkably camouflaged on the ground, yet an endearing blizzard of snowy wings in the air.

Should conditions prove too blustery, take a breather in the belt of pine and birch. In quieter parts of the wood, particularly either side of George Washington Hide, look for muntjac. Squat and short-horned, this non-native deer is as easy to see at Holkham as anywhere. As daylight dims, a familiar sound reaches your ears: the same cackling that kicked off the weekend. Find a good vantage point then sit back and watch another huge chunk of Norfolk's pink-footed geese whiffle down from the skies to slumber on Holkham's damp pastures.

▲ No room at the inn? A roosting flock of knot. (JL)

Practicalities

Where to go: RSPB Snettisham (⊙ TF650328
① 01485 542689 ⓦ www.rspb.org.uk/snettisham)
is signposted west of the A149 at the Snettisham–
Dersingham bypass. Follow Beach Road for 2.5km to
the car park, then walk 2.5km south to the furthest
gravel pit. View the estuary from the seawall and the
pit from the hides. See website for spring-tide times;
arrive two hours before peak water. For **WWT Welney Wetland Centre**
(⊙ TL547944 ① 01353 860711 ⓦ www.wwt.org.uk/visit/welney),
leave the A10 south of Hilgay, following signs southwest through Ten
Mile Bank. See website for swan-feeding times.

The **Wolferton** 'triangle' (⊙ TF669280) comprises the 'scissor'
roads leading west to Wolferton from the A149, 8km south of RSPB
Snettisham. For **Dersingham Bog**, use the car park (⊙ TF663285)
and walk northeast. **Seal trips** to Blakeney Point (1–2hrs) depart
from Morston (⊙ TG005433) or Blakeney (⊙ TG028442) quays. See
September 4 page 160 for operators.

For **Thornham** (⊙ TG727440), leave the A149 at the western
entrance to the village, driving north along Staithe Lane; explore from
road and footpaths. For **Holkham Gap**, leave the A149 at the Victoria
Hotel in Holkham, west of Wells-next-the-Sea; drive north along Lady
Anne's Drive to the car park (⊙ TG891448). Walk north to the beach.
Suggested bases: Hunstanton, Heacham and villages either side
and along the northwest Norfolk coast (ⓦ www.visitwestnorfolk.
com, www.hunstanton-info.com). The **Rose and Crown** (① 01485
541382 ⓦ www.roseandcrownsnettisham.co.uk) is an award-winning
gastropub with rooms, tastefully designed rooms in seaside tones.
Flexibility: Wader flocks congregate at Snettisham August to March;
the largest high-water gatherings are on spring tides September
to January. Pink-footed goose winters October to March, with peak
numbers November to January. Dawn is best at Snettisham; avoid
the five days either side of full moon. Seal trips run February to
November; grey seal breeds October–December. Muntjac can be seen
year round.
Accessibility: ②

50 Hoary and Holy

Northumberland for pale-bellied brent goose, long-tailed duck, Slovenian grebe, waxwing, little auk

> **"Waxwings! With mohican and mascara, these pink punks are posers"**

A perfect winter morning: azure sky, wan sun, crisp chill. Frost encases grass blades, throws hoary armour around berry-laden bushes and fringes a sedge with crystalline comb-teeth. Light so sharp that it slices the air. And air so still... until disturbed by a delicate trilling. Sailing in on triangular wings, a flock of waxwing lands on the cotoneaster and, without ceremony, devours its bright fruits. With mohican and mascara, these pink punks are posers. An aptly Scandinavian start to a Northumberland weekend fresh with northern delights.

In a 'waxwing winter', crop failure forces these berry-eaters to flee northern climes and they head southwards. They may pop up anywhere – from urban centres to coastal hedgerows. So keep alert for waxwings in a weekend of rocky shorelines and sandy bays featuring one of Britain's rarest geese, strings of seaduck and marine mammals. All centered on an island of cultural significance.

The Holy Island of Lindisfarne has been enshrined in Christian history since the 7th century. Its serenity, a result of tiny human population and geographic isolation, renders it as inspirational a location for a wildlife retreat as for its religious equivalent. Tide times govern your visit. The tarmac causeway connecting island and mainland

▲ Waxwings (JL)

is inaccessible for at least the four hours flanking peak water. But don't rush your trip across; the causeway excels for birding, particularly either side of the refuge tower. Waders – notably bar-tailed godwit and grey plover – forage on the sands, and red-breasted merganser, with its spiky coiffure, swim the channels.

The undoubted highlight is pale-bellied brent goose – a separate, scarcer subspecies to brent goose, which occurs both here and more widely (see, for example, *November, 1*). The 3,000 pale-bellied birds emanate from Svalbard's declining breeding population and winter almost nowhere else in Britain.

Holy Island itself combines wilderness and waterbirds, with plenty of areas to explore. The southeast of the island is arguably best in winter. 'Rocket Field' offers close views of brent goose, particularly at high tide. Hundreds of wigeon, teal, common redshank, lapwing and golden plover assemble here, providing more than passing interest to peregrines. A daintier falcon – merlin – also hunts the island, its dashing wizardry bamboozling pipits. You could spot a quartering barn owl anywhere, but will find sanderling only sprinting along shorelines.

From the Heugh, south of the priory, look for grey seal and the odd harbour seal prostrate on sandbanks. Scan sea and harbour for Slavonian and perhaps red-necked grebe, red-throated and great northern divers, long-tailed duck and eider. The last of these is known locally as 'Cuddy's duck' in honour of St Cuthbert, famed local saint. Should the sea be out, fossick in rockpools for anemones, blennies and crabs; the ABC of low-tide life.

▲ A flock of waxwings, Viking invaders pillaging a hedge. (JL)

Back on mainland, explore roads leading to Fenham Flats for pintail by the hundred, brent goose by the thousand, and wigeon by the ten thousand. Wander to Ross Back Sands for Slavonian grebe offshore and snow buntings flitting amidst beautiful dunes. Be sure to scan Budle Bay for shelduck and walk east to Budle Point for further snow bunting and seaduck.

Waters off nearby Harkess (aka Stag) Rocks, below Bamburgh Lighthouse, are good for Slavonian grebe, long-tailed duck, eider, scaup and red-throated diver. A dainty wader more at home swimming on sea than foraging on land, a grey phalarope might pirouette on the flotsam. Further out (bring a telescope!), auks buzz past (sometimes even black guillemot) and a harbour porpoise rolls. The shoreline hosts a flurry of turnstone and purple sandpiper, all surprisingly camouflaged amidst seaweed and rockpool; when the birds have moved on, examine the crescent-shaped Half-Moon Pool yourself for marine critters. Seahouses harbour offers close views of eider, and fishing boats may entice a glaucous gull to scavenge.

A further reason to visit Seahouses is for possible close-up views of marine birds and mammals. Vessels that visit the Farne Islands in summer (see *June, 4* pages 103–6) are largely dormant during winter, but may chunter out (or be chartered!) given sufficient demand. A typical December half-day trip would visit a grey seal colony, enjoying well-grown pups, moulting adults and even the odd pregnant cow.

The excursion would also target feeding grounds for seaduck and divers, auks and porpoises. No peering through telescopes here, but close encounters with marine creatures in their element. Long-tailed ducks in small flocks, males' tails waving as they bicker. Groups of common scoter, the males sooty, the females mud-coloured. Little auks – tiny pied corks – bob in the swell. A black guillemot cloaked in winter garb: almost a negative of its resplendent summer plumage. A lissome red-throated diver, perhaps, or a swarthy great northern. All within photographic range.

As you return to shore, literal and metaphorical memory cards replete, a familiar call causes your ears to prick up: more of those punkbirds with which you started the weekend.

▶ Northumberland is a great county for seeing Slavonian grebe. (JL)

Where to go: For **Holy Island/Lindisfarne**
(NU130430 (W) www.lindisfarne.org.uk), leave the
A1 east at West Mains, following the causeway to the
island. For tide times, see the website and roadside signs.
Rocket Field lies just north of the village–castle road.
For The Heugh, take the path leading southeast from
the village centre, past the pub, through gates and
field to the obvious short path.

    Fenham Flats stretches south of the causeway. Access is via minor
roads (little parking) leading east or north from the A1 to Fenham
(NU088407) or Lowmoor Point (NU097398), and 1km along the
footpath north from Elwick (NU115369). For **Ross Back Sands**
(NU145375), follow the road southeast from Elwick for 400m
then take the first left to Ross. Park at the end then walk onto the
links. View **Budle Bay** from the car park (NU149345) on the B1342
immediately northeast of Waren Mill. For **Budle Point** (NU163360),
walk 2km northeast along road and footpaths; alternatively walk
west from **Harness/Stag Rocks** (NU175359): park on The Wynding,
which leads northwest from Bamburgh; continue to the lighthouse.
Seahouses harbour (NU221321) is 6km southeast of Bamburgh
along the B1342. Billy Shiel's Boats (T 01665 720308 (W) www.farne-
islands.com) and Serenity Tours (T 01665 721667 (W) www.farne
islandstours.co.uk) run occasional winter boat trips. Alternatively, you
can also try Northern Experience Wildlife Tours – see *February 1* pages
21–4, for details.

Suggested bases: Holy Island ((W) www.lindisfarne.org.uk/
accommodation), Amble ((W) www.visitnorthumberland.com/amble),
Bamburgh ((W) www.bamburgh.org.uk) and Seahouses ((W) www.
seahouses.org). The stately **Lindisfarne Hotel** (T 01289 389273
(W) www.thelindisfarnehotel.co.uk) is in Holy Island village and offers
eight sumptuous rooms.

Flexibility: A 'waxwing winter' usually lasts November to March.
Brent goose occurs October to March. November to February is best
for seaduck, grebes, divers and auks. Grey seal is resident but breeds
October to December.

Accessibility: ③ 🕺

51
Ruling the roost

Norfolk Broads for starling roost, rook roost, crane, taiga bean goose, grey seal

Long winter nights are all about sleeping, for birds as well as birdwatchers. While humans tend to 'roost' alone or in pairs, many species congregate in large numbers to doze away the darkness. At the segue between night and day, such mass dormitories offer scintillating sights. Perhaps nowhere is better to experience these than Norfolk's Broadland.

Exploring the Yare Valley on day one, be at RSPB Strumpshaw Fen for dawn to

66 Tens of thousands of rooks and jackdaws stream in from the gloom before cascading into their woodland roost 99

witness the awakening of 50,000 starlings. As the eastern sky glimmers, the chattering commences. The decibel count rises as ever more birds stir. A subset of the roost breaks cover, followed by a second, then a third. A magical murmuration of starlings is soon surging low over the reedbeds and willowing upwards. They are off – and so are you.

Focus the first hour's light on Strumpshaw's mammals. Otters are frequently seen on river and pools, including from Brick and Fen hides, and near the sluice. Chinese water deer is a Broadland speciality: it favours the marshy south of the reserve, at the juncture between damp pasture and fen, *en route* to Fen Hide.

▲ Rooks are energetic, jaunty, vocal creatures. (DT)

Strumpshaw offers a lovely circular walk, taking in several habitats and hides. In alder and willow carr, startle at a Cetti's warbler's explosive outburst. Scan reedbed fringes for bitterns, whether motionless and clandestine or airborne and flying strongly. Aerial predators may include barn owl or marsh harrier hunting for voles or shrews. A strident '*cheeeeek*' heralds a vivid blue flypast from a kingfisher, streaking over gadwall, a smartly vermiculated dabbling duck. At the woodland feeding station, look for marsh tit, brambling and woodpeckers.

As late morning approaches, drift to the downstream reserves of RSPB Cantley and RSPB Buckenham. Your target is taiga bean goose at its only English wintering grounds. Up to 200 birds move between the neighbouring reserves, associating with 200 Eurasian white-fronted goose and a few hundred pink-footed goose.

At Cantley, view grassy marshes flanking the railway line on School Lane or walk the footpath south of Malthouse Lane. For Buckenham, park at the station, traverse the level crossing, walk to the river and follow it southeast. As well as geese, tussocky terrain should be stuffed with grazing wigeon, their whistling a quintessential winter sound, and huddling golden plover. If flocks are put to flight, look upwards for a passing peregrine or hunting harrier.

Darkening skies prompt your departure to Buckenham railway station platform: an unorthodox location from which to savour a remarkable natural spectacle: a pre-roost crowd of perhaps 40,000 jackdaws and rooks. Protagonists in nature writer Mark Cocker's enchanting book *Crow Country*, 'corvids' stream in from the gloom to gather in station-side fields and on telegraph wires. As the remaining light dissipates, the entire cacophony of corvids rises and cascades towards the night's arboreal abode in nearby Buckenham Carrs.

After ensconcing yourself in your own roost, it's time for Broadland proper. Start at the watchpoint at Hickling Broad's Stubb Mill. Again, be there for dawn. And again, use your ears. As night morphs into day, listen for the bugling of cranes before they flap stately to feeding grounds. The height of a seven-year-old, cranes recolonised Britain in the 1980s – here in the Broads – after an absence of four centuries. The wintering population is now 40-plus; Stubb Mill is their most reliable haunt.

At the Norfolk Wildlife Trust reserve at Hickling, Bittern Hide gives another crack at flyover cranes, and, unsurprisingly, your best chance

of the eponymous brown heron. The hide, plus the boardwalk coupling the middle hides is good for bearded tit.

As the sky pales, drive around the Horsey area. Several thousand pink-footed geese winter in the potato and sugar beet fields, their musical calls distracting you from searching the fen edge for Chinese water deer. Looking upwards should reveal the odd raptor: marsh harrier for sure, but also merlin and perhaps rough-legged buzzard.

Take a walk to enjoy grey seals on the beach. During December and January, females venture ashore to pup. From Horsey Gap, walk southeast through the dunes. At intervals you may stumble across the odd resting animal: if so, keep a respectful distance. After 1.5km you reach concrete viewing areas over the main colony. Particularly if pups are present, do not approach too closely: evidence suggests that human disturbance reduces breeding success.

For your roost finale, return to the watchpoint at Stubb Mill 90 minutes before dusk. At this hour, barn owls forsake daytime slumber for hunting. Skeins of pink-footed geese flood overhead. Alert eyes should pick up Chinese water deer, merlin and hen harrier. The morning's cranes cruise by again, usually more showily than at dawn. And the sky should be dancing with marsh harriers – perhaps 40 birds in the air at any one moment. What a curtain fall on an astounding weekend!

▲ Almost mystical: the swirls of rooks heading to their nocturnal roost at Buckenham Carrs. (DT)

Where to go: From the A47 roundabout east of Norwich, drive through Brundall to Strumpshaw and follow brown signs to **RSPB Strumpshaw Fen** (☀ TG341065). From Strumpshaw, follow Stone Road then Station Road to Buckenham train station. Cross the railway to reach **RSPB Buckenham Marshes** (☀ TG351056). From here, continue along the River Yare to view **RSPB Cantley**, or drive east to Cantley village to view from School Lane (☀ TG377038) or Malthouse Lane (☀ TG380036). The RSPB website provides detailed directions for all three sites (☎ 01603 715191 ₩ www.rspb.org.uk/reserves).

Hickling Broad (☎ 01692 598276 ₩ www.norfolkwildlifetrust. org.uk/hickling) lies 4km south of Stalham, off the A149; follow brown signs from Hickling village to the visitor centre (☀ TG428222) and walk from there to the Stubb Mill viewpoint (☀ TG437220). For **Horsey**, park at the mill (☀ TG456223) or drive minor roads to the north, particularly around Horsey Corner (☀ TG460237); scan fields for crane and deer. To reach **Horsey** beach (☀ TG465242), turn north off the coast road at Horsey Corner; park by the coast. Walk southeast towards Winterton to view grey seals. Find birding information at ₩ www.norfolkbirds.com.

Suggested bases: Norwich (₩ www.visitnorwich.co.uk), Aylsham (₩ www.visitaylsham.co.uk), Acle (₩ www.acle-village.info) and Brundall; there is accommodation in villages as well (₩ www. norfolkbroads.com/accommodation). In Norwich, **The Grove** (☎ 01603622053 ₩ www.thegrovenorwich.co.uk) is a stunningly refurbished Victorian villa with spacious rooms and a lavish breakfast.

Flexibility: Any weekend December–January would work. Taiga bean goose is usually present late November–early February. Roosting cranes, harriers, corvids and starlings are present November–February at least, but numbers vary. Grey seals are present most of the year, but pup – December–January.

Accessibility: ③

◀ Taiga bean goose: a Yare Valley speciality
(HT/FLPA)

52 Urban birding

Greater London for red deer, fallow deer, smew, bittern, ring-necked parakeet roost

Beneath a backdrop of rollercoasters, a handful of delicate duck dive for fish in an ice-free wedge of the gravel pit. The location – Thorpe Park, home to adrenalin-pumping rides – may be incongruous, but these wildfowl are worth it. They are smew, a stylish 'sawbill', and southwest London forms the heart of its British wintering grounds. What finer Christmas present for a capital weekend of urban wildlife?

> **" Incessantly vociferous ring-necked parakeets flood in – flock after flock after flock "**

Fewer than 200 smew typically winter in Britain, although more may arrive following a cold snap in the Low Countries. The drake is a 'designer duck', with a minimalist colour scheme of black eye-mask and slashes on a snow-white background, topped off with a punky crest: perfect for posing. Should you fail to catch smew beside the rides, head anti-clockwise round the M25 to Wraysbury gravel pits. Although Wraysbury's halcyon days of scores of smew are long gone, you might still see 'redheads' (females or youngsters) or the odd 'white nun' (male) on pits south of the train station or east of Colne Brook.

Then sally east of London's orbital motorway to Staines reservoirs, walking the causeway bisecting two concrete basins. Using a

▶ Ring-necked parakeet: a splash of colour in London (JL)

telescope, scan the apparently deserted waterscapes to reveal a profusion of waterfowl. Pochard and tufted duck may secrete in their midst goldeneye or even scaup. Great crested grebe is plentiful, but Staines is also a prime winter site for the dinky black-necked grebe. Check cormorants for an errant shag, far from its marine base. Other coastal birds such as great northern diver frequently spend weeks divesting the reservoir of fish. The pre-roost gathering of gulls may include oddities such as Mediterranean gull. The reservoir banks attract wagtails and pipits, including rock or water pipit.

End the day at Staines Moor. A large alluvial meadow, the moor feels remarkably remote for a site circumscribed by urban intensity. With ponds, ditches, marsh, scrub and woodland, it offers plenty for a wander. The north is strewn with nest mounds of yellow meadow ant: revere the ancient landscape of invertebrate citadels. Search for water pipit and little egret alongside pools and the River Colne (plus goosander on the latter). Look for a sentinel stonechat, a red fox stalking, a common buzzard soaring or a red kite gliding. Tread quietly to avoid flushing a common snipe from damp grassland or a slumbering short-eared owl, which hunt the moor's eastern flank most afternoons.

Start day two with the capital's most statuesque mammals. Take advantage of the late dawn to arrive at Richmond Park for first light. The early mist shrouds herds of red and fallow deer, only for the rising sun to wreathe them in golden light. Granted, Richmond's reds are not wholly wild – having been introduced 400 years back – but they don't

▲ Ring-necked parakeets arriving at their evening roost. (JL)

know that. Approach them stealthily, to observe hinds and stags go about their respective business, October's energy-wracking rut is now a distant memory. Before departing, have a butcher's at Pen Ponds for sizeable numbers of gadwall plus a smattering of mandarin, wigeon and shoveler.

Then venture towards central London, visiting Britain's showcase urban reserve. In Barnes, WWT London Wetland Centre has hosted a remarkable habitat transformation, whereby four defunct reservoirs were replaced with a complex of reedbeds, marshy grassland, open water and carr. Last century, it would have been unthinkable that one of southeast England's most important sites for wintering bittern would lie barely 6km from Buckingham Palace. Yet a handful of these reedbed denizens now spend the cooler months here on the fringes of Main Lake or channels near Wildside. Seeing Barnes' bitterns rightly feels special and their presence is testement to conservation foresight.

Numerous ducks – notably gadwall, wigeon and shoveler – graze the marshes, and a jack snipe may bob like a clockwork toy beside the plentiful common snipe. Peregrines often streak overhead, stonechats shuffle between bushes, pipits stride the water's edge and Cetti's warblers skulk in dank vegetation. On a mild day, a drowsy water vole may emerge into Wildside's channels.

Whiling away the day here is an enticing proposition, whether birding, admiring the captive wildfowl, enjoying the interactive exhibits or foraging in the café. But resist the temptation; there's a final urban treat in the post-Christmas store.

Since the decline of the 'Cockney sparrer', no bird is more closely associated with London than ring-necked parakeet. These avian aliens have definitively landed, with 30,000 now domiciled in southeast England. Each evening, parakeets gather in communal roosts, seeing out the night with warmth and company.

Love 'em or hate 'em, watching these long-tailed, fluorescent green and incessantly vociferous parrots flood in – flock after flock after flock – is an unmissable capital experience. So spend dusk watching the central copse at Wormwood Scrubs local nature reserve. A stone's throw from the infamous prison, up to 5,000 birds sleep here, making the trees look like they have a fresh set of leaves. Another incongruous location for wildlife-watching, for sure, but such is 'urban birding'.

Where to go: At **Thorpe Park** (M25 junctions 11 or 13), scan Abbey Lake from the A320 (☀ TQ040681) or walk southeast from Thorpe village to view Manor Lake (☀ TQ034686). Leave the M25 at junction 13 for **Wraysbury gravel pits**, taking the B376 northwest for 3km. Park at the railway station, then either walk west to the footpath that skims the pit's northern shore or walk southeast parallel to the railway line to view Colne Brook Mere (☀ TQ017735). Alternatively, scan Sunnymead gravel pits immediately north of Wraysbury. Return to junction 13, head east on the A30 for 2.5km then north on the A3044. Park after 1km for **Staines Reservoirs** (☀ TQ046729); walk the causeway eastwards. Alternatively, park east of the reservoirs on the B378 (Town Lane).

For **Staines Moor**, continue north on the A3044; take the first left after 2km, then the first left (Hithermoor Road). Park by the reservoir bank. Follow Colne Valley Way south, turning right through a gate after 200m, to reach the Moor (☀ TQ036738).

    Richmond Park (☀ TQ205727 ☏ 0208 332 2730 Ⓦ www. royalparks.org.uk/parks/richmond-park) is southeast of Richmond. The most convenient car parks for deer-viewing are Roehampton Gate: (northeast ☀ TQ214741) and Robin Hood Gate (southeast: ☀ TQ214724). **WWT London Wetland Centre** (☀ TQ225767 ☏ 0208 409 4400 Ⓦ www.wwt.org.uk/visit/london) is 100m east of the A306/ A3003 junction in Barnes. **Wormwood Scrubs** (☀ TQ222818 Ⓦ www. scrubs-online.org.uk) is 1km northwest of the A40/A219 junction, north of Shepherd's Bush. Use car parks off the A219 (Scrubs Lane) or Artillery Lane (between the prison and hospital).

Suggested bases: Richmond is your best bet for **accommodation** (Ⓦ www.visitrichmond.co.uk). In Teddington, **Middle Cottage** (☏ 07775 803664 Ⓦ www.middlecottage.org) offers one Thameside stunning bedroom and private living room decorated with modern art.

Flexibility: Smew occur December to February, bittern and jack snipe late October to early March. Water voles emerge only rarely November to February. Deer are resident, parakeets likewise with the biggest roosts September–February.

Accessibility: ☏

The ancient grasslands of Staines Moor are littered with the nest hummocks of yellow meadow ant. (LD)

opticron
www.opticron.co.uk

Binoculars & Telescopes

Traveller BGA Mg

The Traveller BGA Mg is just one example of our commitment to deliver innovation, quality and value. Designed and manufactured in Japan with a featherweight magnesium body each model weighs just 380g yet delivers high resolution images with neutral colours. Measuring just 98x110mm they will slip easily into a backpack or sling bag and come with the assurance of a 30 year guarantee.
Available in 6x32, 8x32 and 10x32 with **prices from just £269**

Opticron equipment can be tried, tested and purchased at good optical retailers nationwide. To find your nearest stockist, order a copy of our latest **Product Guide** or for product information please phone us on **01582 726522**. Alternatively visit us online at **www.opticron.co.uk**
Opticron. Unit 21, Titan Court, Laporte Way, Luton, Beds, LU4 8EF UK Email: sales@opticron.co.uk

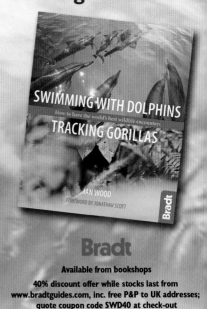

The best birdwatching in North Wales all year round

Black Grouse, Chough, Pied Flycatchers, Hawfinch, Puffin, Dipper ... all the local specialities and many more. As authors of 'Best Birdwatching Sites in North Wales', we know where to find all the birds.

Relaxed paced daytrips, weekends and longer tours, fixed departures and custom itineraries to suit you. Small friendly groups and personal attention guaranteed.

Come and join us...

So you want to see both... and...

	...mammals	...underwater life	...reptiles	...amphibians	...dragonflies	...butterflies/moths	...other invertebrates	...plants	...fungi
birds and...	Jan 1–Mar 2; Mar 4; Apr 2–3; May 2–3; Sep 2; Sep 4; Oct 1–3; Oct 5; Nov 1–3; Dec 1–4	Jan 1; May 2; Jun 4; Aug 1; Aug 2; Sep 3; Oct 2; Oct 5	Mar 2–3; Apr 3–4	Jun 3	Jun 3; Jul 2; Sep 2	Jun 3; Jul 2	Sep 2; Oct 2	Feb 3, Mar 2–4; Apr 3; May 3–5; Jun 4; Jul 2; Aug 1; Aug 3; Nov 1; Nov 4	Feb 2; Sep 4; Oct 5; Nov 1
mammals and...		Jan 1; May 2; Jun 4; Aug 2; Oct 2	Mar 2; Apr 3–4	Apr 4	Jul 3; Aug 4; Sep 2	Sep 1	Aug 4; Sep 1–2; Oct 2	Feb 3; Mar 2–4; Apr 3–4; May 5; Jun 4; Jul 3; Aug 3; Sep 1; Nov 1	Feb 2; Sep 4; Oct 5; Nov 1
underwater life and...			Apr 1		Jul 4		Apr 1; Jul 4; Oct 2	Apr 1; Jun 4; Jul 4–5; Aug 1	Oct 5
reptiles and...				Mar 2; Apr 3–4			Apr 1	Mar 2–3; Apr 1; Apr 3–4	
amphibians and...					Jun 3	Jun 3	May 4	Apr 4; May 4	
dragonflies and...						Jun 3; Jul 2; Jul 4	Jul 4; Aug 4; Sep 2	Jul 2–4	
butterflies/moths and...							Jul 4; Sep 1	May 1; May 4; Jun 1; Jul 1–2; Sep 1	
other invertebrates and...								Jul 2; Jul 4; Sep 1	
plants and...									Nov 1

▼ The now rare water vole is a feature of nine weekends. (TW/FLPA)

222

Further Information

A personal selection of books to accompany *52 Wildlife Weekends*, focusing on identification and locations for wildife-watching.

Birds
Where to watch birds, Britain Simon Harrap and Nigel Redman, Helm 2010.
Collins bird guide Lars Svensson, Killian Mullarney and Dan Zetterström, Collins 2009.
Collins bird songs & calls Geoff Sample, Collins 2010.

Mammals
Where to watch mammals, Britain and Ireland Richard Moores, A&C Black 2007.
Britain's mammals: a concise guide David Wembridge and Claire Poland Bowen, People's Trust for Endangered Species 2010.
Britain's sea mammals: whales, dolphins, porpoises and seals, and where to find them Jon Dunn, Robert Still and Hugh Harrop, WILDGuides/Princeton University Press 2012.

Reptiles and amphibians
Britain's reptiles and amphibians Howard Inns, WILDGuides 2009.

Underwater life
Seasearch observer's guide to marine life of Britain and Ireland Chris Wood, Marine Conservation Society 2007.
Britain's freshwater fishes Mark Everard, WILDGuides/Princeton University Press 2013.

Dragonflies
Britain's dragonflies Dave Smallshire and Andy Swash, WILDGuides 2010.
Butterflies and dragonflies: a site guide Paul Hill and Colin Twist, Harlequin Press 1998.

Butterflies and moths
Discover butterflies in Britain David Newland, WILDGuides 2006.
Britain's butterflies David Newland, Robert Still and David Tomlinson, WILDGuides 2010.

Further Information

Concise guide to the moths of Great Britain and Ireland Martin Townsend and Paul Waring, British Wildlife Publishing 2007.

Britain's day-flying moths David Newland, Robert Still and Andy Swash, WILDGuides/Princeton University Press 2013.

Other invertebrates

Collins complete guide to British insects Michael Chinery, Collins 2009.

Plants

Orchids of Britain and Ireland: a field and site guide. Simon and Annie Harrap, A&C Black 2009.

Britain's orchids David Lang, WILDGuides 2004.

Collins complete guide to British trees Paul Sterry, Harper Collins 2008.

Collins flower guide David Streeter, Collins 2009.

Fungi and lichen

Collins complete guide to British mushrooms and toadstools Paul Sterry and Barry Hughes, Collins (2009).

Mushrooms Peter Marren, British Wildlife Publishing 2012.

Useful websites

In addition to websites mentioned in the *Practicalities* section of each weekend, keep your eye on:

Ⓦ **www.xcweather.co.uk** Arguably the most complete weather site.

Ⓦ **www.tidetimes.org.uk** Check estuary tide times.

Ⓦ **www.atropos.info/flight arrivals** News of migrant insects.

Ⓦ **www.birdguides.com** Up-to-the-minute info on interesting birds.

Ⓦ **www.british-dragonflies.org. uk** British Dragonfly Society.

Ⓦ **www.ukdragonflies.com** Forum for dragonfly observations.

Ⓦ **www.ukbutterflies.com** Forum for butterfly observations.

Ⓦ **www.ukbms.org** An online database of butterfly sites and records.

Ⓦ **www.birdforum.org.uk** A community of wildlife-watchers (well beyond birds).

Ⓦ **www.mammal.org.uk** The Mammal Society.

Ⓦ **www.rspb.co.uk** RSPB (birds and more).

Ⓦ **www.wildlifetrust.org** The Wildlife Trust.

Index of sites

Geopolitical areas (eg: counties in England) are *italicised*; sites are in plain type. Only the first mention of each entry in each weekend is specified. We have omitted from site names both protected area status (eg: 'National Nature Reserve') and site management (eg: RSPB) which are both mentioned in the weekend text.

Index of sites

Index of sites

Index of target species

This index relates solely to 'target wildlife', ie: the five 'highlights' given at the start of each weekend. Scientific names follow each species in parentheses. After each scientific name is a simple descriptor of the 'type' of creature involved (eg: bird, moth, plant) where this is not self-evident from its name or the species is not very well known.

Page numbers in plain type indicate the first mention (only) of the species during a particular weekend; those in **bold** type indicate that the species is one of the 'targets' for the weekend; and those in *italics* relate to photographs.

Index of target species

darter, white-faced (*Leucorrhinia dubia*), dragonfly **118**, *119*

deer, Chinese water (*Hydropotes inermis*) 6, **7**, 101, 207

deer, fallow (*Dama dama*) 5, 10, 35, 62, 114, 146, *157*, **159**, *160*, 184, 189, **212**

deer, red (*Cervus elaphus*) 3, **10**, *11*, 27, **35**, 43, 51, 58, 84, 114, 151, 159, **163**, *165*, **181**, 189, **212**

deer, roe (*Capreolus capreolus*) **10**, 19, 23, 51, 58, 146, 177, 184, 189, 196

dipper (*Cinclus cinclus*) bird 23, **31**, *31*, 35, 46, 74, 126, **180**, 196

dolphin, bottle-nosed (*Tursiops truncatus*) 66, *112*, *117*, **119**

dormouse, edible (*Glis glis*), mammal **145**, *146*

duck, long-tailed (*Clangula hyemalis*) 3, 18, **205**

eagle, golden (*Aquila chrysaetos*) 3, **58**, 89, 188

eagle, white-tailed (*Haliaeetus albicilla*) 3, *17*, **19**, 89, **188**

elf cup, scarlet (*Sarcoscypha coccinea*), fungus **27**

emerald damselfly, southern (*Lestes barbarus*) **143**, *143*

emerald damselfly, willow (*Lestes viridis*) 143, **150**

emperor, purple (*Apatura iris*), butterfly **113**, *113*

filmy fern, Wilson's (*Hymenophyllum wilsonii*) **31**

flycatcher, pied (*Ficedula hypoleuca*), bird **62**, 73, 154

fritillary, high brown (*Fabriciana adippe*), butterfly *x*, **108**, *107*

fritillary, pearl-bordered (*Boloria euphrosyne*), butterfly **84**, **93**

fritillary, snake's head (*Fritillaria meleagris*), plant **62**, *62*, *63*

gannet (*Morus bassanus*), bird **47**, *47*, **79**, *79*, 133, 138, *139*, **153**

gentian, Chiltern (*Gentianella germanica*), plant **146**, *148*

gentian, early (*Gentianella anglica*), plant **66**

glowworm (*Lampyris noctiluca*), insect *145*, **147**

goat, feral/Kashmir (*Capra hircus*) 3, 58, *137*, **139**, *162*, **173**

goose, barnacle (*Branta leucopsis*) **1**, *2*

goose, brent (*Branta bernicla*): dark-bellied (*bernicla*) 39, 176, *184–5*, **185**, **193**, 200; pale-bellied (*hrota*) 19, **204**

goose, pink-footed (*Anser brachyrhynchus*) 18, 22, **26**, **199**, *199*, 209

goose, taiga bean (*Anser fabalis fabalis*) **208**, *210*

goose, white-fronted (*Anser albifrons*): Greenland (*flavirostris*) *1*, **2**; Eurasian (*albifrons*) 15, 22, 39, **197**, 208

goshawk (*Accipiter gentilis*), bird *34*, **35**, **47**, 51, **62**

grape-hyacinth (*Muscari neglectum*), plant **51**, *52*

grebe, Slavonian (*Podiceps auritus*), bird 3, 19, **204**, *205*

grouse, black (*Tetrao tetrix*), bird **57**, *58*

grouse, red (*Lagopus lagopus*), bird *34*, **35**, **46**, 59, 75, 89, 138

gull, glaucous (*Larus hyperboreus*) 3, **15**, *15*, 18, 205

gull, Mediterranean (*Larus melanocephalus*) 15, 18, **22**, 43, 70, 185, 212

hairstreak, brown (*Thecla betulae*), butterfly **146**

hare, brown (*Lepus europaeus*) 14, 38, *42*, **43**, 46, 58, 177

hare, mountain (*Lepus timidus*) **33**, *33*, 58

harrier, hen (*Circus cyaneus*), bird **7**, *8*, 11, 26, 38, 75, 89, 201

hawfinch (*Coccothraustes coccothraustes*), bird **11**, *12*, 31, 51, 62

hawker, Norfolk (*Aeshna isosceles*), dragonfly **99**

hawker, southern migrant (*Aeshna affinis*), dragonfly **141**

Index of target species